Ellsworth on
Woodturning

How a Master Creates
Bowls, Pots, and Vessels

Ellsworth on
Woodturning

How a Master Creates Bowls, Pots, and Vessels

by David Ellsworth

David Ellsworth. *Low Orb*, 2007.
Spalted sugar maple; 4½" high x
8" wide x 8" deep.

Fox Chapel Publishing

1970 Broad Street • East Petersburg, PA 17520
www.FoxChapelPublishing.com

ISBN 978-1-56523-377-5

Publisher's Cataloging-in-Publication Data

Ellsworth, David, 1944-
  Ellsworth on woodturning : how a master creates bowls, pots, and
  vessels / by David Ellsworth. -- 1st ed. -- East Petersburg, PA : Fox
  Chapel Publishing, c2008.

    p. ; cm.
    ISBN: 978-1-56523-377-5
    1. Turning--Technique. 2. Woodwork. 3. Lathes. I. Title. II. Title:
  Woodturning.

TT201 .E45 2008
684/.083--dc22   2008

To learn more about the other great books from Fox Chapel Publishing, or to find a retailer near you, call toll free 800-457-9112 or visit us at *www.FoxChapelPublishing.com*.

Note to Authors: We are always looking for talented authors to write new books in our area of woodworking, design, and related crafts. Please send a brief letter describing your idea to Acquisition Editor, 1970 Broad Street, East Petersburg, PA 17520.

Printed in China
First Printing: September 2008

Because turning wood and other materials inherently includes the risk of injury and damage, this book cannot guarantee that creating the projects in this book is safe for everyone. For this reason, this book is sold without warranties or guarantees of any kind, expressed or implied, and the publisher and the author disclaim any liability for any injuries, losses, or damages caused in any way by the content of this book or the reader's use of the tools needed to complete the projects presented here. The publisher and the author urge all turners to thoroughly review each project and to understand the use of all tools before beginning any project.

A man's wealth is measured by the size of his wood-pile.

—Old New Mexican proverb

Preface

Every book must have a beginning and an end. The end part is easy; you just stop when you run out of things to say. The beginning is more difficult. My style of writing has always been to first set a stage, then introduce the characters and see how the whole thing plays out. This might sound a bit theatrical, possibly even time-consuming. But then, context is important, even in a book about technique.

So, I begin with a discussion on working with green wood and dry wood. Regardless of what we make, the techniques we prefer, or the tools we select, it's the material that binds us together: wood. If this were a book about ceramics, I'd have likely found an embankment on a lonely road somewhere in Utah where I could praise digging out the best stoneware clay...never mind.

A few other things come to mind...

The reader will soon discover I am instinctively and intentionally *low-tech* in my approach to making things. This includes most of my tools and many of my methods. And, while I certainly applaud the wonderful gadgetry developed for turners over the years, I am also a great advocate of using your own natural instincts and common sense to solve problems. Instincts are one of the few things left in life that can't be purchased with a keystroke and a credit card, so I consider them worthy of preserving.

Secondly, I believe in breaking rules, or making up new ones, especially when it comes to the classic "rules of woodturning." So, if you find yourself in a quandary over why I do things one way when other turners do them other ways, consider it a good thing. If we all followed the same path, I suspect our work would end up looking very much alike and we'd all be bored with turning wood instead of being excited. All I ask is that you remain open to all methods. See which ones work best for you.

David Ellsworth, Production work—Salt, pepper, and sugar shaker set, 1976. Walnut and zebrawood; left and right, 2¼" high x 2¼" deep; center, 2" high x 5½" deep.

David Pye, Untitled, about 1990. English sycamore; 2½" high x 17¼" wide x 17½" deep.

Acknowledgments

I would like to thank all of my friends in the community of the creative arts who have become such a huge part of my life, and whose individual friendships and support have contributed greatly to my own survival as a maker and a creative being.

I would like to thank the many students who have survived my methods and philosophy, and who remain a constant reminder that to be a good teacher, I must always remain a good student.

I would like to thank my acquisition editor and old friend, John Kelsey, who persuaded me that after fifty years of working on the lathe, I'd probably learned enough to write a reasonable text.

I would like to thank the hundred-plus creative people whose energies my wife and I live with on a daily basis through the objects they have made, several of which are featured in this book.

And I would like to thank my wonderful wife, Wendy, who has survived, not too painfully I hope, my many hours of absence while I stared at a computer screen trying to translate ideas into a comprehensive text that someone other than myself could understand.

Table of Contents

David Ellsworth, *Maple Pot*, 2006.
Maple; 10" high x 11" wide x 11" deep.
Collection: Jane and Arthur Mason.

Introduction
– The Creative Process

My father, Ralph Ellsworth, was an academic librarian, so it was drilled into me from an early age that the reader has a right to expect a certain amount of wisdom from every book he reads. Now, this might seem ambitious for a book about woodturning, but I'll work on that. My real problem is whether there's an age requirement for wisdom. That said, I have taken the somewhat conventional stance that the creative process, like cell division, is ongoing. If I miss something the first time around, there is always the possibility of a second edition. And were that to happen, I promise to mount my soapbox and wave the flag of wisdom from the very first page.

This book is about developing bowls and hollow forms made from wood and turned on a lathe. This is what I do. And I specifically use the word "develop" because, while I have been a maker of objects since childhood, I was slightly past thirty when I began to establish the focus of my creative energies. Thus, while I intend to provide a complete account of my knowledge on this subject, I also expect those of you who follow my lead to fumble, mumble, and outright fail in many of your attempts at making these objects, especially hollow forms. Failing is good: It's just part of the process. And if you don't blow up a few pieces along the way, you're either taking the safe way out or being entirely too serious about the whole woodturning experience.

The great value of turning objects on the lathe is not so much *what* you make, but the *process* you experience when making it. It is the power of this process—the direct engagement with a material, of making something that is within the mind's eye, and of being totally accountable for successes and screwups—that allows you to evolve from object to object throughout the rest of your life.

What, then, does it feel like to experience a relationship with a material through a process?

David Ellsworth, *Spirit Form*, 2000. Lacewood; 2" high x 6" wide x 6" deep. These low forms are some of my favorites. They evolved from hard-edge low forms I made during the mid 1970s.

David Ellsworth, *Walnut Pot*, 2006. Claro walnut burl; 6" high x 8" wide x 8" deep. I frequently create this type of full-volume form to let the beauty of the wood speak for itself.

Can you learn to laugh, to enjoy that inner pride when something actually does come off the way you planned it, or even when you didn't plan it? Or maybe it's simply that you have created a block of time to be by yourself...just for the opportunity to experience the experience of making.

To help explain what I feel when turning on the lathe, let me tell about a little boy who grew up in two worlds. The first world, his winter world, began in the middle of America—1944, in Iowa, with snowy, gray winters cold enough to chill the bones through *all* of the layers of a woolen snowsuit. Growing up in Iowa in the 1940s and 1950s gave a kid a solid foundation for just about everything. You learned to live by the Golden Rule, you went to church, you got a good education, you knew your friendships would last forever, and your horizons were always in view. Iowa was a good place to grow up, and once you'd moved away, you knew it was a great place to be from.

The boy's second world, his summer world, came with his family's annual trips to their cabin in the mountains of Colorado. This was where things really happened, where his fantasies became reality, and where there was no horizon beyond which imagination could not see. In this world, you didn't just play cowboys and Indians; you *became* cowboys and Indians. His role was to make their toys of battle: bows, arrows, and quivers; tomahawks and slings; knives, spears, whips, and guns. All were created from wood and leather, using the simplest of tools: a handsaw, a knife, a hatchet, and a punch that had been a nail. Here, the boy would explore the forest and the rivers, and challenge the Chinook winds by leaning into them over rocky cliffs. The sounds and the smells, the texture of the land and the light of the darkening sky, became his teachers, and this is where he learned the value of being alone while never feeling lonely.

In the summer world, the boy heard many stories of the Native Americans from an elderly Blackfoot man named Charles Eagle Plume. The story that he enjoyed the most told how a warrior could walk silently through the forest...even at night. And so, he taught himself to move without sound by placing each downward step toe-first, to discover the rising of the earth and how to meet it with equal force. He then learned to reach with outstretched arms to the trees and the rocks, first in the daylight with eyes closed, and then in the dark, discovering their energy, the radiance of their warmth, and their smell. In his many trials, he would mostly fail. And when he finally did succeed, it was only after accepting the presence of his surroundings as an equal to his own.

That boy was my past, and though over the years most of those toys have disappeared, the memories of my childhood interactions with the natural world and of me as a *maker* remained. And yet, it would take many years, long after I had developed my skills as a craftsman, before I realized how these childhood interactions related directly to my experiences in turning wood.

Specifically, I learned to let the tip of the sharpened tool seek the energy of the wood not as a conqueror, but as an equal. And I realized that a successful cut occurred only when I presented the tool to the wood as if the two were shaking hands. I learned to sense the varying densities of my materials, and to adjust the energy of the cuts so that I could work as efficiently at 30" off the tool rest as at 3". Sound helped determine wall thickness, not simply because a thin wall makes a tone when being cut with a tool, but because the consistency of the wall thickness relates directly to the tones produced.

And then there are the smells: the ponderosa and piñon that always seemed to be a part of my surroundings, the fresh-cut sugar maple from the first cabinet shop I visited when I was twelve, the sugar-sweet odor of Brazilian rosewood, and the acrid smell of zebrawood that made me cough and think of camel dung (whatever that smells like).

Teaching oneself a skill without a teacher available is laborious, yet ultimately self-fulfilling. I learned each mistake one day became a learning tool for the next, and swearing was a good thing if it helped me understand that catching the tool in the wood wasn't the tool's fault after all...or the wood's. I learned to make my own tools, to develop my own techniques, and to challenge the limits of my own experiences. Equally important, I learned to become a problem solver. Years later, I would realize all highly skilled craftspeople are also highly skilled problem solvers.

In looking back to my first experiences at turning hollow forms during the mid-1970s, I have come to realize *something* carries us daily from where we have been to where we wish to be, and it goes beyond the beauty of wood, the ingenuity of our tools, or the power, fragility, subtlety, or grandiosity of our objects. It relates to our engagement in the *centering process.* I have heard many other creative people refer to this same experience, whether it involves drawing, throwing a ceramic pot, blowing glass, or beading. I simply refer to it as the process of discovering that wonderful element of personal *mystery.* So, throughout this book, I will do my best to pass on all of my knowledge and skills, but I will not take away your right to discover for yourself the personal sense of mystery that evolves for you through the turning process. This mystery will be your gift to yourself... and so it should be.

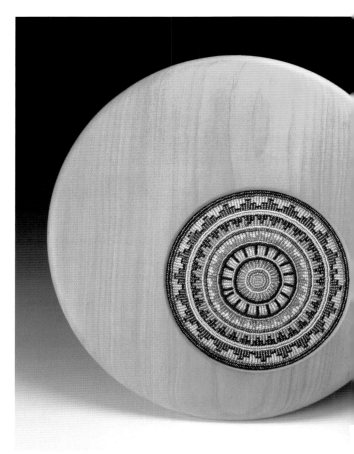

David & Wendy Ellsworth, *Collaborative Mandala Platter,* 1990. Satinwood and glass seed beads; 1" high x 13" wide x 13" deep.

David Ellsworth, Natural-edge bowl, 2008. Poplar; 7" high x 8" wide x 7" deep.

Chapter 1

Working with Green Wood & Dry Wood

The universal law in all of woodworking is that **wood moves**. Dry wood, having released most of its moisture and done most of its moving, is more predictable and stable than green wood, the fibers of which are full of moisture yet to evaporate. Naturally, the processes for working with dry wood and green wood differ, though working with a wood that is either air- or kiln-dried is no guarantee movement will not occur. Whether working with dry or green wood, you can use "wood moves" as a credo; it will help to explain your various aesthetic approaches, design styles, and methods of work.

David Ellsworth, *Hickory Pot,* 2006.
Hickory; 7" high x 8" wide x 7" deep. The pith runs diagonally through this form, creating distortion through the piece.

David Ellsworth, *Bowl*, 2004. Poplar; 4" high x 9" wide x 7" deep. This rough-turned bowl shows rise in pith areas where the shrinking long grain fibers have pushed the end-grain fibers out and up.

You must consider a variety of factors when evaluating a species for your piece. This choice is affected by color, texture, personal preference, and the function of the piece. However, consideration must also be given to the wood's inherent potential to move, as that will ultimately affect things like type of finish and choice of joinery—in fact, even whether joinery can be used at all. Additionally, magnitude and direction of movement often will be inconsistent throughout certain species. This is why you would not generally use madrone burl, eucalyptus, or lignum vitae to make dovetail joints...at least not more than once. Successful joinery depends on appropriately oriented grain, the right glue, and a functional finish. The most beautiful design might fail if the wood movement is not considered. Movement in wood is a critical influence in how you approach design and even what type of objects you design. All of these methods of work not only reflect the processes you use when making, but also accommodate movement of the materials.

Working green wood versus dry wood

It is tempting to draw a line between woodworkers according to whether they use green or dry materials. When working with dry wood, the end result is very predictable and directly reflects the original design. Drawings are almost always required, and, assuming you remember to measure twice and cut once, the finished object will most likely look just like the drawing. In this respect, working with dry materials is in most cases like color photography: What you see is what you get.

By contrast, working with green wood is like diddling with the developing process in the darkroom, trying to get that ultimate black-and-white print. When turning green wood, you can tinker and toy, but you can't guarantee a board will stay flat from dawn to dusk, much less from season to season. You can't make a dovetail joint. You can't sand without gumming up your sandpaper. Finishes don't dry, because the wood isn't dry. Sketches are a great place to start, but detailed drawings are useless. Worse, customers don't much care for that telltale pop when their beautiful new bureau top splits open in the middle of the night.

Why work with green wood?

So what's the big attraction in working with something you can't control?

Well, when I started working with green wood in the late 1970s, I quickly realized *control* was the wrong approach. As soon as I replaced that term with *discover*, I encountered an entirely new path in working with wood. The great challenge in working with green materials is anticipating what direction the movement might take and how much might occur.

In this respect, the turner of green materials works very much like the potter, the glassblower, and the jeweler, in that he must learn the intrinsic nature of his materials—and their movements—in order to become an effective designer and maker.

The distortions in the green-turned bowls shown here are predictable, and therefore, you can easily project these movements into your design. The rim movement in the poplar bowl at left is subtle,

whereas that in JoHannes Michelsen's cowboy hat in madrone burl (below) is dramatic. The hickory pot, shown on page 6, presents the eye with a very unusual shape: the wood movement was utilized simply by orienting the grain diagonally through the form. This sense of movement takes the form out of the realm of bowls and brings it up to the level of a sculpture.

One hazard of turning green wood is a bowl isn't necessarily a good bowl just because its shape is distorted. I have produced a lot of dogs over the years while learning how to manage green materials so that my successes would outweigh my attempts. Each new log or root or burl becomes a challenge, and I am always seeking a balance between what I think I know and what I have yet to learn. One of my early learning experiences was the apple hollow form shown on page 10. At 9" in diameter and 1⁄16" thick, it was a real challenge just to make. After it dried, I realized how

JoHannes Michelsen, *Cowboy Hat*, 2001. Madrone burl; ¾" high x 2" long x 1½" wide. The surface distortions in this hat reflect the internal tensions within the burl during the drying process.

much the distortions in the surface competed with the shape. The hard-edged rim and the undulating top just made the form look strange.

In truth, we "greenies" seek movement in our work, while the "plankers" seek to avoid it. Now don't take offense at these terms, because ever since I started working with green wood, I've been ribbing my furniture friends about their use of dry wood. They, of course, come right back with the notion that my green chest of drawers might be a little difficult to sell. And I respond with, "Yeah, but my old man made a love seat out of green aspen wood back in the '40s, and I am living proof that it worked just fine." And on it goes.

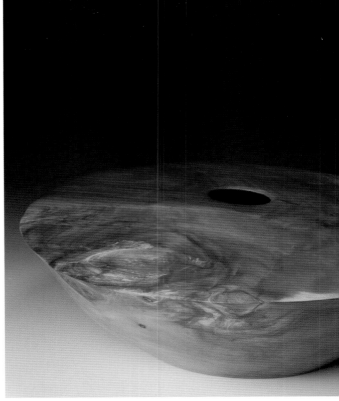

David Ellsworth, *Vessel*, 1978. Apple; 4" high x 9" diameter x 1⁄16" thick. Distortion competes with the hard-edged design of this hollow form, demonstrating that not all green wood forms end up as winners.

David Ellsworth, *Vessel*, 1978. Walnut; 7" high x 8" wide x 8" deep. In this piece, I made the classic mistake of trying to make the biggest hollow form I could out of a block and ended up positioning the pith right next to the entrance hole. It gave the hole an interesting lilt, but I saw these elements as competing within the form. Early experiments are sometimes the best teachers.

An extraordinary wealth of raw material

There is much to say in defense of greenies. We get to work with an extraordinary wealth of raw material that is available to us, most of which is free or very inexpensive. We get to pretend we're real woodsmen and tromp around in the forest listening to the birds and experiencing all the other wonders Mother Nature has to offer. We get to learn what a tree actually looks like, including its shape, color, bark, and leaves. We get to pull the poison ivy vines off downed trees and choose whatever tree part we want to work with, including the trunk, limbs, crotches, stumps, and even the occasional burl. We get a chance to meet the owner of the property where the tree came from, and maybe make a nice trade for a few finished salad bowls. And if we're really, really lucky, we'll also do a bit of trading with our chiropractor at the end of the day.

The main problem in working with green wood, besides the fact it's tough to make a chest of drawers with it, is you can't go to school to learn about it. Instead, you simply have to get out there, get dirty, and do it. Once you've seen that raw color and smelled that fresh odor and watched the patterns of grain in the various regions of the tree—you'll never again look at a bowl or a vessel or a finished piece of furniture without a quiet appreciation. The more you know about your raw materials, the broader your experiences will be, and the more fluid your life as a designer and maker will become.

David Ellsworth, *Black Pot-Dawn* (detail), 2000. 7" high x 3½" wide x 3½" deep. This piece of ash shows the effects of fire. The soft-spring grain fibers show deep etching in the surface from the flames. The result is a striated pattern showing the movement of the grain through the form. For more about using fire, see Chapter 16, "Finishing," on page 218.

Managing Materials

Before you can turn a chunk of green wood, there are a few steps you must take, and a variety of steps you *can* take if you choose. If you're not using the wood right away, you must store it properly. There are ways to create effects in the wood, such as spalting, if you so desire. Additionally, preparing a burl for turning requires some special attention. When it comes to preserving the materials you have, the most important task is to figure out how to minimize change. Before detailing how this can be done, I'll explain the basic elements of what wood is and how it responds to change.

The classic burl features rays extending from the core to the bark, culminating in surface points or pins.

Characteristics of wood

All wood species have three characteristics in common: mass, tension, and a cellular structure. Understanding the subtle relationship between the three elements will influence every aspect of how you manage and preserve these materials.

Wood does not respond well to extreme changes in temperature or humidity. So, while it's important to know the wood's condition when you receive it, it is equally important to consider the climate in which you are going to store, and ultimately use, the materials.

You can learn a lot about the inherent tensions in wood by looking at a piece of dried veneer. There is so little mass in the thin veneer that after it is cut from the green log, the natural tensions within the fibers are quickly released via the elasticity of the fibers as they progress from a green to a dry state. The result is a crinkled or rippled surface. A 2"-thick plank from the same walnut tree will have its own tension, but because of its mass, it must be dried carefully to prevent cracking. In this case, it dried too quickly and cracked.

Some species of wood are packed with resins (cocobolo) and some seem bone-dry (ash). Some have fibers the size of silk threads (boxwood), while others' fibers seem like soda straws (cottonwood).

Metal rods are commonly used to support the crotch of a tree.

Some species will take only a standing finish (lignum vitae), while others will soak up half their weight in oil (poplar). Some contain silica to help dull our tools (eucalyptus), and some cut so finely you hardly have to resharpen (holly). Some trees even come with their own internal support system (above).

Wood tension

Regardless of how a piece of wood is dried, or how long it has been sitting around, fiber tension remains. This bog oak bowl is a good example of the amount of tension wood retains, even after several thousand years of being buried in a peat bog. Imagine what happens when you take an antique table from Philadelphia to Phoenix. It's no wonder it opens up.

David Ellsworth, *Bog Oak Bowl*, 2003. Irish bog oak; 2" high x 7" wide x 5" deep. Tension exists even in this very old piece of bog oak.

Preserving materials

The question is this: What do you do to preserve your materials once you have them? This is where the furniture makers have it over us turners. They can select their boards well in advance and stack them in almost any enclosed space where the temperature and humidity are reasonably constant. Turners–especially those of us who turn green wood–often face a feast-or-famine situation where we have to contend with entire logs, roots, or burls. How do we control the cracking or rotting that occurs in the time it takes to turn up an entire log?

The easy answer is to invite a bunch of friends over and share the log. This is a common practice with the turning clubs that exist both privately and as affiliates of the American Association of Woodturners. Opening up a tree is like cutting a hole in the roof of your house: Nasty things can happen. So, short of leaving the log whole, the first thing you want to consider is what you wish to do with the material.

The most common practice is to block up the log into desired shapes using a chainsaw and then coat the end-grain surfaces with a couple of coats of wood sealer, such as Anchor Seal. Painting or waxing the ends of the blocks doesn't work very well, because as the wood shrinks over time, it pushes moisture out of the end grain, which lifts the paint or wax right off the surface. This is not a problem with wood sealer, as it both sticks to the wood and breathes to slowly let the moisture through.

The next step is to store the blocks in a cool, neutral climate, out of the sun and wind. Garages and barns are ideal because they're easy to back the truck up to. Air-conditioning in any space is evil for both green and dry wood, as it will draw moisture too quickly out of the wood.

If your intent is to turn the blocks up within a few weeks or months, wrapping them in plastic bags is another good solution because it completely isolates the blocks, not allowing any moisture to escape. If you're bagging fresh-cut green wood, be careful not to leave the blocks too long, or mold and rot can occur.

In hot, dry climates like the desert, bagging is the only way to save solid green blocks. Some people will even buck up a tree and bag it on site just to keep it from cracking in the truck on the way back to the workshop. Others will spray the bagged blocks with water while they're turning the form just to keep moisture levels high. The constant heat and aridity is why so many turners in these climates have gone to making segmented turnings. Tiny pieces of wood that are already kiln-dried and glued together don't exhibit any significant change in shape, with the result that any overall form movement in these extreme climates is very minimal.

In colder climates, freezing the logs is the best option. My first experience with freezing wood was when I lived in the mountains of Colorado from 1977 to 1981. This was the period when I began working with green wood. It was obvious that solid green blocks and logs (when I could find them) wouldn't last long in the dry and frozen winter climate at 8,500 feet. My answer was to pack them in snowbanks during the winter and dig them out as I used them.

Where I now live, in the more humid climate of Pennsylvania, I am blessed with dense hardwoods. I can leave my logs whole under the canopy of the forest, where they don't get much direct sunlight; they'll stay in good turning condition for quite a few months. An added plus for me, because I enjoy working with spalted wood (see "Spalting wood" on page 16), is that the combined heavy leaf cover, moist climate, and high humidity make it easy to spalt wood in a few months. The difficulty I have is woods like silver maple spalt so quickly you can hardly get through a tree before the whole thing rots. But the exciting part is while I'm working my way through the log, the designs of the pieces I make vary as the wood's condition changes—the first piece being made from fresh-cut wood and the last from heavily spalted wood.

"When it comes to preserving the materials you have, your most important task is to figure out how to minimize change."

Spalting wood

Spalting is Mother Nature's way of turning trees and other organic materials into the forest floor. Spalting is a natural process in which fungi attack the living cells of organic material. This process occurs in dead or dying trees, leaves, or any other compostable material. I have been told the fungi exist throughout the earth's surface, but they only manifest in areas where there is both heat and moisture. I guess that eliminates the Arctic and most high-altitude or desert regions.

The spalting activity decomposes the cells in wood, with the result that it also reduces the natural tensions or growth stresses within the material. The reason it's important to me is I know I will get somewhat less overall form distortion when turning a spalted piece of wood compared with a non-spalted piece. In fact, some spalted pieces are so decomposed there is no tension left in the wood and, therefore, no distortion in the finished piece, even though the wood was dripping wet when I turned it.

The reason most turners use spalted wood is that the material can be intoxicatingly beautiful. The dark graphic markings left by the spalting activity— technically known as melanized pseudosclerotial plates, but commonly called zone lines—record the progress of the spalting activity as it migrates through the wood along the long fibers. The zone lines come

Dark zone lines, which are created by spalting activity, are destructive to sharp tool edges but can be very beautiful when incorporated into a piece.

in various colors from brown to black, depending on species. They are also wickedly destructive to any sharpened tool edge—like those of chain saws and band saws, for example—as they are no longer part of the wood, but made of a carbonized, iron-based composition.

Whether working with these active spores is safe is an unanswerable question. I've posed it to my students who are doctors and I get a very consistent answer that sounds something like this:

"The active spores in spalted wood don't actually cause a definitive lung disease, but like all wood dust, they certainly will fill the sacs in lungs, which can lead to lung disease." And then, "For some people, there may also be an allergenic problem with mold." My solution is to be cautious and wear dust protection when working with spalted wood and especially when sweeping out the workspace.

Other times, when I take down a tree, I'll cut the log into rounds with lengths corresponding to the height or the diameter of what I'd like to make. I then

Creating effects in the log

I've discovered a variety of ways to help Mother Nature create interesting effects in logs of my choosing. For example, some years ago, I inadvertently left a section of an ash log sitting with the end grain directly on the ground. I forgot about it until, one day a year later, I turned it over and trimmed off the mud to discover that capillary action had drawn the minerals out of the soil and turned the log from the original ash white to a rich gray–honey brown. I've had mixed results when trying the method with other woods like maple and oak; in most cases, I would simply get spalting activity, sometimes mixed with a little rot. The lesson is this: Don't be afraid to experiment if there's a certain effect you're seeking. Who knows what Mother Nature will cook up?

leave the log on the ground with just the space of the saw cut between the rounds. Depending on rainfall, sunlight through the trees, and maybe some beer, and a little yeast, I'll get spalting entering from both ends of each round.

On the other hand, if I want spalting only on one side of the finished piece, I'll cover one end of the round with plastic and leave the other end exposed to the elements. The effects can be interesting—sometimes quite dramatic, sometimes junk. It's worth using your imagination and experimenting to see what comes about.

On occasion, I will turn a vessel form to a finished shape, then wrap it in plastic with a few shavings from a heavily spalted piece of wood. After a few months, the vessel's surface will begin to spalt, and I can trim the shape and hollow it out. The result is a spalted surface exactly where I want it. To stop the spalting process and kill the fungi, simply dry out the wood.

In the late 1980s, I wanted to introduce some gray tones to the sapwood of a piece of redwood lace burl I was working on. To get the gray tones, I tried to spalt the sapwood area by wrapping it with some spalted maple shavings that contained a good dose of powder post beetles. I hoped this would advance the spalting process through the holes the beetles would drill into the wood. It worked, but it took a year and a half because I'd forgotten how resistant redwood is to bug and bacterial decay. That was the longest amount of time I ever spent making a piece! (See photo on page 20.)

Experience becomes a huge factor when working with green wood, but I think the most important lesson is to understand the wood *is* going to change. By learning about changes and remaining open to them, many new design opportunities have opened up to me. I also have learned about changes in myself that have allowed my design aesthetic to grow, the most important being to keep an open mind and not to get stuck with any rules about what I think I'm *supposed* to do, but rather remain open to what is possible.

Spalting your own wood

Sometimes, Mother Nature doesn't spalt in the area of the logs where you want spalting. That doesn't mean you can't help her out. To help your logs spalt, try leaving them outside and open to the elements if you live in a humid area. I like to leave a small space between the logs. Add beer or yeast if you wish to speed the process along. If you live in an arid climate, try bagging the logs with shavings from spalted logs.

Leave the logs on the forest floor to spalt. Allow a small space between the logs, and feel free to sprinkle yeast or pour beer over the logs to accelerate the process. Shavings from a spalted log will help, too.

After a few months, remove the ends of the logs to check on the condition of the spalting.

As you can see, the experiment has been a success; spalting has spread throughout the logs.

Working with burls

I've never heard a satisfactory explanation of why burls form, which is probably why there's so much misinformation about them. The best story I've ever heard came from an old New Englander who said that if you whacked a tree on one side in the early winter, a burl would start to grow on the other side in the spring. Sounded pretty good to me!

I don't have much faith in the idea of burls being cancerous growths, as their growth patterns are quite regular rather than random, and certainly not destructive to the host tree unless there is a bark opening that will absorb moisture and induce rot. That said, it is possible to mistake a branch overgrowth for a burl, as they often look alike in older trees. Mature overgrowths are bulging elements that surround a broken branch and there is always a hole in the face of them. Maybe that's what causes the confusion.

It is possible for some trees, like this Norway maple, to explode in one continuous burl.

Burl delivery

Sometimes burls come in trucks, and often in boxes. There is nothing like having a few tons' worth of redwood burl shipped to you directly from California...

A boxed-up black ash burl being pulled from the back of a tractor trailer. My long and winding driveway is not navigable to trucks, so instead, I rope up with my truck and jerk the burls off. In the case of extremely heavy burls, I lock my truck down, and the driver of the semi simply drives off, leaving me with a lump in the road.

A redwood lace burl I shipped from California in 1986, shown in the back of the tractor trailer. It weighed 7,300 pounds.

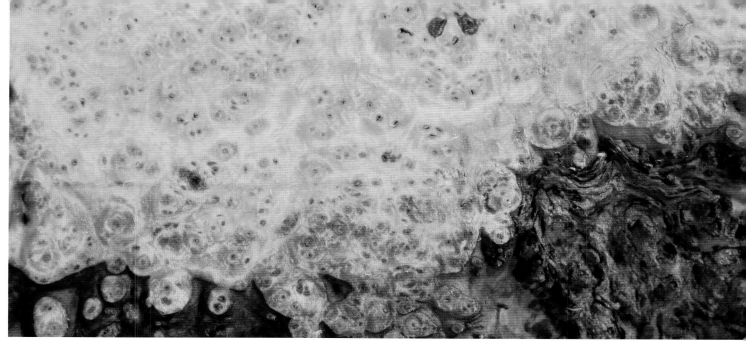

The cut surface beneath the pins shows the classic "eye" burl grain patterns.

Types of burl growth

There are two fundamental types or patterns of burl growth that seem to be consistent within each species, meaning different species of trees will have one or the other type, but not both. The first type is the "classic," or "pin," burl; the second type is what I call an "onion" burl.

The classic, or pin, burl: The classic, or pin, burl is what most people are familiar with. In this pattern, the burl begins as a series of tiny sprouts all coming from one location near the tree's center. As the burl develops, these sprouts form lines, or "rays," that extend to the surface of the burl and are crossed by layer after layer of annual rings of the tree's growth. This cross-grain structural pattern makes the burl wood extremely strong (you can't split a burl), but I don't believe it is any harder than the trunk wood.

If you cut a burl parallel to these rays, you can see how these rays extend from the burl's core to the surface and how they are crossed by the annual growth rings. It looks rather like a July 4 rocket explosion in the sky. But if you cut the burl across these rays, you get the classic "eye" configuration that you see so often in furniture veneer. When turning hollow forms, you get both patterns in the same piece.

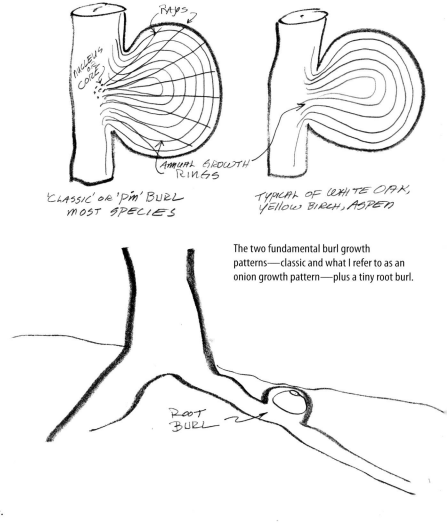

The two fundamental burl growth patterns—classic and what I refer to as an onion growth pattern—plus a tiny root burl.

David Ellsworth, *Redwood Burl Vessel*, 1990. Redwood burl; 13" high x 15" wide x 15" deep. Collection: Robyn & John Horn. The holes in this piece were created by powder post beetles.

David Ellsworth, *White Oak Pot*, 2001. White oak; 13" high x 8" wide x 8" deep. This piece is made from what I call an onion burl. The piece was oriented with the top near the center of the burl and the base near the bark. This positioned the annual rings of the burl horizontally as they circled the form.

The onion burl: The second type of growth pattern is constructed somewhat like an onion, in that growth rings are arranged in a series of layers, one ring for each year of growth—just like in the trunk. This pattern is typical in white oak, yellow birch, and aspen burls. I once thought it would be fun to cut a burl in half and boil it up. If I could then separate each ring, I'd have lots of beautiful thin-walled bowls, one for each year of the burl's growth. Never tried it.

Working with burls

Burls come in any number of sizes, shapes, and species, but the fundamental objective when working with burl materials is to remove all of the parts you know you don't want so you'll be left with what you do want.

After plunge cutting with the chainsaw, I've created a reasonably round blank to turn. Sometimes, the designs inside a burl will jump out at you.

Bowls and hollow forms can be located in a variety of positions in burls. Here are a few suggestions to get you started.

Dissecting the burl

The wonderfully rounded mushroom-cap shape of the broadleaf maple burl pictured at top right demanded me making one single hollow form. Trimming the excess with plunge cuts produced a circular form 19" in diameter, just the right size to clear the bed on my 20"-capacity lathe.

When dissecting a burl, I will often circle all the primary nodules with the tip of the chainsaw, then start working in from the burl's end, where I can cut trunk sections away without damaging the burl areas I wish to use. I then work my way through the log, undercutting each lump and extracting them one at a time. This type of cutting requires numerous plunge cuts between each lump. These are dangerous cuts unless you have plenty of training and experience, but this is the only way to properly work through the burl without wasting material.

I don't recommend this type of activity when dissecting a burl with a chainsaw, so if you don't want to look, don't look. The chunk I am working on is about a quarter of the original redwood lace burl.

A Norway maple burl partially dissected. The shape of the tree burls were set up ideally to make nine or ten finished pieces.

Chapter 3

Why Turning Tools Work

Every time I pick up a woodturning catalog, the number of new tools available just knocks me out. Compared with the simple scrapers and gouges available when I started turning, today's lot is a vast improvement. It is also vastly complicated—especially for beginning turners—trying to figure out which tool will work best for a given task. Will it work on green wood as well as dry? With balsa as well as rosewood?

Over time, most turners develop a working familiarity with their tools, or at least a certain confidence in knowing what a tool is supposed to do and how to make it work. But when it comes to understanding *why* a tool works (or doesn't work), that's when many people begin to scratch their heads. It just seems a lot easier to say, "This is my favorite tool," instead of "This is why my tool works." So, it's that "why" part that I'd like to address.

Bent tools are used for hollowing. They can be made in many sizes and angles to reach any part of the interior of a hollow form.

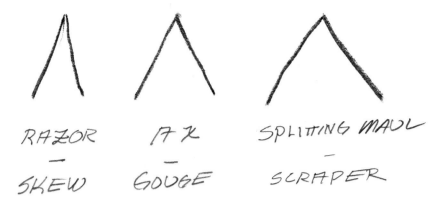

RAZOR   AX   SPLITTING MAUL
—   —   —
SKEW   GOUGE   SCRAPER

Observe the cross sections of the razor (skew), ax (gouge), and splitting maul (scraper). Skews are sharpest, but lose their edge the fastest. Scrapers hold their edge longest, but cannot get very sharp due to the angle of the edge. The compromise is the gouge, which is not as sharp as the skew, but holds its edge longer.

Turner's phrases defined: If you don't "ride the bevel," the tool can "back up on you"

The bevel is the curved area on the end of a gouge that intersects with the flute to form the edge. It's the bevel you sharpen when you go to the grinder. When making cuts on the wood with a gouge, you rest, or rub, the bevel against the wood and advance the edge forward to begin the cuts. This is also called "riding the bevel." In effect, the bevel stabilizes the edge as it flows through the wood in the same way a fence stabilizes the wood when working on a table saw or jointer. Without support of the bevel (or the fence), the wood would become unstable and the cut inaccurate, if not outright dangerous.

You also ride the bevel when working with a skew chisel on a spindle. And as most turners have experienced, if you inadvertently raise the bevel off the wood during a cut so that only the edge is in contact, the edge will catch and the skew will travel backward instead of in the forward direction you'd intended. While this is not usually dangerous to the turner, it does leave a rather deep, flowing spiral groove on the wood, the beauty of which is generally matched only by the intensity of the language that follows. This action can be referred to as the tool "backing up on you" or "catching the tool on the wood."

The mechanics of sharp

Let me begin with some very basic concepts of tool design that affect *all* tools, the first stage of which is learning the *mechanics of sharp*. Without understanding what a tool is designed to do, and what it looks like, you won't have a clue about how to shape it, sharpen it, or put it to work on the wood.

For instance, let's say you get up in the morning, eat breakfast, grab your razor, and shave. Then you fetch your ax and go out and cut down the tree you want to make some bowls from. After lunch and a nice nap, you buck up the sections of the tree with a splitting maul. The razor, the ax, and the maul are all cutting tools in some form. They are very efficient tools, but each has a specific function, and none can be used to perform the tasks of the others...at least not very efficiently.

From a woodturner's perspective, look at the cross-section sketches of the tools shown at left and think of the relationships between the razor and skew, the ax and gouge, and the maul and scraper. They all have two surfaces, or planes, that join to form an edge, and each has a certain amount of mass that supports (or doesn't support) that edge—the razor having the least amount of mass, the maul the most.

The skew has a sharper edge, but because there is so little mass behind it, the edge doesn't stay sharp for very long. It lacks durability. In effect, the less mass a tool has to support the edge, the less *durable* that edge will be when cutting the wood.

Scrapers, on the other hand, have plenty of mass behind the edge, so they're good at holding their edge. Of course, they never get very sharp because of the broad angle of the two planes that form the edge, which is why you apply a burr so they will cut the wood.

Gouges, then, are the compromise between these two types of tools. With their moderate amount of mass behind the edge, they sacrifice some of the sharpness of the skew, but they gain the durability of the scraper.

Cutting versus scraping

There are two basic types of cuts in woodturning: cutting and scraping. The easiest way to picture the process of scraping is fingernails on a blackboard, while cutting is more like whittling on a stick.

Cutting occurs when the edge is raised up while the wood is coming down (see illustration at bottom left). As a process, cutting can be subtle or aggressive, all depending on how much tool edge is exposed to the wood. The beauty of the cutting process is it "slices" the fibers rather than chopping them off. As a result, you don't tear the fibers below the surface, which, subsequently, reduces the amount of sanding needed. Cutting removes a lot of material and can get out of control unless the tool is correctly positioned.

Scraping occurs when the edge of the tool engages the wood's surface at approximately 90° (see illustration at bottom right). Scraping tools are most effective when used on fine-grained dry woods, whereas the burr edge tends to grab the softer fibers in green wood.

Scraping tools have an advantage over cutting tools—gouges—in that some turners find it easier to make long, flowing curves in the bottom of open bowls with scrapers. On the other hand, gouges are more efficient cutting tools, so they reduce sanding considerably. My experience is regardless of which tools are used, the flow of the curve of a bowl is directly related to the flow or movement of the person holding the tool. When I first came into turning in the mid-1970s, there was a raging battle between the gougers and the scrapers. I found it quite amusing watching these otherwise mature men railing on one another, as it didn't seem to matter *what* they made, but what *tool* they used. As I recall, the ones who made the most noise also made the worst-looking bowls, possibly because their bodies were too tight to move with whatever tools they used. Another anecdote to this division between gougers and scrapers is woodshop teachers invariably taught scraping because they thought it was a safer method for their students. Fortunately, with early authors and teachers like Peter Child, Russ Zimmerman, Dale Nish, and many others, the benefits of both methods have been preserved and improved upon.

"The easiest way to picture the process of scraping is fingernails on a blackboard, while cutting is more like whittling on a stick."

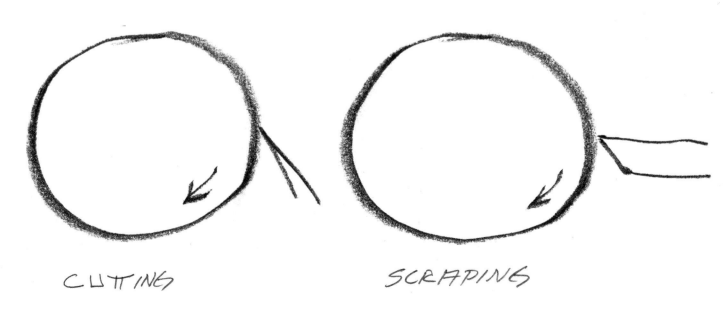

CUTTING

Tools cut when the edge is raised up against the wood (A).

SCRAPING

Scraping occurs when the tool contacts the surface of the wood at 90° (B).

Friction and abrasion

Friction and abrasion will cause any tool to lose its sharpness, although the various grades of high speed, powdered, and cryogenic steel available in today's tools will extend the life of their edges to some degree. But some woods are so abrasive that they'll quickly whack the edge off any tool. Dulling woods include root burls, which usually contain pockets of sand; eucalyptus, many species of which contain silica; and any tree with bark where the little crevices have been packed with dust by the wind while the tree was growing.

And then, of course, there are spalted woods, which are a nightmare to a freshly sharpened edge. This is because the black zone lines in spalted wood are not really wood anymore. Instead, they are mineral-based deposits left over from the spalting process as the fungi crept through the wood, destroying cell structures in their wake. As far as the tool is concerned, cutting these zone lines is more like turning seashells. One good slice, and the edge of your favorite tool is gone. That is the reason I never run spalted wood through my band saw. Sharpening the teeth on my chainsaw is lesson enough.

Spindle versus faceplate

Spindle turning is quite likely the oldest form of shaping something on the lathe, because it would have been easier for primitive cultures to trap a stick between two points and spin it than to dangle a bowl blank off the end of a shaft. And that is basically the difference between the two methods of shaping wood on the lathe. For example, chair legs, porch posts and pens are all spindles and turned between centers, while bowls, vessels, and vases are turned off the shaft supported by either a faceplate, glue block, or chuck. The three basic tools used to form spindles are the skew, gouge, and parting tool, while bowl and vessel turning primarily involves using gouges and scrapers.

Specific tools

Now let's look at some practical applications of specific tools and see how this relationship between sharpness and mass applies to efficiency in cutting the wood.

Skews

The skew, or skew chisel, is a spindle-turning tool used to rough-out and finish the surface of cylindrical forms like pens, tool handles, and bats. The only time I use a skew on my hollow vessels is when I'm turning the outside surface of an end-grain form—similar to a vase, which is simply a large-diameter spindle. The skew is not designed to work on cross-grain forms like bowls and vessels, as the long edge would be drawn into the end-grain fibers and cause a horrible and dangerous catch.

The cross section of the edge of a skew can be of various angles, but it is generally much thinner than the cross section of a gouge. For this reason, the skew edge has great sharpness, but limited durability. Skews are generally honed after shaping on the grinder in order to produce a super-smooth surface on the wood.

Traditional skews come with a straight line for an edge, but my preference leans to a slightly rounded edge profile, often called a radius skew. This puts slightly less of the edge in contact with the wood, yielding a more precise cut and less opportunity to get a catch.

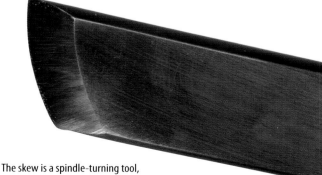

The skew is a spindle-turning tool, rarely used in hollow turning except for doing the outside of end-grain forms. Note the long edge, which is very sharp but has limited durability. I lean toward the radius skew with its slightly rounded edge profile because less of the edge is in contact with the wood, which makes for a safer and more precise cut.

Parting tools

Parting tools are primarily used in spindle turning to define specific locations on a cylinder before the turner begins to shape the object with gouges or skews. Examples of these locations would be the left and right ends of an object, the maximum and minimum diameters of areas such as coves and beads, or any distinguishing element of the design that will help the turner understand the shape before turning it. However, I have adapted their use in making vessels when I am working in the lower quadrant near the foot of the form at the junction of the glue block, faceplate, or chuck.

One of my old **standard diamond-shaped** parting tools with concave surfaces above and below the tip is shown at top right.

The **"barracuda"-shaped** tool I use today (second from top right) has a convex surface below the tip and a concave surface above the tip. The reason for this choice was simply to introduce more mass below the cutting tip to make it more efficient and cut with less vibration.

The **thin-bladed** parting tool designed by Chris Stott (second from bottom right) has a similar feature to the barracuda-shaped tool: The slight chamfer below the tip gives it more stability during the cut.

And what I call "**the beast**" is simply an old round-nose scraper recut into a parting tool (bottom right). I made this back in the late 1970s after Ed Moulthrop explained to me that by dropping the edge below center, vibration would be greatly reduced.

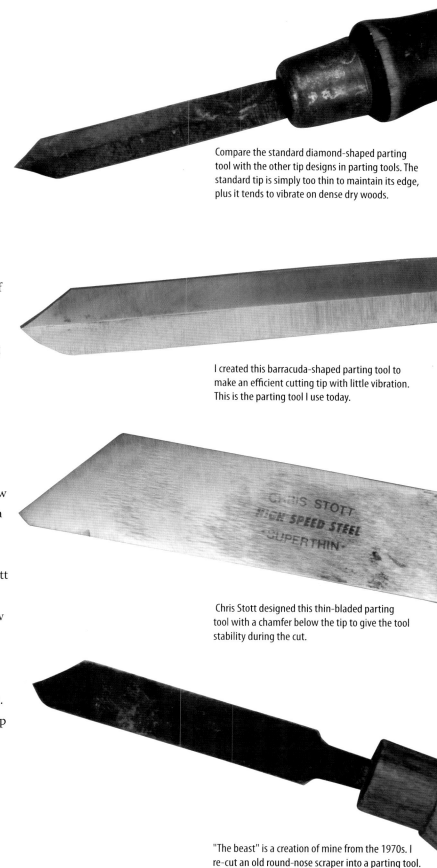

Compare the standard diamond-shaped parting tool with the other tip designs in parting tools. The standard tip is simply too thin to maintain its edge, plus it tends to vibrate on dense dry woods.

I created this barracuda-shaped parting tool to make an efficient cutting tip with little vibration. This is the parting tool I use today.

Chris Stott designed this thin-bladed parting tool with a chamfer below the tip to give the tool stability during the cut.

"The beast" is a creation of mine from the 1970s. I re-cut an old round-nose scraper into a parting tool. Dropping the edge below center reduces vibration.

Hollowing tools

All of my hollowing tools are scraping tools rather than cutting tools. I work at great distances from the tool rest and through very small openings with relatively small-diameter tool shafts. If I used a cutting-type tip rather than a scraping tip, the cutter would be too efficient for the diameter of the shafts, and I wouldn't be able to control the cut. In effect, the cutting tip would be *too* sharp. However, the principles described above relating to edge sharpness and mass still apply. In fact, they are more dramatic.

The tools I use today are more sophisticated than my earliest tools of the 1970s. The tips are now 10% cobalt high-speed steel instead of bent and sharpened bars of 0-1 drill rod. The shafts are round instead of square so I can rotate them on the tool rest. The bent shafts carry the mass of the shaft closer to the tip of the tool for greater support. I use a burr edge right off the grinder with an 80- to 100-grit wheel. Honing the edges with a diamond hone works, but I find the honed edge burnishes away quickly, leaving a smooth surface that simply won't cut the wood.

There are six principles that explain how hollowing tools work. A basic grasp of these principles is necessary to know whether the tools are working properly, especially since you can't see the cutting going on inside the form.

Two of my earliest hollowing tools: The larger is ½" square stock drill rod from 1976; the smaller is a hard-to-see tip of high-speed steel brazed to a ¼" square shaft drill rod with a lot of wear, from 1977.

My current hollowing tools have evolved to 10% cobalt high-speed steel tips set into rounded shafts that rotate easily on a tool rest when I need to maneuver the tips inside the pieces. The tips are glued into a hole in the end of the shaft with superglue.

Why use a parting tool to shape bases?

Viewing the photos at right, you can easily see how confined the region at the base of the piece is and why my large gouge won't fit. By using the parting tool, I am able not only to shape this region, but also to shear the lower surface of the form with the top edge of the parting tool. There's nothing special about this edge except that its angle when meeting the wood is elevated to approximately 45°, which makes it ideal for making a brief shear cut in this narrow location. This edge comes right off the grinder, and its sharpness is limited to only a few cuts. But it does an excellent job.

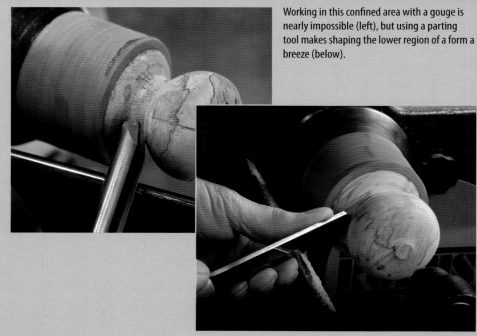

Working in this confined area with a gouge is nearly impossible (left), but using a parting tool makes shaping the lower region of a form a breeze (below).

Principle #1: Cutting with the shaft horizontally positioned and the edge of the tip at the centerline of the work piece will produce the most efficient and controllable cuts. Cutting below the centerline causes the edge of the tool to drag on the wood, and cutting above this centerline can cause the tool to skip or pull into the wood, which invariably causes a catch.

Principle #2: The greater the amount of surface area of a tool's edge that makes contact with the wood, the smoother the cut will be.

However, greater surface contact also means greater drag of the tool's edge on the wood, often resulting in a catch. It is for this reason I use ¼"- and ³⁄₁₆"-wide tips on my straight and bent tools, respectively. In fact, I never go larger than a ³⁄₁₆"-wide tip on my bent tools, because even the ¼"-wide tip creates so much drag on the wood it can cause excessive vibration when cutting at depth in a hollow form.

Principle #3: Extending the tool tip further and further from the support of the tool rest makes it harder to control the tool when cutting the wood.

I'm sure this last statement sounds a bit obvious, especially since part of the challenge in doing hollow forms is to be able to cut at some distance from the tool rest. However, understanding this principle is critical. It relates to every aspect of the design of every cutting tool that has ever been used.

When turning wood, the deeper you try to work off the tool rest, the longer the tool needs to be. This means longer handles to create enough balance so the front end of the tool won't drop down when cutting the wood. Similarly, when going deeper into an object, the shaft of the tool needs to also be proportionately larger in diameter.

Unfortunately, there is no specific formula for determining what exact diameter and length of tool will cut at various distances off the tool rest. And if there was a formula, all you'd have to do is change the density or dryness of the wood and the numbers would go out the window. This is where trial and error and good old-fashioned common sense become your best guides. And as usual, it's always best if you err on

Bevel angles affect the sharpness and edge durability of a tool. The left tip is very steep, making it sharp but weak. The middle tip isn't sharp enough, and the bevel could rub against the surface of the wood. The right tip solves these problems by using a 65° edge. This tip is both sharp and durable enough to cut with efficiency and control.

the side of greater rather than lesser when it comes to support. If the tool shaft starts to flex or vibrate on the wood, you should use a larger diameter, longer shaft, smaller-diameter cutting tip, or all three.

Principle #4: The bevel angle on interior-scraper tips determines the efficiency of the cut.

The ideal angle for the bevel is approximately 30° back from vertical (right tip in the photograph at top). If the angle of the bevel is cut back too steeply, say, 45° (left tip), the edge will of course be sharper. But this is also a weaker edge that will tend to vibrate on the wood, particularly dense or dry woods. In effect, there isn't enough mass behind the edge to support it when making the cut. Conversely, if the angle is cut too vertically, say, 85° (center tip), the edge may not be sharp enough to efficiently cut the wood. In most cases, this will cause you to push the tip harder than necessary against the wood to get the cut to start. Unfortunately, once the edge finally does engage the wood, it is quite likely it will rip uncontrollably into the fibers rather than cutting smoothly through them.

This principle will be magnified when you are working on forms with very thin walls where the surface can flex under the pressure of the edge pushing against it.

Principle #5: If you happen to be working at some length from the tool rest on a thin-walled vessel and you accidentally make too deep a cut, the bent tool will kick the tip down and *away* from this thin surface, thus preventing it from ripping through the wall. Conversely, because the tip of the straight tool is so well supported by being positioned directly in-line with the shaft, it will rip through the thin wall before you have a chance to retract the tip from the wood. I find it an interesting phenomenon that when using bent tools in thin-walled hollow forms, the tip that does the *best* job for interior-finishing cuts is also the one with the *least* support from the shaft that holds it.

Principle #6: Creating triangles throughout the body is the most efficient way to create good support for the tools. Triangles also help to maximize the energy to the cuts and minimize muscle fatigue. For more on how to set these triangles up, see Chapter 8, "The Body," page 98.

If you put the principles together, what you come up with is a basic understanding of the meaning of the term *support*. That is, a combination of an edge that's supported by a certain mass in the tip, a tip that's supported by a certain mass in the shaft of the tool, a tool that's long enough for the turner to support the cut at long distances off the tool rest, and a body that is comfortably triangulated for balance in support of the tool. All of these factors need to be working together to provide efficient, safe, and vibration-free cuts.

The straight boring bar is used to initiate cutting the interior of a hollow form. Cuts are made from slightly left of center toward the center in a plunging movement. This will create a cavity of some depth that is then widened in order to make room to introduce the bent tool.

The bent tool is used to remove additional mass from the interior and to establish the finished surface at whatever wall thickness is desired.

Hook and loop tools

Hook and loop tools have been used for centuries, primarily in Europe and Japan, and are used almost exclusively for end-grain turning in bowls, vases, and hollow forms. These are cutting tools as opposed to the scraping tools that I use, and they work off the fibers from a central hole drilled in the forms. The primary reasons I do not use these tools is because virtually all of my forms are cross grain, but also that the entrance holes I make in my pieces are too small to get the shafts of these hook tools inside.

The straight boring bar is used to make the first interior cuts in a hollow form and do the bulk of interior cutting.

The bent tool is used after a central opening has been bored with the straight boring bar. The bent tool will be used to cut and define the final thickness of the walls.

The gouge

There are many types of cutting tools that come under the generic category of gouges. These include spindle, bowl, deep-fluted, roughing, and detail gouges. Some will overlap in their functions, as most good tools are prone to do. But all gouges share the common attribute of being cutting tools rather than scraping tools (see illustration on page 25).

My emphasis on the gouge's bevel angles relates to each tool's ability to function effectively for the types of cuts you make on bowls and vessels. There's no question all gouges cut the wood. It's just that all gouges don't necessarily work well in all conditions. The traditional gouge, with a 45° bevel angle, is extremely efficient, but it is not as versatile as the side-ground gouge at 60°. Similarly, an 85° gouge won't do what the traditional and side-grind gouges will do, but it will reach those tight areas on the inside of open bowls that the other two gouges won't.

What is commonly referred to as a **traditional** or **conventional gouge** is recognized by its U- or V-shaped flute and where the cutting edge is located—at the intersection of the surfaces of the flute and the bevel. These gouges are primarily used for making spindles, open bowls, and the outside surfaces of bowls and hollow vessels.

The ⅜" **detail gouge** is one of the hidden wonders of a woodturner's armament. I was first introduced to this type of gouge by Rude Osolnik back in the late 1970s, and then later by Michael Mode, whom I met when I moved to Pennsylvania in 1981. I'm sure they both invented it on their own, which is often the case with a good design, as I know neither knew the other at the time. Today, Michael Hosaluk uses a similar tool that is larger in diameter for most of his spindles and bowls.

The photo at right shows a simple ⅜"-diameter spindle gouge I have converted into a detail gouge by adding a continuous convex bevel rather than the straight-surfaced bevel you'll see on traditional gouges. The advantage is there is no sharp trailing edge from the bevel's bottom to compress the fibers as the gouge passes through a cut.

Note the U-shaped flute and the cutting edge at the intersection of the flute and bevel surfaces on the traditional gouge. Gouges are cutting tools.

Not unlike the skew, the two planes that form the tip come together at an acute angle—around 10° to 15°—so the edge is predictably very sharp, but not terribly durable.

The secret in using this gouge is to always begin with the bevel against the wood and the tip of the tool in a vertical position when entering the wood. Once the cut is started, roll it to around 10° to 30° off vertical (axially) as you progress into the cut. You must also always keep the bevel against the wood throughout the cut; otherwise, it can back up on you, just as a skew can.

I use the tiny radius of the tip as a detail tool on something like the bowl's rim or foot. Or I use it as a regular spindle gouge by placing the bevel against the wood and then using the side of the edge to cut from the peak of a bead to the base of a cove. It doesn't take a skew's place, but when doing small-diameter beads and coves, it's a terrific tool that doesn't kick back on you the way a skew can.

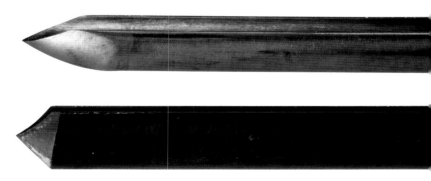

I created the ⅜"-diameter detail gouge (top) from a ⅜"-diameter spindle gouge (bottom). Note that this has a continuous convex bevel, not a straight-surfaced bevel. There is no sharp trailing shoulder on the bottom of the bevel to compress the fibers while the gouge is cutting.

Making bead jewelry with the ⅜" detail gouge

I remember spending an entire month back in the mid-1990s making beaded jewelry for my family just in time for Christmas. Every bead was made with the ⅜" detail gouge. It was fun matching beads left and right, and trying to get the right length and diameter of each bead was fairly easy. The hard part was getting a full volume in the curve of each bead. I think the smallest bead was ⅛" diameter, so it was a great challenge and a lot of fun. I made a total of five necklaces and two sets of earrings.

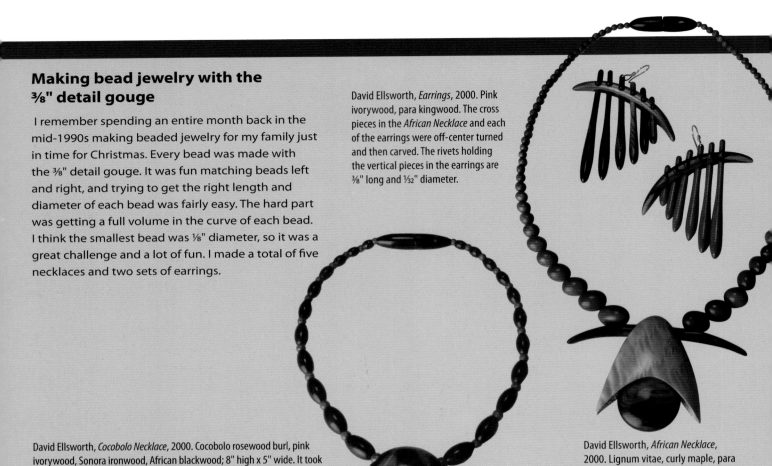

David Ellsworth, *Earrings*, 2000. Pink ivorywood, para kingwood. The cross pieces in the *African Necklace* and each of the earrings were off-center turned and then carved. The rivets holding the vertical pieces in the earrings are ⅜" long and ¹⁄₃₂" diameter.

David Ellsworth, *Cocobolo Necklace*, 2000. Cocobolo rosewood burl, pink ivorywood, Sonora ironwood, African blackwood; 8" high x 5" wide. It took a few attempts to get my skew chops up to speed and to gear down to this scale. The difficult part wasn't actually turning or matching the beads left and right; rather, it was getting the fullness of the curve in each bead.

David Ellsworth, *African Necklace*, 2000. Lignum vitae, curly maple, para kingwood, pink ivorywood, African blackwood; 11" high x 5" wide.

The **deep-fluted 85° bowl gouge** gets its name from the angle of the bevel measured off the shaft's base.

This gouge is used for making cuts across the inside base of an open bowl, the inside of a very deep goblet, or around the belly of a bowl whose rim is narrower than its major diameter. Because of the extreme projection of the bevel, the shaft doesn't strike the rim of the form, which makes it an indispensable tool for these types of cuts. It can be used either on face grain or end grain, so it's excellent for cutting the final surface inside a goblet.

This gouge really illustrates the importance of riding the bevel when going through a cut, without which the cut wouldn't work. It's really a beautiful cut to make. The handle sweeps nearly a third of a circle as the cut shifts from the left side of the edge to the center of the edge.

Two types of 85° gouge: deep-fluted (top) and a modified Ellsworth side-ground Signature gouge (bottom). Note that the angle of the bevel on the end of both tools is 85°.

How the 85° gouge works compared with the Signature gouge

The 85° angle allows me to reach areas in bowls with narrow rims not accessible with other gouges, such as the Signature gouge. I've cut a bowl in half to illustrate how these tools work. With its flute pointed straight up, the 85° gouge begins the cut with its left-side edge, shifts to the center of the edge in the curve of the bowl, and then to the right side of the edge to finish the cut across the bottom. By comparison, the 60° bevel of the Signature gouge is too steep to maintain contact through the cut on this narrow-rimmed bowl. For more on the Signature gouge, see page 34 and Chapter 9, "Turning an Open Bowl with a Cut Rim," page 108.

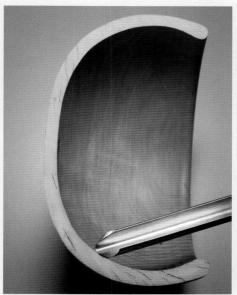

Using the 85° gouge, I insert the gouge with the flute pointed straight up. The edge on the left side of the tip will begin the cut.

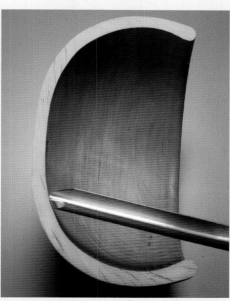

The cut then shifts closer to the center of the tip in the lower curve of the bowl.

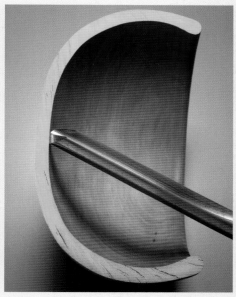

Finally, the cut rolls to the center of the tip as it continues cutting to the center of the bottom of the bowl. Notice that in the progression of these cuts, the 85° bevel prevents the shaft from striking the rim of the bowl.

This attempt to cut with the left side of the tip using the 60° bevel on the Signature gouge only works going down the inside wall of this narrow-rimmed bowl.

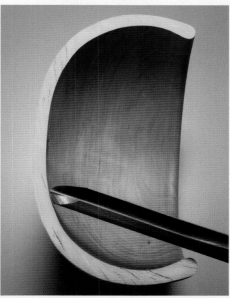

Notice that in the lower curve, the bevel lifts off the surface because the rim is in the way of the shaft.

The Signature gouge cannot keep contact when cutting across the bottom of the bowl. Here, and also in the lower curve, I would use the 85° gouge as described above.

The back hand generates the force of the cut, while the front hand simply keeps the shaft pinned down to the tool rest. In effect, the back hand pushes the bevel directly into the wood, which forces the tip to cut to the right, as guided by the bevel, and through the fulcrum point on the tool rest. In the meantime, your feet need to be broadly spread apart and the knees unlocked so the handle is free to make the full sweep without the body being in the way. It's very exciting. And it takes a little getting used to. But it's easy to develop confidence as long as you keep the bevel pressed against the wood.

Another nice thing about this gouge is you can use almost any brand and almost any flute shape except a shallow flute from a spindle gouge. Just be sure there's plenty of length and mass in the shaft and the bevel is kept at 85°. When making a bowl, it's not uncommon for me to hang the tip as much as 4" to 5" off the tool rest, so I use a minimum ⅝"-diameter gouge to gain maximum stability for the cut.

The **Ellsworth Signature gouge** is my own design, inspired by the designs of several other turners. The basic difference between my Signature gouge and conventional or traditional bowl gouges is its versatility, particularly the slicing and shear-scraping cuts that are made possible by the side-ground edge. There are also differences in the approach to the cutting process, specifically pulling the tool through the roughing and shaping of a form rather than pushing it, thus reducing fatigue and increasing efficiency. Finally, this tool allows for a very fluid approach to cutting the wood that allows for more movement of the entire body and, therefore, less fatigue. The Signature gouge can perform five cuts: the roughing cut, the slicing cut, the scraping cut, the shear-scraping cut, and the interior-finishing cut. In most cases, it is possible to turn an entire bowl using only the Signature gouge. I also turn the exterior of all of my hollow forms, large and small, with this tool.

To give a little background, I first experienced the side-ground–style of bowl gouge in 1982. Liam

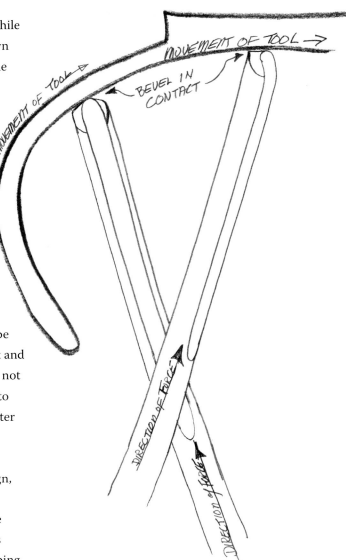

To make the interior cut, the 85° gouge moves from left to center in the bowl, with the bevel always in contact with the surface of the interior. Note the shifting in the direction of force through the cut.

O'Neill of Ireland showed it to me, although Michael O'Donnell of Scotland, Ray Key of England, and Richard Raffan of Australia had also made variations of this tool design. In fact, at the time, I jokingly accused each of them of screwing up the grind on their traditional gouges and coming up with something new and better. In any case, I modified the shape of Liam's tool tip so that the tool would perform more effectively for my own needs and provide a variety of cuts.

Also note that what I call the Ellsworth Signature gouge refers to a side-ground edge ⅝"-diameter (16mm) bowl gouge with an uninterrupted parabolic flute. I do not recommend using a ½"-diameter gouge, for the simple reason that while you can get almost the same length of edge on both of these tools, the ½"-diameter gouge has considerably less mass in the shaft. This reduction of mass results in vibration when trying to perform the various cuts on dense or dry woods, especially the shear-scraping cut, plus a loss of control when extending the tip over 2" off the tool rest. On the other end of the spectrum, a ¾"-diameter gouge would put so much more edge into the wood it would be very difficult to control the cut. As such, the relationship between the length of the cutting edge, the diameter, and the weight of the tool can make a huge difference in overall performance.

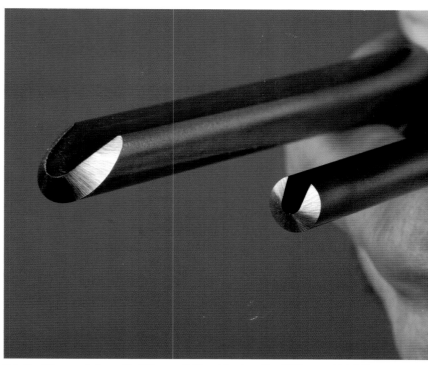

Note the differences between the 85° gouge (left) and the deep-fluted 85° gouge (right). The shapes of the flutes are different, but the 85° angle of the bevels at the tips of both tools is the same. As such, they pretty much do the same thing, although the deep-fluted gouge might be best for the interior cuts across the bottom of smaller forms like goblets.

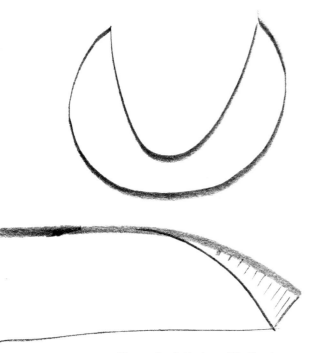

These end and side views of the Signature gouge show the parabolic flute. The convex curve to the edge is what allows the gouge to make five distinct cuts.

Also important to the design of the Signature gouge is the flute's shape (see illustration at left and photo above). I prefer a uniform parabolic shape with an uninterrupted surface. This gives me a progressive convex curve to the edge that maximizes each of the five primary cuts the gouge will make.

The Signature gouge is designed to make these five primary cuts so it will work with equal efficiency on the outside of hollow vessel forms, plus the outside and the inside of open bowls. I don't recommend using it for spindle turning, simply because it wouldn't be as efficient as a skew or a spindle gouge. But I certainly encourage people to experiment by using tools for a broad variety of applications, as long as they feel safe in doing so. In this respect, tool design is like language: It evolves with time and need. The history of the gouge is surrounded with experimentation; who knows what other turners might come up with?

For more detail on the five cuts and how to use the Signature gouge, see Chapter 9, *Turning an Open Bowl with a Cut Rim*, page 108.

Chapter 4

Making Tools & Tool Handles

Today, making tools—especially hollowing tools—approaches maximum coolness. You know exactly what you need and how to get there. You quickly learn about the physical dynamics of how a tool works or does not work. You discover new applications for tools and new shapes upon which to use them. You sometimes need to invent jigs to make the tools, not knowing that someone, somewhere, has already made that jig for another purpose, but that doesn't matter. You can become so totally engrossed in creating the tool that you often forget about the object you're trying to make. Frequently, the tools are made so late at night there's no one around to notice. Often, homemade tools are ugly as hell, but when you first put them to the wood, it's like walking through cheesecake with a hot chainsaw. I've been using ugly tools for so long that they've become beautiful to me. What could possibly be more satisfying than that?

With the aid of a propane torch and a vise, you can make your own bent hollowing tools.

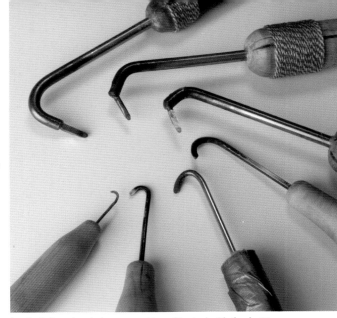

I make J-shaped tools from screwdrivers (the tool with the duct tape wrap), Allen wrenches (the rest of the small-handled tools), and 0-1 drill rod (the three on the top) to cut recessed openings in my *Homage Pots*.

Making tools comes from having a need. If you look at the history of tool design in woodturning since around the late 1970s, it's pretty clear we are a needy group. What a joy! With the exception of the standard gouges, skews, and a few parting tools, all of the specialty tools you see today have been designed by living makers, and most are made and marketed by those individuals.

I love making tools because it gives me a particular satisfaction to know that when I have a problem, I can create something to solve it. Often the problem involves reaching an area inside a hollow form that cannot be reached by an existing tool without sacrificing some design element... like enlarging the opening hole to get a bigger tool inside. I did that once, and it ended up such a lousy piece that I heated my studio with it for the better part of about five minutes.

Most turners haven't a clue how to make a tool. New turners don't yet have the background or experience to know what they actually want in a tool. Besides, it's easier to pick up a credit card, make a few keystrokes on the computer, and buy something, assuming the seller has the tool you need. Some do; some don't.

When it comes to making hollowing tools, logic and simplicity are the secrets to success. When I came up with the recessed-opening design in my *Homage Pot* series, I wasn't going to sacrifice a good idea because I didn't have the right tool. I made seven tools from Allen wrenches, some drill rod, and a screwdriver (that's the one with the duct-tape wrap in the photo at top right). My philosophy is don't make the piece to fit the tool; make the tool to fit the piece. Trust me, it grows on you!

Getting started

The average time required to make an average tool? A bit more than an average Internet visit. The more tools you make, the less they cost, because you already own the important stuff. The handles are free because you walk outside and cut some off a small tree, or you go visit your local friendly furniture maker and beg or trade some of your bowls for some of his scraps. Neither one of you actually *needs* either one of them anyway, so it should be an equal exchange.

If you don't like how the tool works, if the handle is too short or too long, if the angle of the bend is too little or too great, keep making the tool until you get it right. But save the first tool, because you'll always find another use for it down the road. You can't fail. There are no bad tools, just ones you don't use as often.

In fact, without experience, you can't know how a tool is going to react on the wood until you try it. It's that trying part, the figuring out what a tool does and doesn't do, that helps you solve problems and guides you in new directions. If the tool doesn't work on dry wood, try it on green wood. I have some bent tools with ½"-thick shafts and severe bends extending as much as 4" past the bend that work better than thicker ⅝" bars of the same shape. Why? Usually, when the cutting tips receive *less* support from the shaft, they become *more* sensitive to the surfaces I'm cutting. Logic says more support would be better. In this case, logic is wrong.

To drill a hole in a tool shaft to hold the tip, secure the rod in your vise and use a twist bit slightly smaller than the diameter of the rod.

Making tool shafts

Making tools is something everyone can do, and I believe it's the best way to get totally involved in the making process. The general steps you will use when creating a turning tool aren't hard to follow, either.

1 Cut the steel to the length you want with a hacksaw and grind the end of the rod to receive a drill bit.

2 Using a standard twist drill bit, drill a hole where you want it in the end of the bar to match the size of your high-speed cutting tip.

3 Grind your cutting tip in half on the edge of the grinder (now you have two tips) and shape the ends.

4 Glue one tip into the hole in the bar. Save the other for another tool.

5 Turn a handle, drill a hole in the end, and glue in the shaft.

6 Tie a ferrule around the end of the handle.

7 Sharpen the tip of the cutter, and you're ready to go.

Materials and tools

For those of you adventurous enough to make your own tools, here is a list of the materials and tools you'll need. You may already have many of the required tools. If that's the case, you won't have to invest much money at all.

- A couple of 36"-long 0-1 drill rod steel bars of various diameters
- A couple of 10% cobalt high-speed cutting tips, ³⁄₁₆" or ¼" square
- A couple of standard drill bits (³⁄₁₆" and ¼")
- A set of long-stemmed Allen wrenches
- A good bench vise
- A propane shop torch
- A hand-held power drill
- A pair of vise-grip pliers
- A grinder
- A hacksaw
- A tube of superglue

Making a bent shaft

Begin making a bent-shaft tool by cleaning the shavings off your workbench so you don't burn down the studio when heating the rod. With a hole already drilled in the rod, place it in the vise so the area to be bent is at least 2" above the jaws of the vise to help prevent the metal in the vise from draining heat away from the shaft.

Next, heat the shaft until it is slightly red and slip a larger rod with a hole drilled in it over the end. I have a couple of these larger rods with different size holes drilled in them for tool rods of different diameters. This is easier than grabbing the end of the heated rod with a vise grip. Now you can bend until you get to 45°. If the tool rod cools down during the bend, reheat it and keep going.

Cool the rod by dunking it in water or air drying. There is no need to temper the shafts. I've never had one bend on me during use. Finally, glue in the tip with medium-density gap-filling superglue (cyanoacrylate) and you're done. Well, almost. It's best to use your grinder to score up the surface of the opposite end of the shaft where it will go into the handle. Score 1½" up from the end of the rod for small tools up to 7" long, and 2¼" up the shaft for longer tools up to 12" long.

Choosing a tool angle

I do make some bent tools with an angle greater than 45° for reaching difficult areas, but using an angle less than 45° creates problems with tool skipping on the wood.

Making a bent shaft

These photographs show how I create a bent shaft. Try using MAPP gas instead of propane. Though MAPP will cost around $10 a tank instead of $3.25, it's a hotter gas, so it takes less time to heat the bar.

Drill the hole in the end of the shaft. Secure the rod vertically in your vise. Heat the area on the rod that you want to bend until it is red.

Using a rod that has a hole in it larger than the rod you are bending, grab the hot rod, and bend the end to a 45° angle.

Making a tip

The tips I make are of two sizes: ³⁄₁₆" square for all of my bent tools and ¼" square for my straight boring bars. The tips come in 2½"-long sticks, so first cut them in half. This can be done by placing the center of the stick against the corner of the grinding wheel and cutting a V in one side, about three-quarters of the way through the stick. I then break the stick in half, which leaves a very nice angle on the end of each stick that can be integrated into the tip of the tool.

Step two is to round the stem to fit the hole in the shaft. I have a series of jigs set up for this, but it's easily done in a home workshop. Using vise-grip pliers, grind each of the four corners of one end of the tip separately, starting at the top of the wheel and working down to the base of the wheel. The stem needs to be from ³⁄₈" to ½"-long. With practice, it's easy to cut a nice round stem. It doesn't have to be perfect, just round enough to go into a hole of the same size as the tip. Epoxy or gap-filling superglue will make up the difference. Do not overgrind the stem or it will become weak.

The final step is to drill the hole in the shaft using a standard twist drill and glue in the tip.

Recycling tips

As the tips of my hollowing tools grow shorter with use, I find I use them for different purposes. For example, a steeply bent tool is good for use in the shoulder of a hollow form, but as the tip wears away and it becomes shorter, I remove it and place it in a tool with a shorter bend so I can use it more as a roughing-out tool. When the tip becomes really short, I grind the end down so it becomes a straight tool for boring in the center of a smaller form.

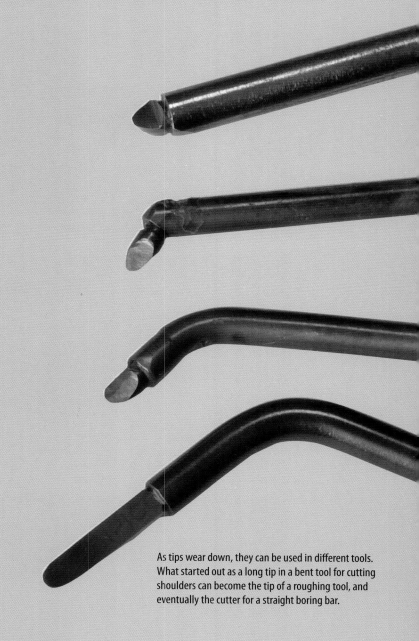

As tips wear down, they can be used in different tools. What started out as a long tip in a bent tool for cutting shoulders can become the tip of a roughing tool, and eventually the cutter for a straight boring bar.

Making a tip

To make a tool tip, try cutting your 2½"-long 10% cobalt high-speed cutting tip in half on the grinder at a 45° angle.

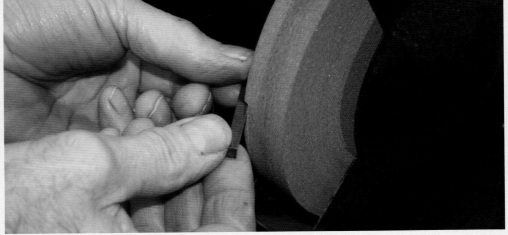

Grind the cobalt tip almost the whole way through the middle by using the corner of your grinder. Be sure to maintain a 45° angle.

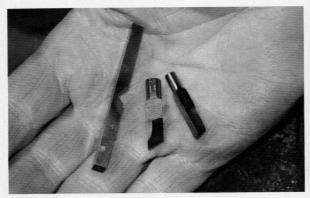

The tips will still be attached when you are done with the grinder.

Use your vise and vise-grip pliers to break the tips apart. Bend toward the V angle you have cut.

Grind each corner of the squared end of the tip until the base fits in the hole of the shaft. Start at the top of the grinder wheel and working down to the bottom. The rounded base of the tip should be ⅜" long.

Secure the shaft of the tool in your vise, then drill a ³⁄₁₆" hole to receive the tip in this ⅜"-diameter shaft.

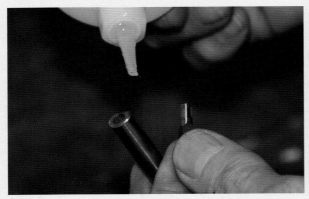

Apply superglue into the shaft's hole. Spray the hole and stem with accelerator.

Insert the tip into the hole. Be sure the top surface of the tip is aligned (parallel) with the line of the chamfer on the end of the rod just above the hole. Doing so ensures this and any successive tip used in this tool always seats in the horizontal position in the shaft.

Creating hollowing tools from other tools

When you turn smaller forms, you'll find you already have the materials to create small hollowing tools in your workshop: screwdrivers, Allen wrenches, and nails. I've been using screwdrivers and Allen wrenches to cut the interiors of my smaller hollow forms since the late-1970s. They're accessible, inexpensive, and efficient, and most turners already have them. I can bend them with a propane torch, shape the tips as I wish, and make handles in shapes to fit my needs.

Screwdrivers

Screwdrivers are nearly ready-made for the job. Either Phillips or slotted will work, and I shape the tips into a simple round nose or a fingernail-shaped scraper. Screwdriver handles are too small in diameter for my hands, so I wrap them tightly with several layers of foam rubber and duct tape. With use, the imprint of my hand settles into the foam, and then I always know when the tip is horizontal by how the handle fits in my hand.

With slotted, or flat, screwdrivers, it's best to cut the tip back at least ½" so the tip's thickness will be at least half the shaft's diameter to prevent vibration when cutting.

Allen wrenches

Allen wrenches, like screwdrivers, aren't the hardest steel in the bin, but they do hold an edge remarkably well. After they're shaped on the grinder, I use a diamond file to maintain the edge. I cut the tip end back to about a third of its original length unless I need the full length to reach a specific area in a small hollow form. I then use a shop torch to heat and bend the tip to the required shape. It is important to keep these tools sharp, or they'll simply rattle against the wood.

Irish concrete nails

The only really exotic tools shown here are the Irish concrete nails (3.5mm x 100mm). Irish concrete nails are long, smooth, and very hard, and I haven't found anything like them in the United States. Screwdrivers with a ⅛" diameter would also work, but you'd miss the trip to Ireland to get the nails, where they're available at lumber stores.

Shaping the bevel on repurposed tools

As with all scraping tools, the angle of the bevel can range from around 75° to 85°, depending upon your needs. But, if you cut this angle back to 45°, the tip won't have enough mass behind it and will vibrate on the wood.

Making a tool handle

Ergonomics plays an important role in designing turning tools, especially for handles. I've been using oval handles on my larger hollowing tools since the early 1980s, when I got into making larger tools to turn larger forms. I realized I was overgripping the back of the handles on my round-handled tools, and my right hand was really throbbing. I'd wake up at night and my whole forearm felt like pins and needles. What to do?

I remembered a time when I was making handles for ceramic pots back in the early 1970s. As I was pulling the clay handles, they naturally became oval in cross section and fit my hand beautifully. Then, I remembered the old oval wooden screwdriver handles, and how much force they provided when screwing those dreadful slotted screws. Imagine trying to frame a house with a round hammer handle. You wouldn't last half an hour before the hammer would start slipping in your hand. Oval is in. Our hands aren't designed to hold perfectly round objects, so why should our tool handles be round? The answer is that round handles are easy to fabricate.

"Often, homemade tools are ugly as hell, but when you first put them to the wood, it's like walking through cheesecake with a hot chainsaw."

Turning a tool handle

To get an oval-shaped handle on my hollowing tools, I first turn the handle round, then offset the back of the handle in the tailstock ¼" and use a gouge to shave off some of the extra meat at the back of the handle. This produces an oval shape in the area where I have to grip the tool with the greatest strength. You can trim the area to fit your hand. If you overcut, you'll end up with a round shape, offset from the rest of the handle by ¼".

I run the oval around 6" up from the back of the handle, but people with shorter arms might want to go 12" just to give them more of this area to grip when they're cutting at shorter distances in a hollow form.

I also leave a rough surface on my tool handles to give my hands some traction. I've seen a lot of pretty handles in people's shops over the years, with fancy woods and slick surfaces. They're a nice tribute to a good tool, and a lot of fun to make, but I wonder how efficient they are in terms of hand slippage—you might have to grip them tighter to make them work. It comes down to personal choice. My handles are intentionally crude.

Finally, I cut a ⅛"-deep recess 1½" long on the business end of the tool handle to receive a wrapped ferrule after the shaft is glued in. I also roll over the end so it fits comfortably in my hand.

Drilling a hole for the shaft

To drill the hole, I mount a Jacobs chuck in the headstock and the back end of the handle in the tailstock. I use either a multispur drill bit or a flat spade bit the same diameter as the shaft, because regular drill bits will wander as they go deeper into the end grain of the handle. I mark the bit with tape at the depth to which I want to drill and grab the handle with one hand, turn on the lathe, and wind the tailstock handle forward. When I'm at the desired depth, I let go of the handle, reach down, and turn off the lathe. This way, I'm in no danger if anything goes wrong while drilling.

Turning a tool handle

One overlooked value to making your own turning tools is you get to make your own handles. You can turn the handles from branches or dimensional hardwood. The handle's diameter should be whatever is comfortable to your hands, and the length depends on how you're using the tool. For hollowing tools, I like to use a 15"-long handle for a 6"-long shaft, and a 28"-long handle for a 12"-long shaft. Try creating handles from 8/4 dry square stock or a small tree limb.

Place the gouge in the slicing position in preparation for roughing the handle. Shape and smooth the handle.

Turn a recess ⅛" deep to receive the ferrule. Roll the left edge of the handle.

Move the back end of the handle about ¼" on the tailstock—it doesn't matter which way, as long as it is off-center.

Shave off some of the back end of the handle to create an oval shape. Make sure the oval shape runs at least 6" up the handle, though you may want to go to 12" if you have shorter arms. Grab the handle and see if it feels right in your hand.

Roll over the end so it will fit more comfortably in your hand while you're turning.

Attach a Jacobs chuck in the headstock and hold the butt of the handle against the tailstock. Mark the depth of the cut to 2¼" on the drill bit with duct tape

Turn on the lathe and wind the tailstock forward. Hold the handle stationary while drilling. When you have drilled to the desired depth, let go of the handle and turn off the lathe. Check to be sure the hole is centered.

Attaching the shaft to the handle and tie a ferrule

These steps show how I attach the shaft to the handle and create a ferrule.

If you choose to use epoxy rather than superglue to secure the shaft, try drilling a ⅛"-diameter exit hole into the side of the handle, just above the base of the large hole, to allow excess epoxy to escape and give the shaft a proper seat at the bottom of the hole.

I like to tie the ferrule either while the handle is mounted on the lathe or holding the handle in my lap. Try both and see what works best for you.

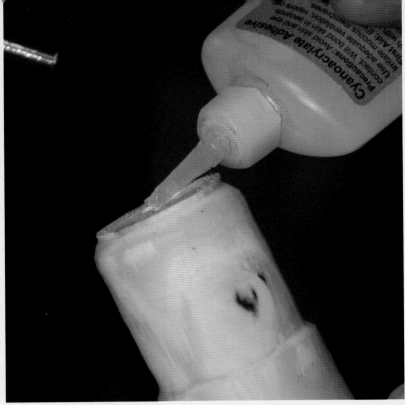

Mount the shaft in the vise so the tip is in a horizontal cutting position. Apply superglue into the hole in the wooden handle. Spray the end of the shaft with accelerator.

Push the handle onto the shaft with both hands. Make sure your right hand is on the back of the handle where it would be while you were turning to ensure the tool is put together as you will want it while turning.

Make a loop with nylon cord and place it on the recessed area. The end of the cord should extend a few inches past the handle. Make sure the loop end extends past the recessed area.

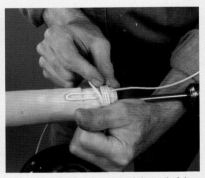

Begin wrapping the cord around the end of the handle, making sure you keep the wraps tight.

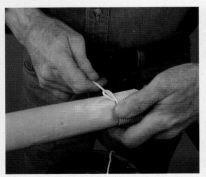

When you finish wrapping the cord the whole way along the recess, cut the cord, leaving a few inches. Thread this end through the loop.

Pull the end of the cord on the shaft end. This will pull the loose end under the wraps.

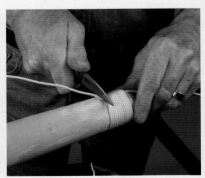

Cut off the ends.

Attaching the shaft to the handle

Gap-filling medium-density superglue is a perfect solution to fixing a shaft in a handle. If I'm using a fresh-cut limb and the wood is still wet, I must move quickly after pouring glue in the hole in the handle and spraying the shaft with accelerator. There is about five seconds before the glue sets. I put the shaft into my vise with the tip horizontal, so I always know it is horizontal inside the form when the handle feels good to my hand. I then dribble the glue in the hole, spray the end of the shaft, and ram the handle on with my hand at the back of the tool where it feels comfortable on the oval shape. Epoxy works just as well, although it's smart to drill a tiny hole into the side of the handle at the location of the bottom of the large hole to let the epoxy escape; otherwise, the shaft may not squeeze all the way down into the hole.

Tying a ferrule

Next, make the ferrule. I use nylon cord instead of brass or copper pipe because I work with so many diameters in my handles that I'd have to buy out the store to be sure I always had the right size pipe. Instead, I use a hangman's noose and coat it with superglue. The glue is a bit modern, but the knot is the oldest ferrule known to man and I *always* have the right size available.

A lot of the ferrules I see on homemade and commercial tool handles are too small in diameter to do their job. One ferrule I saw allowed only ⅛" of solid wood between it and the shaft, and I doubt that it would have held under stress. I don't believe a ferrule is supposed to keep the handle from breaking away if you get a severe dig in the wood. It's there to keep the shaft from flying out of the broken handle. If that's all it does, that's a good thing. I've often thought a nicely woven herringbone pattern on the ferrule, with multiple-colored threads, would dress up my tools a bit. I'm just a little afraid they might be too pretty to use.

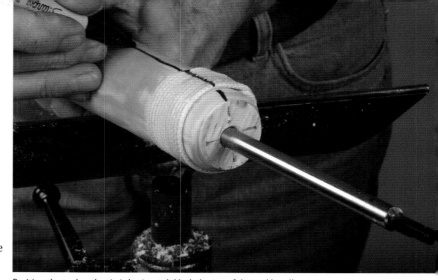

Position the tool so the tip is horizontal. Mark the top of the tool handle with a long black line so you know when the tip is in the horizontal cutting position inside a form. Mark a red line to the side of the black line.

Marking the tool handle

Another important part of my tool design is to mark the handle with black and red lines so I can tell if the tip is horizontal when I'm working inside a pot. Black line up, everything's fine; red line up, trouble on the line.

Making large tool handles more comfortable

When I'm working with large bent tools, I often wrap the handle's back end with foam rubber and duct tape. When gripped, the foam provides additional comfort and takes on the imprint of my hand to provide another reference for when the tip is horizontal.

ROTATION

8" GRINDER

TWO SPEED

1725/3450 R.P.M.

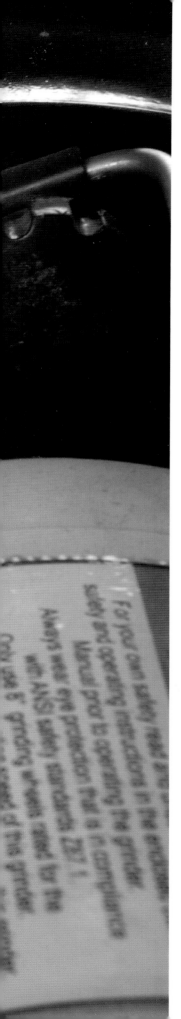

Sharpening

Anyone who has had the opportunity to watch a skilled woodturner as he works on a bowl or a spindle will notice how relaxed and efficient he is with the various cuts, and how fluidly he moves from one cut to the next. This is especially true with spindle turners, as they're constantly working with lengthy objects where they need to move equally both left and right.

It is much the same with sharpening. Once you learn, you'll wonder why it took so long to do so while at the same time crying, "Oh, my God, just look at all the time and money I've spent butchering my tools!"

Keeping your tools sharp is one of the most important parts of turning. Without sharp edges on your tools, your making process will be plagued with frustration.

Fear not. We can all develop sharpening skills and begin enjoying the pleasures of the process instead of the pangs, and the only downside is a few years in therapy and a daily whack upside the head. Sharpening *is* a pleasure, especially knowing that your efforts make a tool that functions the way it is supposed to and that you have accomplished a process often surrounded by mystery and confusion.

There are two basic stages in learning how to sharpen a tool. The first is learning about the *mechanics of sharp*, which I discussed in Chapter 3, "Why Turning Tools Work," on page 24. The second stage is learning how to *practice the processes* of sharpening without fear of screwing up the shape of the tool or overgrinding. This chapter is about practicing the sharpening processes.

"Don't GRIND the tool...
　　　　simply dress the bevel."

Sharpening concepts

Just as furniture makers have adopted the mantra "Measure twice, cut once," woodturners might easily consider a similar approach of "Practice twice, sharpen once." In fact, once a tool is properly shaped, it generally takes only a stroke or two over the wheel to refresh its edge. While that may sound a bit daunting to the beginner, consider that when you go to the grinder, you're not trying to GRIND the tool. Instead, you're simply trying to dress the bevel.

I emphasize *practice* because, from working with students since the mid-1970s, it's clear most beginner-level turners don't really understand what it means. Practice is much more than just standing at the grinder repeating the same motion. In fact, that's a great way to learn just about nothing except how to grind away your tool. It is easy to practice poor sharpening techniques without realizing it. You could have the wrong stance, the grinder at the wrong height, or your feet too close together, which all are going to create areas of tension within the body that translate directly into a poorly shaped or multifaceted edge.

Four common problems resulting from tension

Problem	Result	Solution
Overgrinding and overheating from too much pressure of the tool against the wheel.	A waste of your energy and money for both tools and wheels.	Approach the grinder not to grind the tool, but to sharpen or dress the bevel.
Multiple facets on the bevel.	Uneven cutting on the surface of the wood.	Use smooth and fluid movements while sharpening. Take care not to linger in any areas.
Misshaped tip.	A tool that doesn't work, which creates additional tension.	Return to basics by referring to the photos of the tip to understand any problems in shape. Correct where needed.
Slipping off the face of the grinding wheel.	Grinding the face of a sharpening jig if you're lucky, or grinding your fingers right down through the tendons if you're unlucky! Very dangerous.	Breathe, relax, and sharpen in a fluid, even movement.

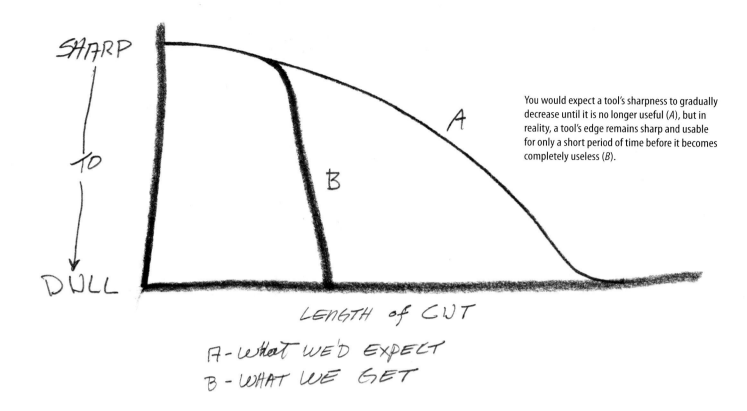

SHARP

↓

TO

↓

DULL

A

B

LENGTH of CUT

A - WHAT WE'D EXPECT
B - WHAT WE GET

You would expect a tool's sharpness to gradually decrease until it is no longer useful (*A*), but in reality, a tool's edge remains sharp and usable for only a short period of time before it becomes completely useless (*B*).

Body tension

Nearly *all* accidents on the grinder are directly related to having too much tension in the body. Tension comes from being nervous, and nervousness comes from a lack of experience. Accidents on the grinder can be as simple as pushing too hard against the face of the wheel so that the gouge slips off and a big V is cut on the gouge from the corner of the wheel. Worse—and it's only a millimeter away—you slip a little farther and scrape the top of your knuckles. Worse yet, you keep slipping and run a finger or two below the wheel, sucking it down between the wheel and the wheel guard, taking a lot of skin off. My point is, it's worth learning how to relax when grinding a tool. The chart at left describes four common examples of how tension manifests at the grinder.

The curve of sharp

Before I go further, let me first address a few more elements that relate to this general question: What is sharp?

It would be wonderful if tools dulled over a long period, as seen in the illustration above (*A*). You would have greater use of the tool's edge over a longer period before it needed to be resharpened. Unfortunately, such is not the case. Instead, the edge is efficient for a short period of time—the usable zone—and suddenly goes over the hump and becomes useless (*B*). The difficulty most turners have is they get so wrapped up in turning that they continue trying to cut with a useless tool, even when it's obvious nothing productive is happening. It is a paradox because no one would tolerate the pain of continuing to shave with a dull razor. And yet, although you can almost hear the wood saying, "Please, go sharpen the tool," most turners continue anyway.

Honed edge versus burr edge

To hone or not to hone? That is a good question and seems to be one of the more intriguing, lingering controversies in turning. Let me try to unravel some of the controversy. Any time a turning tool is sharpened on a grinding wheel, a burr is formed on the edge that corresponds to the size of the grit of the wheel used. Under magnification, this burr can look like anything from miniature saw teeth to the bicuspids of a hungry bear. Honing is a rather simple method of removing this burr in order to create a smoother edge, and is done by stroking the edge with either a whetstone or a diamond file. A honed edge cuts better than a nonhoned edge, which is why the American cowboy preferred his hot suds and a honed razor over a Bowie knife, except, perhaps in the movies. The problem is you don't get much durability out of a honed edge. Abrasion, heat from the spinning wood, and lack of mass behind the edge are the primary problems. That is why you must constantly hone both a razor and a skew to make them work properly.

Furniture makers have always honed their plane blades. It was natural for turners to hone their tools as well, especially their skews and spindle gouges. The bowl gouge, however, is different. Referring to page 24 in Chapter 3, you'll clearly see the cross section of a bowl gouge's edge is broader than that of a skew or a spindle gouge. This gives the bowl gouge a more durable edge, while sacrificing some sharpness as compared with the skew and the spindle gouge. The bowl gouge needs extra durability because it cuts into both end grain and face grain with each revolution of the wood. Skews and spindle gouges only need to cut across the fibers of the face grain when shaping a spindle.

Basically, a bowl gouge is not a skew, so it may be unnecessary to treat it with the same attention as the skew. After all, you don't hone your scrapers or parting tools. You either give them a burr edge or use them straight off the grinder. What would happen if you sharpened your gouge and your skew with a 60-grit wheel instead of a 120-grit wheel? If you honed the edges, wouldn't it produce a different kind of edge? Absolutely. I suspect the edge off the 60-grit wheel would be pretty coarse even if it were honed.

When it comes to the tools you use, one size does not necessarily fit all. So the question of whether you should hone your bowl gouges might be better stated this way: Which edge will perform better for the job you need to do?

With my work, I use the burr. However, I am using 100- to 120-grit aluminum-oxide grinding wheels, so I'm producing a very tiny burr in order to get a very clean surface on the wood. A 60-grit wheel produces a large burr that is quickly knocked off, leaving behind a jagged edge that causes streaks in the wood. A 60-grit edge without a burr also loads up with dust and stalls the cut on the wood. Similarly, a honed edge burnishes very quickly and leaves me with nothing to work with.

I have also learned that without the burr, I can't perform the shear-scraping cut—the most important finish cut I use before sanding. The burr edge will wear to a burnished surface just as the honed edge will. But the tiny burr I use tends to last longer than a honed edge.

I also turn a lot of spalted wood, which has black zone lines that simply whack the edge right off any tool, honed or not. My answer is to line up five or six freshly sharpened gouges on the bed of the lathe and take a finish cut of no more than 1" to 2" along the surface with each gouge, blending the areas together as I go. If I try to cut more, the zone lines burnish the edge so quickly I end up tearing the fibers instead of cutting them.

So am I saying you should no longer hone your bowl gouges? No. I'm suggesting we work with an enormous variety of new technologies that were not available to traditional turners of the last century, including harder and more durable steels, new tool designs, and new cutting approaches. We need to be more flexible in our acceptance of new concepts and discover what works best.

Diagnosing dullness

How do you tell when a tool is getting dull? The simple answer is that either the tool stops cutting or you find yourself pushing the tool harder than necessary into the wood. In softer woods, a dull edge tears up the fibers. In most situations, the tool vibrates very slightly on the surface of the wood. A tool even slightly less than sharp no longer cuts the end-grain fibers as efficiently as it can the face-grain fibers. The result is end-grain fibers cause the edge of the tool to bounce off of them.

How can you test the edge for sharpness *before* you commit to making a cut? Simple: Sharpen one side of the tool. Carefully stroke both sides with the thumb in the same direction to compare and learn to feel the difference. Just be careful.

Grinders and grinding wheels

In my workshop, I use standard 8" grinders with 80-grit aluminum-oxide wheels for coarse work, and 100- to 120-grit wheels for my Signature gouge and hollowing turning tips. These wheels are designed for use with the harder steels found in modern turning tools. Don't use silicone carbide wheels, which often come mounted on grinders, because they are meant for softer metals like bronze and aluminum, and even for plastics.

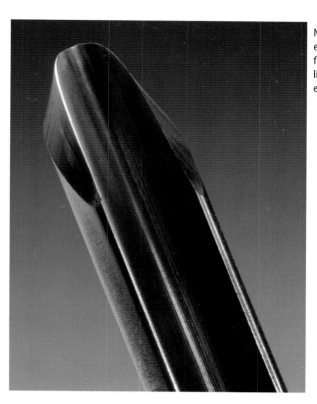

Notice how the dull edge on the left has a flat surface that reflects light, while the right edge is sharp and thin.

There are several types of grinding wheels on the market today. They come in various colors, and with various grits from around 40 to 120. Color designates the type of grit used. Green is silicon carbide; white, pink, ruby, and light gray are aluminum oxide; dark gray is carborundum; and blue is ceramic. The grit numbers refer to the size of the grit: 60 grit being very coarse and 120 grit being very fine. And then, there are the letter ratings—G, H, J, K, and L (I don't know what happened to I)—that indicate the hardness of the bonding agents used to hold all that grit together. Figuring out what kind of wheel to get can be confusing.

In general, the softer the wheel (the lower letters), the cooler it cuts—meaning it causes less friction—and the faster it wears out. The finer the grit (the higher numbers), the smaller the burr that forms on the edge of the tool. If you do a lot of grinding and reshaping of various types of steel, you might prefer a higher-speed grinder (think 3,450 rpm) with a coarser-grit wheel—or better yet, a variable- or two-speed grinder so you can do it all. Most turners I know today have gone to an 8"-diameter wheel. This is because 8" wheels have more surface area, so you can get more use out of them.

Key to SKETCH: CUTTING GRAIN

ROOT STUMP
DIRECTIONAL LINES of GRAIN
HURRICANE
ROTATION
ROUGH WATER
EASY SAILING
SUPER SMOOTH

If the tool you are using is dull, you will find the entire turning experience a little rough. The end-grain area, especially, will be very difficult to cut.

Many people are afraid of burning their tools on higher-speed grinders. Heat is obviously an important factor when sharpening, as overheating or "burning" a tool will cause it to lose its temper and, thus, its ability to properly hold an edge. Because the metal in our turning tools comes with different alloys and in different compositions, the acceptable heat range for each tool is different. Traditional turning tools were high in carbon and had a very low heat range or burning point. Too much pressure on the grinding wheel would easily turn the edge blue or red, so it was common to frequently cool the tip in water while grinding. Most modern turning tools use high-speed steel (HSS), which incorporates many alloys that both harden the steel and push that burning point very high—and dunking a red-hot HSS tool in water can cause the tool to fracture internally. You can blue these modern tools on the grinder and only reach around 750° F, while the heat required to exceed the temper is in the range of 1,400° F. My experience is that a hair more pressure on the grinding wheel will jump the temperature quickly from the blue color to the red range, so care must always be taken not to over-grind any tool. Prudence and a more thoughtful approach to the entire grinding process will solve all these overheating problems.

> "Practicing is much more than just standing at the grinder repeating the same motion."

And finally, professional turners often have their favorite type and style of grinding wheel, and they rarely agree on one. That is of little help to beginning turners trying to set up shop on a budget. My suggestion is not to buy on recommendation, but go to a couple of trade shows or woodturning conferences and try various wheels until you find ones you like and fit your grinding needs.

Note: Before beginning any grinding, be sure your wheels are properly balanced and dressed. If there is any vibration in the grinder, or if the face of the wheel is full of grit, nothing good will come of it.

The basic sharpening stance

Approaching the grinding process without fear or intimidation is extremely important. Equally vital is how you stand, how you hold the tool, where your head is located, and how your body and hands move. Follow the description to learn the basic sharpening stance. Once you master it, you will be able to hand sharpen any turning tool.

The first step is to turn the grinder OFF and set the tool on the bench. Then, place your feet slightly wider than shoulder-width apart. Put your hands on your thighs and unlock your knees so they can flex easily (see photo at near right top). Keeping your feet stationary, rotate your body to the left until the line of your shoulders is 90° to the bench—on the same plane as the wheel (see photo at center right top). Continue this rotation equally to the right, always moving in slow motion so you can feel the effects of any tension building in the legs, feet, or hips (see photo at far right top). Close your eyes and repeat this movement in slow motion through several more rotations. With your eyes closed, focus on your body—your toes, your calves, your knees—so you become acquainted with how these movements feel. If you feel any muscles binding up, reposition your feet until you learn to relax those muscles. Learning how and where to place your feet through this movement is a way of establishing a base of support from which all of your grinding and turning activities begin. This is also a way to learn how to get comfortable and build confidence *before* you grab a tool.

Grab a tool to be sharpened and bring the tool to the grinder. With your feet spread and the machine turned off, pretend you are going to grind the tool. Notice the position of your head in relation to the grinding wheel. If your head is dipped so much you can see the bevel making contact with the face of the wheel, you will soon get a stiff neck and overgrind the tool. Any time your body is out of balance, you overcompensate with additional muscle. The result is you no longer move gracefully and put too much pressure on the tool against the wheel. Instead, raise

The basic sharpening stance

In order to sharpen properly, it is helpful to have an understanding of the basic stance to use while sharpening. Take a look at the stance I'm using in the photos below.

With your feet slightly more than shoulder-width apart, unlock your knees, and place your hands on your thighs.

Rotate your body to the left so your shoulders are perpendicular to the bench and parallel with the wheel.

Rotate your body to the right, moving slowly and relaxing any tension that you feel in your muscles.

Do not bend down so far that you can see the bevel being sharpened. You will get a stiff neck and overgrind the tool.

If you are standing properly at the sharpening wheel, your head should be raised and you should only be able to see the top of the tool.

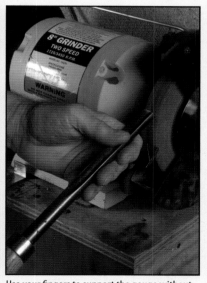

Use your fingers to support the gouge without gripping it. Use only the weight of the tool against the wheel to avoid overheating the tip.

Rest the handle against the side of your leg. Hold the end of the handle with just the tips of your fingers and gently rotate the handle evenly left and right. This will sharpen the gouge evenly on both sides of the tip.

> "The difficulty most turners have is they get so wrapped up in the turning process that they continue trying to cut with a useless tool even when it's obvious nothing productive is happening."

your head and stand more vertically so you can see *only* the top of the tool rather than the bevel against the face of the wheel. In a more vertical position, you can flex your knees and become more fluid in your movements while grinding. When I'm dressing the bevel to sharpen a gouge, I can't see the bevel making contact with the wheel. But I know that I've reached a sharpened edge when I see sparks coming over the edge and running down the flute.

With your hand on the tool rest and the tool through your fingers, only the tool's weight should be against the wheel. Don't grab the tool. It will only put tension in this hand. I use the tips of my fingers and thumb, not my full hand, to hold the end of the handle. In this position, I can fully rotate the tool equally from left to right. I then rest this hand on my leg at a height that gives me the desired angle of the bevel against the wheel. In effect, I turn myself into a sharpening jig so I can make equal cuts in all areas of the bevel without experiencing body stress. You can adjust the height of your hand on your knee to get the desired angle on the bevel. Spindle gouges ride higher on the wheel, so that would put your back hand lower on your leg. You would raise your back hand a bit to sharpen deep-fluted bowl gouges, and a lot for the 85° gouge described in Chapter 3 on page 32.

I consider the stance described above to be a basic sharpening position. From here, you can modify your feet and hands as needed to sharpen other tools, like skews and parting tools. Address the grinder with your head up and your torso erect. With a slight amount of flex in your legs, you can relax throughout the grinding process. Don't worry about not being able to see the bevel flush against the wheel. By delicately rotating the gouge through the full motion

left and right, you can easily see the bevel as it rises on either side through this rotation.

When sharpening a tool, there are a few processes worth practicing before you get started. Leave the grinder off, position your body comfortably, support the tool firmly but lightly in your hands, close your eyes, and begin rotating the tool with your fingertips. You are practicing the fluid motion of the movement of the tool with your hands, and how your entire body moves as a unit to support you through the grinding process. You can easily learn the movement with your eyes closed, because there are no distractions. When you do open your eyes and turn on the grinder, continue to focus on the movements and avoid letting the distractions of noise and sparks take over.

If you feel any tension building in your body, shut the grinder off, close your eyes, practice the movement again, and make adjustments. The problem will usually be in your feet, but it might also be you've dropped your head to see what you're doing. This is a natural instinct, but also a total distraction to your progress. You don't need to see it. Learn to feel it.

Finally, check your grinder's height, as it might be too low or too high on the bench. Different professional turners have different preferences for grinder height. We're all built differently. A standard cabinet height for your bench might not be the right height for you. A spindle turner and a hollow vessel turner do things differently, so there's no reason to think they need a grinder at the same height. If there were a magic measurement for grinder height, it would be wrong for half of us. What you're looking for is your own comfort zone. Spread your feet wider to drop your body a few inches, or you could stand on a couple of my books and raise yourself up. Whatever feels good is what works for you.

Sharpening individual tools

Here are some suggestions on sharpening the tools I use, with emphasis on discovering and dispelling some body tensions that make sharpening difficult. These methods are best practiced individually to understand what is actually happening in the body, muscle by muscle. Once the methods are linked, you should have a more relaxing and efficient experience at the grinder.

Conventional bowl and spindle gouges

Conventional gouges can be sharpened with one of the many grinding jigs available on the market today. If you're just starting out and don't have or don't want all the gizmos and gadgets, don't panic. All tools can be sharpened by hand using the basic sharpening stance. Using a grinding jig does not mean you can't mess up the grind on your tool. You can. The important thing is to understand what the tool should look like before you begin. If it starts to look strange, you'll know it's time to back up and solve the problem.

The ⅜" detail gouge

You can make a ⅜" detail gouge from any ⅜"-diameter spindle gouge except a deep-fluted bowl gouge, because it simply won't work.

Round out the existing bevel by positioning the gouge perpendicularly to the plane of the wheel so the side of the tip touches the face of the wheel. Point the flute straight up, and beginning with the edge, roll the gouge *away* from the edge. Repeat until you have a nicely shaped convex bevel on half of the gouge tip. Reverse the direction of the gouge and repeat the process. Be sure that the flute is pointing up so you will be cutting *away* from the edge. If you start on the bevel and work toward the edge, you'll over-grind the edge and end up regrinding the whole tool, which can take as much as ¼" off the end.

Balance the shape on both sides, then switch to a 150-grit sanding wheel to even out the facets. Move on to 400 grit to polish the surface. This surface will prevent resins from the wood packing against the bevel. To maintain the edge, I use a round diamond hone inside the flute. Do not roll the edge over, or you'll need to regrind the entire tip.

Making the ⅜" detail gouge

You can create a ⅜" detail gouge from most gouges. In order to convert a gouge to a ⅜" detail gouge, it is important to round out the existing bevel.

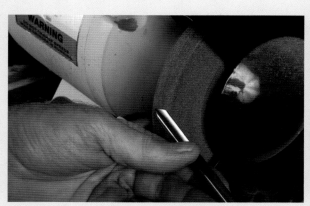

Place the gouge, with its flute upward, perpendicular to the wheel plane. Touch the side of the tip to the wheel and roll it away from the edge, not toward it to prevent overgrinding the edge.

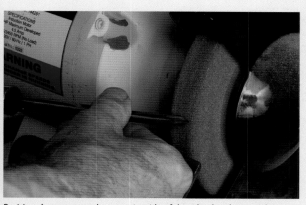

Position the gouge on the opposite side of the wheel and repeat the grinding process. Be sure to begin with the flute pointing upward.

The top view of a properly sharpened ⅜" detail gouge will appear balanced (top), while a malformed tip will appear unbalanced (bottom).

The Ellsworth Signature gouge

This versatile tool used to be a pain in the neck to sharpen because there is much more edge to sharpen than with a conventional gouge and because it goes through so many changes of angle from one side to the other. It requires a lot of extra body movement to reach all areas of the edge. So, to all my students over all those early years who endured my lessons on sharpening this tool, I do apologize. At least they got a firm understanding of the hand-sharpening process, because if you can sharpen this tool by hand, you can sharpen anything.

That's why I came up with the Ellsworth Signature gouge sharpening jig, which makes the process a pleasure. I use it all the time, both in my own workspace and when I'm on the road. It gives me a perfect shape every time and takes only a micro amount of steel off the tool. Looking back at the way I used to sharpen it—by hand—I can see I favored the right side slightly more than the left. The result was I had to occasionally cut off a lot of steel to get the tip back in balance. It was a good lesson that I was still using too much pressure against the wheel.

To satisfy the needs of both hand sharpeners and jig sharpeners, I've included some methods on both sides of the fence so you can sharpen the tool and begin having fun with it. I love all of the controversy about how "real" woodturners learn how to sharpen by hand instead of relying on a jig, which reminds me of the old days when "real" woodturners only used scrapers, while the other "real" woodturners only used gouges. Personal preference should take the reins. Use the method that helps you build confidence so you can get on with why you opened the cover of this book: to learn to turn wood.

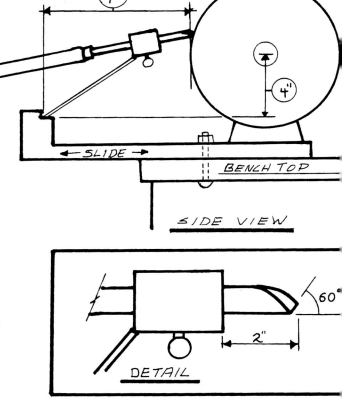

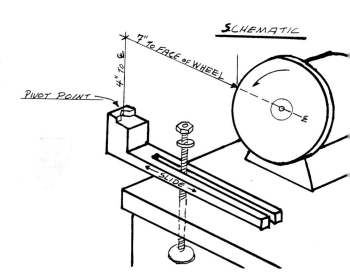

To set up the Signature gouge jig, make sure your pivot point (where the jig's stem rests) is 7" from the face of the wheel horizontally and 4" from the center of the wheel vertically. Whatever you use for your pivot point should be movable, as the diameter of the wheel will change with use.

To sharpen the Signature gouge by hand:
Follow the step-by-step closely and make sure you understand the steps below.

Holding the gouge with the flute pointed up and the bevel's right side against the wheel's face, position your head to the *left* of the wheel so you can see directly across the face. What you're looking for is flush contact between the bevel on the tip of the tool and the wheel's face. Next, hold the gouge lightly with both hands, and rotate it until you reach the tip and lift the tool off the wheel. Repeat this motion for the left side of the gouge, always lifting the tip away from the wheel at the end of the cut. If needed, stand in front of the grinder and blend the two sides of the gouge at the tip area.

To sharpen the Signature gouge with the jig: The pivot point must be set 4" below the centerline of the wheel, 7" from the face of the wheel (measured on a vertical plane), and the tip of the gouge must be projecting 2" from the jig's front surface. I prefer to work with a 60° angle on the end of the tool, but between 55° and 65° will work, too. A sharper edge with less bevel exposed requires 55°, while a 65° angle will give more bevel exposure for deeper open bowls with only a slight reduction in sharpness. The length of the sides of the bevel depends on personal preference. Anything from ¾" to 1⅛" long will work. Be aware the longer the edge, the more likely it is the sides will become flat or concave instead of convex. Unless you are using the side of the gouge as a scraper, there is really no advantage in having it longer than 1⅛". I generally work at about 1".

Stand slightly to the side of the grinder instead of straight in front of it as you would with a conventional gouge. Then, identify the 2" extension of the gouge tip beyond the front of the jig and tighten the set screw.

Hold the jig with the fingertips of *both* hands, as shown at right. Do **not** hold the shaft or the handle of the gouge. Let the jig do its job of flailing the gouge back and forth where it needs to go. If you do hold the gouge, tension will build in your hands and you

Sharpening the Signature gouge by hand

Though I usually sharpen my Signature gouge with a jig, it is possible to sharpen it by hand. Try following these steps to do so. Note: I have shown why watching the bevel could be a mistake, but in this case, it is important to ensure flush contact with the wheel.

Hold the gouge with the flute pointed up and your head to the left of the wheel. This way, you can see flush contact between the bevel and the face of the wheel.

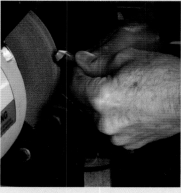

Start at the edge of the tip and rotate toward the center. Be sure to maintain flush contact between the bevel and the wheel.

Rotate the gouge toward the tip and be sure to lift the tool off the wheel when you reach the center of the tip.

will overgrind the sides of the tool. In the sequence on page 59, notice I am holding the jig equally with both fingertips, giving me an equal amount of pressure against the wheel on both the left and right sides of the gouge. With the machine turned off, place the lower part of the long edge of either side of the gouge against the face of the grinder and rotate the tool up with a sweeping motion toward the tip. Pull the tip away from the wheel and shift to the other side of the tool and repeat this process. Always lift the gouge away from the wheel when you reach the tip, because you do not want to overgrind it.

Practice the process repeatedly until you can keep the gouge in the center of the wheel when stroking both sides of the tip. If you slide off either edge of the wheel while the machine is running, nasty things will happen to the gouge, the jig, and possibly to your hand. When you feel comfortable, close your eyes and repeat these movements. Again, go very slowly so you can feel any body tension that would prevent a fluid sweeping motion. If tension occurs, open your eyes and figure out how to correct the problem. It will generally be with the feet being too close together, or the knees being locked, or—most often—the hands having a death grip on the jig. Figure out ways to relax, and don't hurry.

When you turn on the grinder, focus on the movement of your hands, wrists, and legs. With some practice, and using only your fingertips to support the jig, you will be able to cover both sides of the gouge without moving your shoulders or head. With practice, you will be able to sweep from the bottom of one side and down the other in one fluid motion.

Tips and trouble spots

The tip of the Ellsworth Signature gouge should be shaped with a nice even radius with slightly arched or convex sides. Grinding the tip too much will produce a recess, which will form wings on either side, and you won't be able to safely enter the rim of a bowl or perform interior-finishing cuts.

Grinding too much on the sides will drop the edge from a convex shape to concave, producing wings just behind the tip and you won't have an edge available to do the exterior shear-scraping cut. I recommend working from the base of the edge up to the tip because it is easy to overgrind the sides of the edge if you begin with the tip and work down to the base of the edge. Turners often get nervous, their bodies get out of balance, or they simply can't see what they're doing. As a result, they linger in one area of the tip and end up overgrinding.

If high wings do appear, knock them down by stroking *only* the wings on the grinding wheel to avoid overgrinding the adjacent areas of the edge. Once the wings are gone, gently sweep the entire tip again to even everything out.

All of these elements are important to get the full functional use of the tool, but you can avoid problems by paying attention to pictures of the tip shape in this book so you'll know what it's supposed to look like. The nice thing is any change to the tip shape will generally occur very slowly, not all at once. So if you do see something going amiss, it is important to discover the reason behind the problem before it gets so out of whack that you have to reshape the entire tip of the gouge.

A properly sharpened Signature gouge will have an even radius on the end of the tip and slightly convex sides.

An improperly sharpened Signature gouge could have wings on it that will cut unsafely.

Sharpening the Signature gouge with the jig

Using the jig is another option for sharpening the Signature gouge. Try following these steps to see how I do it.

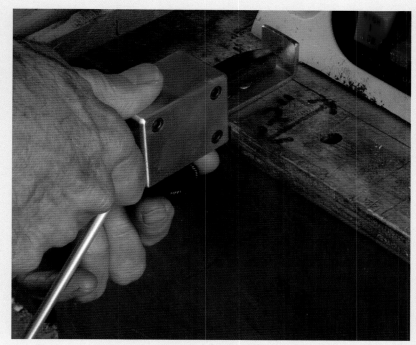

Make sure the tip of the gouge extends 2" in front of the face of the jig. To make this measurement consistent, I have used an L-shaped piece of metal cut from an angle bracket and attached to my workbench as pictured.

Another method is to drill a 2"-deep hole into the edge of your workbench and glue a nickel in the back as a stop for the gouge... whatever works for you.

Hold the jig gently with just your fingertips. Try to avoid a death grip on the jig because it will give uneven pressure on the gouge.

With the grinder turned off, practice moving the gouge against the face of the wheel, starting on either lower end of the bevel and moving toward the tip.

Move to the other side of the bevel and sweep it toward the tip. Be sure not to linger on the tip, or you will overgrind it.

Sharpening a parting tool

When sharpening a parting tool, I find it helpful to create a concave shape to the upper part of the tip and a convex shape to the lower area.

The side view of a properly sharpened parting tool, as presented to the wood, will have a concave surface above the tip and a convex surface below the tip.

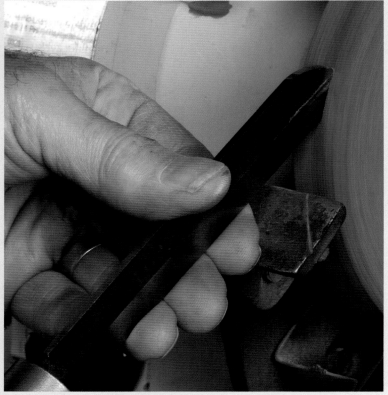

To create the concave surface on the parting tool tip, hold the edge lightly to the radius of the wheel.

When shaping the convex surface, lower the handle slightly to ride up the face of the wheel.

The parting tool

This parting tool is used horizontally, with the concave surface positioned up and the convex surface down. Sharpening a parting tool requires positioning the shaft vertically and bringing the upper and lower areas of the tip to the wheel to sharpen. Using either a 6"- or 8"-diameter wheel makes little difference with parting tools, as the radius of the concave surface is not critical to how the tool performs on wood.

With the tool held upside down, form the concave surface by holding that surface lightly to the surface of the wheel. To shape the lower convex surface, ride the tip up the face of the wheel. Start with the surface just below the tip and lower the handle to move the surface up the face.

Use a diamond wheel dresser to put a slight radius on both corners of a 100- to 120-grit wheel.

Hollowing tools

The straight boring bars and bent tools I use for hollowing my forms are scraping tools with ¼" and ³⁄₁₆" square cutters, respectively. Sharpening the straight and bent hollowing tools are very similar processes: I place a round nose shape on the tip of the cutters and cut the angle of the bevel back to approximately 20° to 25°. Sharpening the small cutting edges can be difficult because the tools themselves are usually large and unwieldy, making

it easy to over-grind the tips. Here's what I do to simplify the process.

Using a diamond wheel dresser, I cut a slight radius using both the right and left corners of a 100- to 120-grit wheel. I find the finer grit raises an ideally sized burr on the tool tips that lasts a long time. It is possible to hone these tips if you use a diamond hone on them between sharpenings on the wheel.

To sharpen the left side of a bent tool tip, keep the tip pointed parallel to the plane of the wheel and touch the tip to the right corner of the wheel.

To sharpen the right side of a bent tool tip, touch the tip to the left corner of the wheel while keeping the tip parallel to the plane of the wheel.

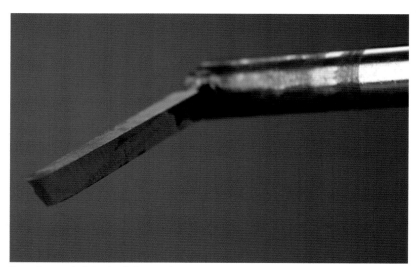

If you sharpen the left side of a bent tool tip further up the side—possibly even to the joint with the shaft—you will be able to cut the surface right under the top of a hollow form.

To sharpen a straight boring bar with a ¼" square, 10% cobalt high-speed steel tip, follow the description below. The directions I give are for right-handed turners. If you are left-handed, reverse the directions.

Hold the handle on your thigh with your right hand. Place your left hand on the tool rest and support the shaft of the tool with the fingers and thumb. Be careful to only use your fingertips to hold the shaft and not to grip the shaft, or you'll put too much tension in your hand and overgrind the tip. Position the tip so it is parallel to the plane of the wheel, then bring the side of the tip to the right corner of the wheel. Rotate the handle slightly clockwise a few degrees so you'll put a slope on the side of the tip. Pull and push the left side of the tip very delicately over the right corner of the wheel (see photo at top). Repeat on the left corner of the wheel to sharpen the right side (see photo at center). Rotate the handle a few degrees counterclockwise to produce a slight slope on the right side of the tip. Avoid touching the tip to the face of the wheel, because it will grind a flat spot that will interrupt the flow of the curve.

To sharpen a bent tool with a ³⁄₁₆" square, 10% cobalt high-speed steel tip, review the concepts covered for sharpening the straight hollowing tool—the steps are very similar.

The only difference is you place the handle of the tool on the left side of your body and hold the shaft with your right hand. Then, as you would with a straight tool, point the tip parallel with the plane of the wheel and work on the left and right corners of the wheel to get an even grind on both sides of the tip. Be sure to rotate the handle a few degrees left and right to give a slight slope to both sides of the tip. As with the straight tool, avoid touching the tip to the face of the wheel.

On some bent tools, you may wish to sharpen the left side of the tip further up, possibly all the way to the joint with the shaft (see bottom photo). This allows you to cut and smooth the surface directly under the top of a hollow form and around the inside of the entrance hole.

Sharpening a straight boring bar

Sharpening a straight boring bar as I do utilizes both sides of the grinding wheel. Try to keep each side of the tool parallel to the grinder sides.

Use both left and right edges of the grinding wheel to sharpen the tip of the straight boring bar.

Use the right corner of the wheel to sharpen the left side of the tip by gently pulling and pushing.

Use the left corner of the wheel to sharpen the right side of the tip, making sure to rotate the handle slightly counterclockwise to cut a gentle slope on the tip.

Chapter 6

Chucks, Glue Blocks & Faceplates

In a lecture at the Minneapolis Institute of Art in 2001, turner and sculptor Mark Lindquist said, "the most important technological achievement in woodturning since the mid-1980s has been that we've finally learned how to attach the wood to the lathe." I totally agree, and anyone who has turned objects in excess of 50 pounds will know exactly what I mean. Why the mid-1980s? That's when New Zealand's Teknatool, creator of Nova tools, first came out with a four-jaw chuck with circular jaws that would safely hold a bowl blank. Before that, we had only glue blocks, faceplates, and a few screw chucks. If we were really lucky, we might find an old three- or four-jaw chuck from a metal lathe lying around. The problem was that the chucks were designed to grab metal, not wood, and if we took too deep of a cut or caught the edge of a tool, an airborne event followed that only a Frisbee player could fully appreciate.

Glue blocks (left), four-jaw chucks (middle), and faceplates (right) are the three primary methods of attaching your block to the lathe for turning.

Today, we have a full complement of chucks, glue blocks, and faceplates, which brings up this question: When do we use which method of securing an object to the lathe, and why? I'll soon give some examples. I always have tried to impress upon my students that there are advantages *and* disadvantages to every tool and mechanical gizmo we use in woodturning. That could not be truer or more important than when it comes to the devices we use for properly securing objects to the lathe. The alternative is the wood will fly off and smash whatever is in its way—your foot, a window, a spectator...you get the idea. There is another interesting aspect about these attachment devices that may not be so obvious: Because each device has its own particular limits, we can often become limited by what they will or won't do for us. The growth in your woodturning experiences may very well be stalled if you get stuck using only one of the devices available to you. Use them all! That way, there are no limits to your personal growth.

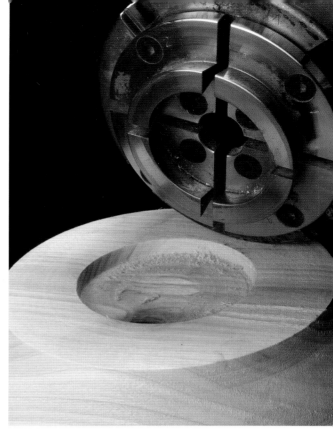

In addition to being capable of grabbing a chunk of wood *inside* its jaws, a chuck can be expanded into a recessed hole in a bowl blank to hold the blank with the *outside* of its jaws.

Modern mechanical chucks have jaws that function somewhat like fingers to grab objects. The jaws are either tightened around a spigot—a chunk of wood protruding from the blank—or expanded into a hollow created in the wood for that purpose. There are many sizes of four-jaw chucks available.

Chucks

I'll begin with a discussion on chucks, because they have opened up an eight-lane freeway of new ideas for what woodturners can make. Chucks grab objects by tightening the jaws down onto a spigot or by expanding them into a drilled or turned cavity. Chucks are relatively safe and easy to use, so it's a wonder turners didn't discover them sooner. The metal industry has been using chucks for decades, plus we do have two hands with fingers on them that are pretty well designed for grabbing stuff and operate similarly to a chuck. I guess we just weren't looking in the right places.

Pros of the chuck

Chucks are versatile. With a little modification to the blocks you wish to turn, such as cutting a hole into the bottom of a thin plank or turning a spigot on the base of a bowl blank, you can now turn a variety of platters, bowls, and hollow forms without annoying screw holes or glue lines. Chucks even allow you to safely grab the end of a long piece of square stock and turn a candleholder, a wine goblet, or a pool cue.

Cons of the chuck

The downside of using chucks comes when the objects you make start getting bigger and taller, and especially when they're made from green or spalted wood.

The first problem with a chuck is any time you make cuts at any distance from the headstock, you introduce the potential for vibration. Vibration not only causes poor-quality cuts on the wood, but it can whip the piece right out of the chuck and into your body, face, or head. Imagine trying to turn an 18"-long spindle held with a chuck with no tailstock for support, and you get my point. Similarly, most larger chucks made today are approximately 2½" tall, which means the foot of *any* object you're turning is now 2½" away from the mass of the headstock. Any time you begin to lose support from the mass of the headstock, vibration will occur.

The problem in working with green wood is not a design flaw of the chucks themselves. The jaws are clamping down on a spigot composed of elastic green fibers. In effect, the jaws from the chuck not only crush these fibers, but they also crush them more in the softer face-grain areas than in the denser end-grain areas. The result is objects can come loose in the chuck while you're working on them or get thrown completely out of the chuck. Clamping down tighter on the jaws usually throws the object slightly off-center. Because of their soft fibers, many spalted woods are almost impossible to hold with a chuck.

Incorrect spigot length can be an issue. Be sure the front surface of the chuck jaws reaches the bottom surface of the blank. If the spigot is too high, the chuck will not be secure, and the spigot could snap off. It's easy to snap a spigot right off if you make it too small in diameter for the weight and size of the work piece. This can happen just as easily with dry wood, so common sense and caution need to be applied with *every* piece you put into a chuck.

Here are some solutions for these problems: tighten the chuck frequently; cut a larger-diameter spigot; support the object with the live tailstock center as long as possible; and take it easy with when using a gouge...especially my Signature gouge.

A chuck can easily and securely grab a spigot like this one.

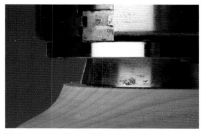
Make sure the front of the chuck is flush with the base of the blank.

Beware: If you cut the spigot too long, the front surface of the chuck jaws will not reach the bottom surface of the blank.

Mounting a piece in a chuck

In preparation for using a chuck, I use the gouge tip to make two slicing cuts in the base of the form. The first cut establishes the diameter and height of the spigot. For most chuck designs, the cut needs to be finished off with a 90° inside corner. If I use a chuck with dovetail-shaped jaws, I use a pointed scraper or a tiny-tipped gouge to cut a taper on the spigot's slope. A skew laid flat on the tool rest works great, too. The second cut is the base cut. Lastly, position the spigot in the chuck so the chuck is flush with the base cut. Tighten the chuck.

I use a gouge to make the spigot on the base of the form in preparation for mounting in a four-jaw chuck.

Glue blocks

Glue blocks date back...well...to when glue was invented. As I recall, everything we turned in my high-school shop class was done with glue blocks. We'd lather up a bunch of maple, oak, and walnut boards with Elmer's Glue, and then stick a piece of plywood on the bottom, with some butcher paper in between. The paper was there so we could split the joint later with a mallet and chisel. Of course, being boys, we'd tighten the clamps with a lot of boy force, meaning we starved the joints by squeezing out most of the glue. Then we'd screw one of those skinny little 3"-diameter pot-metal faceplates onto the glue block, and finally, checking the lathe to make sure the guy before us hadn't "accidentally" turned the speed up to max, we'd hit the switch.

In most cases, everything worked fine...which means the starved glue joints didn't open up, the three skinny little wood screws holding the faceplate didn't rip out of the glue block, the glue block didn't split apart, and somehow...somehow...we remembered to ram the tailstock point against the whole thing so that when we jammed that big old scraper into the end-grain fibers, the block didn't take off like a rocket looking for a plate-glass window. In the end, assuming we were able to complete the bowl as planned, we'd go ruin a good sanding disc trying to get all that glue and paper off the bottom of the bowl.

The hazards I described are as serious today as they ever were. The way we now use glue blocks makes them supersafe and superefficient for holding a range of objects to the lathe. A variety of pieces can be created with a glue block, thanks to superglue (cyanoacrylate), without which we'd still be boy-forcing those clamps and starving the glue joints.

> "Glue blocks are the perfect choice when using spalted wood, because the entire glued surface becomes a uniform driving surface for the object."

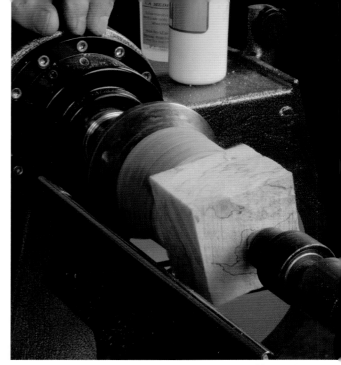

Glue blocks are useful for securely holding materials that wouldn't work well with chucks or faceplates, such as green wood, spalted wood, and exotic materials that you wouldn't want to crush or put holes in.

Pros of the glue block

Consider first what you can make with glue blocks. It is possible to turn very tiny objects—like my miniature hollow forms—with a chuck or a single-screw faceplate holding the glue block. Glue blocks are perfect for spalted wood because the entire glued surface becomes a uniform driving surface for the object. And think of those superexpensive materials you don't want to drill holes into, or exotic materials such as alabaster, bone, and acrylics. All of the green woods—some so fresh they're dripping wet—can be easily stuck to a dry glue block with superglue and be ready for roughing-out in thirty seconds.

Oh, yes. I forgot the part about gumming up the sanding disc when finishing off the bottom of your bowl. There has never been a good way to hold the bottom of a bowl steady enough against a sander to get it flat. The bowl always leans to one side. Instead, cut down on the diameter of the glue joint with a parting tool, snap or chisel the object off after you've turned off the lathe, and then mount it in reverse direction on a jam chuck and turn off the rest of the glue joint. Or, support the object with a jam chuck and cut the entire glue block away...including the glue joint (see Chapter 14, "Jam Chucks & Vacuum Chucks," on page 190).

Cons of the glue block

There are two cautions to observe while using a glue block. First, be cautious when using superglue: Smelling the stuff when used with accelerator increases heart rate, often dramatically. It can also cause headaches, dizziness, and lethargy, which can become very severe with prolonged usage. I have become so sensitive to superglue that I can't even walk by an opened bottle of the accelerator without taking an involuntary detour. So the answer is... CAUTION! Ventilate. Use exhaust fans. Do whatever needs to be done to protect yourself, including *not* sniffing the cloud of chemical smoke that drifts up from the wood's surface when filling cracks or voids.

Another hazard you want to avoid is using plywood or other cheap woods for your glue blocks. Plywood is designed to separate, and you only have to lose one object to get the message. Instead, use good-quality woods like kiln-dried birch, maple, oak, and walnut. I don't recommend cherry, because it has resin pockets in the growth rings that can cause it to split. If the necessary woods are difficult to locate, find a furniture maker in the phone book and rummage through his off-cuts. Trade him a bowl...make friends...or you might even find a convert.

Preparing a glue block

The methods I use when preparing a glue block are quite simple. I thread the block onto a screw chuck, flatten the surface using the scraping cut, and burnish this surface with the side of the gouge to reveal any high spots.

Next, I lock the spindle, put the object block against the glue block, and mark an impression of the tailstock point. Then, I smear the superglue onto the face of my object, touch it to the face of the glue block, back the object block off and fix the point of the tailstock into the impression, give the glue a shot of accelerator, roll the tailstock forward until the two surfaces make contact, and finally, give the piece a slight twist as I tighten the tailstock. The last twist ensures the two surfaces are flush and secure.

To be sure there is no glue leakage, I put a small bead of glue over the entire exposed area of the glue joint, spray it with accelerator until it's dry, bring the tool rest up next to the piece, and then stand aside, and turn on the lathe. If there is any spray on the tool rest, I know I need to spray again and am thankful the droplets are on the tool rest instead of in my eye.

Creating a glue block

I prefer to use good-quality wood, such as maple or kiln-dried birch, for my glue blocks.

Thread the glue block, which is made of quality hardwood and not plywood, onto a screw chuck.

Flatten the surface of the glue block by using a scraping cut to ensure good contact between the block and the object to be turned.

Be sure the face of the block is flat. Hold the side of your gouge lightly against the surface of the glue block as it spins—high spots will show as burnished rings.

Preparing a glue block

Here's one way to attach an object block to a glue block. The contact surfaces of both blocks must be flat, or you risk losing the object block.

Place the work block against the glue block, lock the spindle, and tighten the tailstock against the work block so it leaves an impression.

Back the tailstock away and smear the bottom of the object block with superglue.

Briefly touch the super-glued surface to the face of the glue block.

Match up the impression on the object block with the tailstock point and hold the block there. Give the glue a shot of accelerator.

Roll the tailstock toward the glue block until the two surfaces make contact, then give the object block a slight twist to be sure the two faces are flush.

Put a small bead of superglue around the glue seam. Spray with accelerator until the glue is dry. Bring the tool rest up next to the piece, turn on the lathe, and stand back. If there is any spray on the tool rest, apply accelerator again.

Faceplates

Faceplates seem to have gone somewhat out of fashion since the introduction of mechanical chucks...and that's too bad. One reason is that people no doubt spend so much money for wood these days, they're afraid to stick a bunch of screws in it. And who can blame them? Another reason is that, because beginner-level turners are always the majority in a growing field like woodturning, most of the work produced will be small-to-moderate in scale. At this scale, mechanical chucks are ideal, while using faceplates might be cumbersome. Conversely, look at the size of the lathes being used. Capacities of 20"-diameter are the norm, 25"-diameter machines are commonplace, and my custom-made Thompson lathe will handle 33" x 60". What I'm suggesting is as our field grows, people become better turners faster. And for those who have the equipment, it's natural they would also want to make bigger objects—and faceplates are perfect for large pieces.

Be creative. Old tractor chain gears, like this 10"-diameter one, can be used as very sturdy faceplates. Just be sure the waste area of the object being turned is larger in diameter than the teeth on the gear so that you don't get nibbled.

This 38"-long redwood burl vase form is being supported by a 1¼" x 9"-diameter faceplate. I would not suggest any other method of attaching the piece to the lathe in this case. Faceplates are strongest.

Faceplates can also be used delicately. This hollowed spalted-maple piece is spinning at 800 rpm.

Pros of the faceplate

One of the nice things about using faceplates is there's no common sense required. If the piece of wood is tall or heavy or out of round, or if it looks like it would smash your foot instead of just crunching a toe, don't even think twice—just stick it on a faceplate. The bottom line is that nothing holds a piece of wood to the lathe stronger and with less vibration than a faceplate.

When using faceplates, the object is positioned so it picks up the support of the headstock mass, and there will be little or no vibration off the tool as the piece is turned. But if you were to move the wood further away from the headstock, as it would be if held by a chuck, vibration develops immediately.

Another thing that affects vibration is the faceplate's mass. Cast-iron and solid-steel plates are best, especially if they have a large hub between ⅜"- and ½"-thick. Aluminum faceplates are fine for small work. What's important is the transfer of mass from the headstock to the wood without breakdown.

Cons of the faceplate

It is possible screw holes can ruin a piece if not properly positioned. Notice in the illustration at right how the screws securing the 3" faceplate get in the way of the object being turned. However, if you switch to a 6"-diameter plate and put the screws in the outer ring of holes on the faceplate, the screws go into the waste block and don't get in the way of the base of the form. I use 1"-long #14 self-tapping sheet-metal screws, which are fatter than the standard #12s and don't need to go so deeply into the wood to do their job. Unlike wood screws, sheet-metal screws have deep, sharp threads, and they're made from hardened steel. I'll talk more about how to turn off this base area of the form in Chapter 14, "Jam Chucks & Vacuum Chucks," on page 190. From the illustration (right), it's clear you can easily make use of the height of the wood by using a larger faceplate and positioning the foot of the form inside the ring of screws.

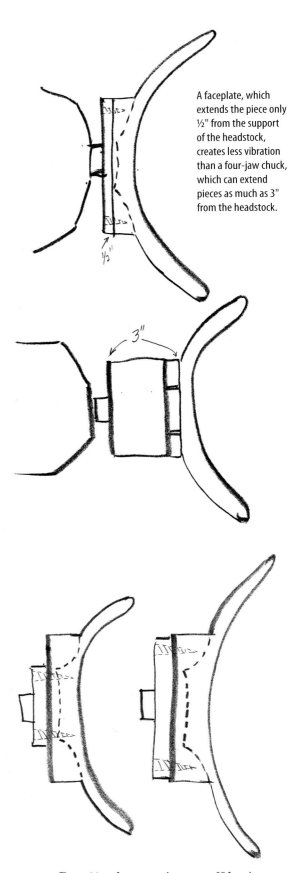

A faceplate, which extends the piece only ½" from the support of the headstock, creates less vibration than a four-jaw chuck, which can extend pieces as much as 3" from the headstock.

The position of screws used to secure a 3" faceplate get in the way of the object being turned. However, the screws used to secure the 6" faceplate are screwed into the waste area of the block.

Mounting a piece on a faceplate

When the base is either flat or slightly concave (according to your preferences), turn a base cut onto the block. To attach a faceplate, position the center of the faceplate over the center of the base and screw in as many #14 self-tapping sheet metal screws as there are holes for.

Helpful tidbits for modifying faceplates

Finally, here are a few tidbits of information that will help in selecting faceplates, or in modifying the ones you already have.

Countersink the holes on the *face* of the plate. Screwing directly into green wood raises fibers off the surface, which will cause the faceplate to rise off the surface of the wood and weaken the contact of the plate to the wood. Countersinking the holes gives the fibers somewhere to go, and maintains a strong bond between plate and wood. Caution: The object *will* loosen on the plate if flush contact isn't maintained. This isn't a problem with dry wood, because the holes would be predrilled. A standard ½"-diameter drill bit in a handheld drill works great for countersinking

To attach a faceplate to a piece, simply center the plate and screw in as many screws as the faceplate has holes.

Countersink the screw holes on the face of the faceplate so that green-wood fibers have somewhere to go when the screws enter the wood. Otherwise, these fibers will lift the plate off the surface of the wood.

Rusting the faceplate gives the wood fibers more traction than on a smooth metal surface. The less slippage, the better.

these holes. And you don't have to drill deeply into the faceplate, just to the diameter of the ½" bit.

Rust the surface of the plate to give it some traction. The faceplate's surface is not intended to look or feel like the surface of a table saw or band saw. It provides a nonslip surface that will give better traction to the wood. Rusting the surface gives the faceplate the roughness of heavy-grit sandpaper. Imagine the traction of that rust being forced into the wood fibers under the pressure of the screws—there's not going to be much sliding. Sticky-backed 40- to 50-grit sandpaper also would work, if you don't mind getting the faceplate surface a little gooey. When working with softer or green woods, the traction of a modified surface actually takes some of the pressure off the screws.

Remember that screw choice is very important when using a faceplate—the screws are what holds the piece to the plate. I use #14 self-tapping sheet-metal screws, 1" long or longer, depending on the size of the wood and the number of screws being used. If

Pros and cons of block attachment methods

Method	Pros	Cons
Four-jaw mechanical chucks	Relatively safe and easy to use. Versatile.	Turning heavy and tall pieces can be dangerous. Distance from headstock encourages vibration. Green and spalted woods can be difficult to hold due to their elasticity. Spigots can snap off.
Glue blocks	Can make very small objects. Best choice for punky and spalted woods. No drill holes needed, so good for expensive or exotic materials. Works well with green wood.	Glue blocks made from plywood or other cheap woods can separate. Superglue fumes can be hazardous to the heart and skin.
Faceplates	Strongest way to hold wood to lathe. Minimize vibration. No common sense required.	Can be cumbersome for small-to-moderate-size pieces. Screws can get in the way of bases if not properly laid out.

These are general guidelines. If something doesn't feel right to you, stop and reconsider the attachment method you've chosen.

Not all screws are created equal. From left to right: drywall screws, wood screws, concrete screws, and self-tapping sheet-metal screws, my favorite.

there are six holes in the plate, I use six screws—the more the better. If your plate doesn't have six holes in it, get out your drill. Unlike wood screws, self-tapping screws have very deep, sharp threads for super gripping power. They also are hardened steel, so the #3 Phillips driver won't strip out the cross slots in the head.

Another quality screw is the cross-threaded concrete screw, which comes in great colors and is available at any lumber company. Try not to get them too long, as they're sometimes difficult to get out. Drill out the holes in the faceplate to ¼" diameter to accommodate the larger-diameter #14

screws. Never use drywall screws, as they are too thin and will strip out of green wood, and are too brittle to be used with dry wood.

What I'm focused on here is support and versatility. Good support at every stage will reward you with vibration-free cuts and accident-free operations. For versatility, become comfortable with each type of attaching device. One size does not fit all, and I know turners who get stuck using one method. There is a world of wonderful objects out there that *need to be turned*. If you use only one attaching device, you'll never have an opportunity to find out if you can make them.

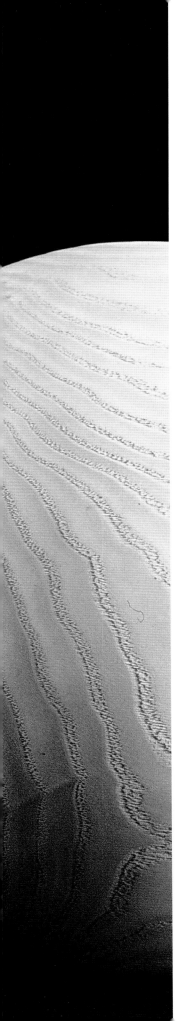

Design

Sometime back in the late 1980s, I noted design was the "fear word" of the turning decade. Turners were deep into learning the technical aspects of woodturning, but overwhelmed by designing a form. I still see design fear frequently when teaching workshops. A student will go through preliminary stages of roughing-out an odd-shaped lump of wood, get to the stage of designing a shape, and then say, "OK, I'm on the train, now where am I going?" I even had one student say on the first day of class, "I'm here to learn everything you know. Just don't teach me anything about design!" That seemed like an odd way to start a class. It was also a clear indication of how big an impact the term *design* can have. But why?

David Ellsworth, *Reflections*, 1997. Ash; (left) 14" high x 14" wide x 14" deep, (right) 11" high x 11" wide x 11" deep.

Look at the demographics of woodturners. Since we started actively teaching woodturning in the late 1970s, the majority of woodturning students have been hobbyists in the 50-plus age range who have come to woodturning with great desire but little or no prior experience in art fields. It was akin to putting a bunch of people in a room and asking them to converse in a language they didn't understand. The desire was there, and so was the skill of language—just not the language that works. Additionally, many colleges and universities established programs in ceramics, jewelry, and fiber after World War II, but woodturning stayed in high schools where it was safely ensconced in its industrial base. Unfortunately, without a workable vocabulary in the arts or exposure to design, woodturning had little opportunity to develop into a creative art form. The picture began to change around the mid- to late 1970s, as momentum toward more creative work in woodturning began. Riding the coattails of the success of the studio craft movement in other media fields, and inspired by a rejuvenated craft show and gallery marketplace, studio woodturning began an upward surge in both concept/design development and creative/artistic credibility. Because of this, all the primary woodturning design styles we see today—bowls, platters, spindles, segmented forms, architectural forms, totems, hollow forms, and sculpture—became fully mature by 1982.

Today, we fortunately have a dozen or so academic programs with woodturning as an integral part of a woodworking curriculum. We're now developing a much broader base for opportunities for learning about design methods within woodturning. Still, the question remains: how do we help entry-level woodturners develop design skills without having to enroll for a college degree? Or, how do we help those who look at design from the perspective of "I'm not a creative person; I can't even draw a straight line"? I believe part of the answer is we need to redefine our objectives and pay close attention to the methods we use in achieving our desired goals.

Appreciating the process

From a practical approach, the first objective is to appreciate the value of the process on a par equal with the value of the finished product. It's not always easy to appreciate intangibles, but doing so has merit. It's the difference between fishing and fish catching.

There is nothing wrong with joy in completing a successful venture. Our friends and relatives love everything we make, and while they may not be our best critics, their praise is important. Once we've given our work away, what we are left with is the experience of making, which becomes a building block for the self-confidence we need to advance as creative beings. And we are creative beings. All of us.

When I look at the work of woodturners, I find a succession of ideas that all relate to one another, but are not necessarily the same. Someone's first bowl and current bowl may look completely different. If I follow that person's work through each phase of development, I can generally see how each group of ideas inspires the next. Personal growth can be seen as an evolution of ideas that occurs over time through the process of making. Step back a bit and remember to give these ideas time to evolve. This is one reason no one starts out making dynamic, fully mature work.

Experiencing the process means learning how to see what you're looking at internally. The paths you follow while making are a direct reflection of who you are as the creator. When you address the question of how to learn about design, what you are looking for is a glimpse of yourself through these objects as you think, act, react, and evolve through the process of making.

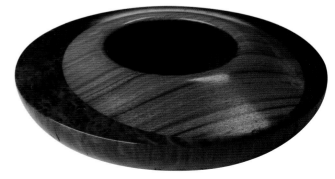

David Ellsworth, *Bowl*, June 1976. Redwood burl and pau ferro; ⅔" high x 7" wide x 7" deep. My first "successful" hollow form turned with bent tools.

Improving your design skills

There is a point at which each of us asks the question, "How can I make my forms look better?" When it comes to improving your design skills, this is *the* most powerful question you can ask. The key words in this question are "how," "I," and "look."

The "how" part indicates a curiosity of method, evolving from your early learning experiences at the lathe, which probably began with a lot of glitches and bangs. Since then, you've progressed to a level of confidence where objects actually come off the lathe somewhat as you'd planned, or at least in one piece. Either is OK, and from this stage, everything is looking up.

The "I" part indicates a relationship between the maker, the material, and the process. You've reached the point where you say, "I really can do this." Turning wood is generally a solo endeavor, not a team sport: "I am responsible for what I am doing." Finally, the clincher: "What do I do if I want to make my forms a little different?"

The "look" part is the final link. This is where you investigate the "self" in self-expression. You recognize that from birth onward, each of us has been surrounded with objects that have profoundly shaped our lives. It doesn't matter what gender you are, what culture you come from, or what backgrounds you have pursued in life to bring you to the present. The moment you begin to consciously look at objects that surround you with any sense of curiosity, you begin to see your world from a different perspective. It is from this new viewpoint that your work begins to evolve with a sense of confidence and direction. The designs you are looking for come from within.

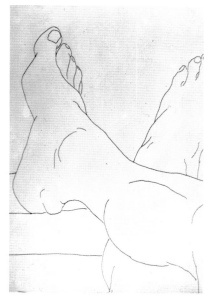
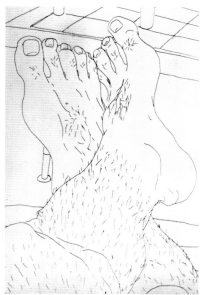

David Ellsworth, *Feet*, 1970. Even sketching something as normal as your feet can help you gain a greater appreciation for form, perspective, and design.

David Ellsworth, *Hairy Feet*, 1970. Small details can make a world of difference, even in a simple sketch.

Learning what you like

As to methods, we are all different, so we experience our world in a different way than everyone else, which is a good thing! It means that if you can appreciate how you experience our world, you can learn to translate those experiences into the work you do. This is a chance to step back and look closely at your objectives. The best way to establish your own design ideas is to figure out what you do and do not like, and you can only do that by trying things.

Make drawings

If I were asked a group of students to grab a pencil and pad and begin to make drawings, most of the group would say they can't draw. They actually can draw, because all it takes is to hold the pencil against the paper and push it around a little. That's a drawing. It may not be a drawing of what they see or what is in their minds to draw, but it is a drawing.

If the objective is to draw a finished drawing you "know" you can't make, you're sunk before you get started. If your objective is to enjoy the process of scribbling on the page, you can learn to enjoy the process of drawing and let images emerge naturally from what is in front of you. And who cares what it looks like? After making two or three drawings, you can look at them side by side and select the one you prefer.

I filled numerous sketchbooks while studying sculpture and drawing in the 1960s and 1970s, although this was before I got into turning full-time, so none of my sketches involved turned objects. Even sketching something as simple as my own feet provided a greater understanding of the relation between form and volume, something that relates directly to the work I do today in turning. Another relationship between sketching and turning is my method of working involves using the gouge as my pencil as I work directly on the wood, allowing each design to evolve as I progress through the turning process. From here, the skill of drawing grows as a means of expressing your ideas visually instead of verbally.

Make shavings

It's the same with turning. If you want to learn to turn wood, stick a log on the lathe and make lots of shavings. Don't make anything except a huge pile of shavings. If you want to learn to design a bowl, make a dozen bowls and see which ones you like. After fifty bowls, you'll make more you like and fewer you're uncertain of or don't like. With additional confidence in the skill of turning, you progressively train your mind's eye as to what shapes appeal to you.

Another method of training both your technical and design skills is to take a bunch of branches (12" long x 4" or more in diameter) from a downed tree, rough them into cylinders, and begin to make shapes. Don't make things; that requires thinking. Just make shapes—any shapes—with no thought involved. Try a gouge; try a skew. Make a dozen shapes, number and date them with a black marker, and throw them into the corner. Do it once or twice a month for six months, then line the pieces up in numerical order. Notice the increase in quality of both the turning skill *and* the design skill. The time it takes to make each shape shrinks, and the curves become more fluid. Making without thinking is the best frame of mind to be in when you're designing something.

By shifting your objectives from the product to the process, you lose the burden of achievement and pick up the natural design skills that exist within all of us. Learning how to train the mind's eye is just a way of learning how to truly see what you're looking at. This is an integral part of helping to develop a design skill that reflects your own personality and interests.

Don't worry about whether you can turn wood or not...just make shavings!

The two primary ways of designing

There are two primary ways of working that lead to designing objects on the lathe. The first is designing an object on paper and then selecting wood for the design. The second is to bring the wood to the lathe and design the form as it is being cut and shaped.

Designing at the beginning

In the first method, design occurs in the initial stage of the object's development. The wood, if already chosen, must be stabilized in some manner so it doesn't change over time, though different woods can be substituted while the drawing remains the same. Here, the turning process, whether simple or complex, is the mechanical stage of the object's development and is directly related to the turner's skill. This design method is typical of spindle turning, which represents the historical and industrial roots of woodturning. It is also used in segmented turning, where objects can be designed from small pieces of wood into anything from spindles to bowls, vessels, and sculpture.

Design development

The second method has always been my method of choice, because it fits my life experiences and personality. It provides me with a great sense of creative freedom and a high level of risk. The freedom comes because I can alter a shape or an idea during the turning process. Changes can be based on almost anything, including the discovery of unusual characteristics within the material, reflection on an idea from another object I have seen, or my mood that day. The risk comes in never knowing what I will end up with or where I'm going with a form when I begin. I think of this as design development, and I accept the risk as part of the excitement of making. I am free to learn about the wood with which I'm working and myself as the object evolves.

Trusting your instincts

There have been several past cases when I finished a hollow form and it didn't settle well with me. Either I didn't fully connect with it, it seemed somehow unrelated to the direction in which my work was headed, or I didn't understand it. I have learned to stash such pieces away and look at them later... sometimes years later. At some point, I'd invariably stumble onto one of them buried in some closet and realize the idea or the memory or something about the piece had been influencing other pieces I'd been making all along. The first lesson I learned from this experience was that it was actually *me* I didn't understand when I made the piece. The realization brought with it a second lesson: to learn to trust my instincts, wherever they might lead.

> "In consideration of instincts—things we all have but don't necessarily understand or know how to trust—I've also learned there are reasons we each select certain objects or designs over others."

In consideration of instincts—things we all have, but don't necessarily understand or know how to trust—I've also learned there are reasons we each select certain objects or designs over others. It's not important that we do or don't understand the reasons. What is important is we begin to look at our design choices with critical awareness. Why did I choose this couch over that one, or this dress, or this set of dishes, or that tool? Cars, of course, are one of the most common and revealing design considerations we all make. My point is every decision you make in your daily life is, in part, a design decision. And each decision is a direct reflection of who you are. We often pass these decisions off as simple likes or dislikes, or even a reflection of personal taste. But they are design decisions—creative decisions—that reflect how we see ourselves, decorate ourselves, and feel about ourselves.

Inspiration and evolution

My intent is not to provide answers, but to help you learn to ask the right questions. The objects you see in the books of private and public collections on woodturning may appear to be beyond the skill sets of a beginner-level turner, and they are. Inspiration is a wonderful thing, and each of the makers of these objects began with some form of inspiration. It then took many years to develop both themselves and their skills before their work achieved the level of their aspirations. Over time, those aspirations changed, and so the maker and the methods changed and matured. It is the way of making. It could be the making of craft or the making of art, but you can never know when you first begin. It's only important that you begin.

What is it about design that is so mysteriously intriguing, so simple yet complex, so fundamental to the balance of life, and so seemingly unachievable? Is it as simple as a lack of experience with an unfamiliar language? Is the ego too heavily involved to feel comfortable when revealed? Probably, it's both of these and more.

I think of design as a culmination of a person's entire being, including his psyche and aesthetic, pulse, and purpose. The best way I can illustrate is to give examples of how I've created dialogues with myself while making specific objects. I've provided some of my very own evolutions and inspirations in design, documented in photographs and prose. I hope it will encourage you to attempt a similar approach. Besides, it's a lot more fun than saying, "I like this, but don't like that," or "This is a good design, but that is not." Both are one person's opinion, and we can't learn much from either.

Sikyatki pottery: Inspiration from an inspiration

The roots of my early bowl and vessel designs came from Sikyatki ceramic pots of the late nineteenth and early twentieth centuries—specifically, the work of Nampeyo, a Hopi-Tewa potter who lived from 1860 to 1942. The pottery Nampeyo saw at the Sikyatki excavation site in Arizona in the 1890s inspired her. According to oral tradition, Sikyatki was a Hopi pueblo destroyed by a neighboring pueblo. The pottery at the site was circa 1375 to 1625 and was decorated with multicolor designs. Nampeyo utilized both the vessel shapes and painting style she observed on those forms.

As a child, I was exposed to Native American art—pots, rugs, jewelry—but Nampeyo's pots were more than just functional ceramics. The design and construction were daring and seemed to possess their own internal energy—a pulse.

In observing prehistory ceramic vessels from the early 900s to the present, and including vessel forms from ancient world cultures, we can clearly see that the narrow neck, high shoulder, belly, and foot design concept is universal and a direct reflection of the ultimate vessel—the human form.

Hohokom bowl, c. 950. 4" high x 7" wide x 7" deep.
Salado pitcher, c. 925. 7" high x 4½" wide x 4½" deep.

#1: Toward hollow forms

It is easy to see with the Brazilian rosewood bowl, done in March 1977, how my interest in making hollow forms evolved directly from making open bowls (right). The bowl is awkward in shape and proportion. The cracked and wormy rosewood is not the best quality. The piece seems to be trying to find an identity somewhere between an open bowl and a hollow form, but it's not sure in which direction to go. It was a transition piece based on what I knew at the time. I also noticed the original slide had a $100 price listed on it. That would have been a heavy price in 1977, so I guess my ego must have been in transition, as well.

The bowl done in December of that same year shows a distinct shift in my design and technical abilities, including the selection of materials (below). It is a far riskier design, more skillfully turned, and has a sense of unity, as if it feels more comfortable in its own skin. You can see how the shape evolved from the previous piece—simply extend the walls upward. This piece won the Colorado Artist Craftsman award that year, which was my first award ever, and it gave me great incentive and confidence for continuing down this road into hollow turning.

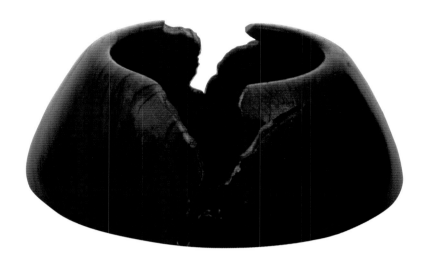

David Ellsworth, *Bowl*, March 1977. Brazilian rosewood; 3" high x 6" wide x 6" deep. This transition piece is somewhere between an open bowl and a hollow form.

David Ellsworth, *Bowl*, December 1977. Brazilian rosewood; 3" high x 5½" wide x 5½" deep. The design of this piece was inspired by the earlier bowl shown above. You can see how the design is definitely more a hollow form than a bowl. It has resolved its identity.

#2: Natural edges

Another example of reaching out was my exposure in the early 1980s to the wonderful varieties of burl wood available to me after the move to Pennsylvania. While other turners had made natural-edge bowls dating back to the early 1950s, it was Mark Lindquist, with his robust bowl and sculptural forms, who brought this design motif onto the woodturning stage in the mid-1970s. Because I was working with thin walls in green wood, my approach integrated the natural edge as a complement to the distortions I could achieve in the surface of the forms, which resulted from the tensions within the fibers going from green to dry.

David Ellsworth, *Vessel*, 1983. Walnut sapwood burl; 5" high x 6" wide x 6½" deep. I created this early vessel as an exercise in exploring my options.

David Ellsworth, *Red Oak Pot*, 2007. Red oak burl; 8" high x 8" wide x 8" deep. This late vessel shows more direction than the earlier piece.

I love the juxtaposition of the two forms shown here. The first was created from a walnut sapwood burl during a time in my life of major aesthetic and technical exploration (see photo at top). It was a time when "anything goes," and everything went in the direction of free expression. The word that would have characterized my life at the time was "charge." The red oak burl piece, made twenty-four years later, shows a similar design approach and a definite freedom of movement within the form (see photo at left). Yet, it is executed with more refined skill and greater knowledge of material use. The earlier piece is searching for direction; in the later piece, I am directing the search.

#3: Form shapes and opening sizes

This succession of pieces demonstrates how my tools and techniques became more sophisticated between 1978 and 1981. The openings in my forms became smaller, and with that change, they also became more technically challenging and visually dynamic. These early forms were very angular, with hard-edge rims and flat bottoms. There was an understandable struggle on my part toward design development and technical virtuosity that contributed to my forms being somewhat sophisticated, but conceptually tight.

The second and most important change occurred over the following two years. I was no longer locked into the hard-edge "line as shape" designs from the previous years. The newer forms evolved into "line as volume," and the new approach to vessel forms indicates a significant amount of design freedom, almost as if I was reaching out for new ideas and directions.

During this period, my life began to gear up and settle down all at the same time. My 1977 divorce was now emotional history, my work was being shown and accepted on a national stage in both galleries and craft shows, and a wealth of new and challenging materials came into my life because of friendships with other woodturners. The most significant change was my marriage to Wendy in 1980 and our move in 1981 from the mountains of Colorado to the woods of Pennsylvania. With this union, I inherited two young boys, Isaac and Adrian. The addition of the two boys gave me three children, including my own daughter, Kate. I was suddenly a family man, a property owner, a house and studio designer, and builder, and, lest I forget, a maker, photographer, teacher, and marketer of my artwork. I was also in my mid-thirties and maturing fast, both personally and creatively. Some might say that it was about time!

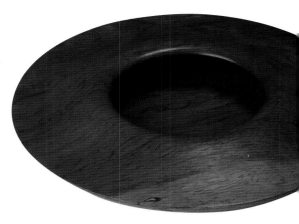

David Ellsworth, *Bowl*, October 1978. Bubinga; 1¾" high x 13" wide x 13" deep. Notice the hard-edge look to this design.

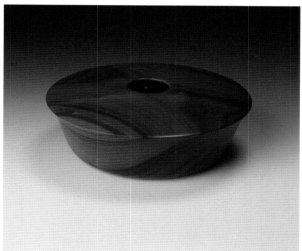

David Ellsworth, *Bowl*, October 1978. Putumuju; 2½" high x 6½" wide x 6½" deep. This piece exhibits a smaller opening and a deeper shape.

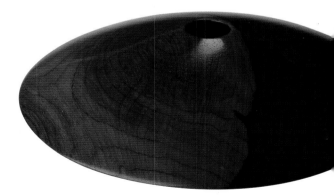

David Ellsworth, *Bowl*, June 1979. Brazilian rosewood; 2¼" high x 8¾" wide x 8¾" deep. This piece is a much more sophisticated and mature form.

David Ellsworth, *Vessel*, 2007. Ponderosa pine; 6" high x 9½" wide x 9" deep. This most recent piece demonstrates the latest in my design evolution toward a shape that is showing "line as volume."

#4: Surface textures

Another Lindquist influence on my work was exploring surface textures. This trio of white oak pots from 1991 (see photo at far right bottom) began as a challenge to myself: Could I design for simple, common woods instead of relying on the beauty of the burls I had worked almost exclusively throughout the 1980s and 1990s? The surfaces are left straight off the gouge and unsanded, a practice I began in the late 1980s.

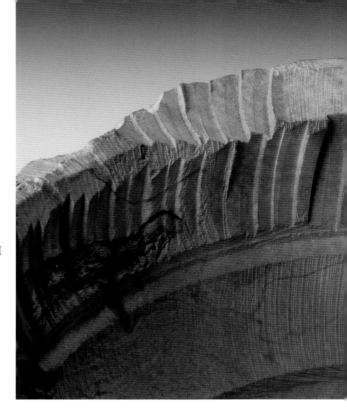

I created *Chaco Pot* from a block of heavily spalted maple given to me by a student. My first attempt at turning this pot has a chunk missing from when it became disconnected from the glue block.

David Ellsworth, *Chaco Pot*, 1994. Spalted maple; 4½" high x 5" wide x 5" deep. Collection: Detroit Institute of Art. Gift of Robert Bohlen. The surface of *Chaco Pot* is sandblasted.

Mark Lindquist, *Bowl*, 1982. Sugar maple burl;
5" high x 9½" wide x 9½" deep. Lindquist's
robust forms exhibit delicate chain saw textures
that bring volume and visual excitement to the
surface, as seen in this bowl.

My feeling was you reach a point with every object when you must decide that it is done and finished. One day, I got to this point, started to pick up my sander, and suddenly said, "Wait, wait... they're already done." The naturally coarse texture of the oak had a wonderfully raw, woody look. When touched, a sound was produced that was like stroking a raku ceramic pot. In fact, this series had so many references to ceramic pots in both form and feeling that I realized I was making wooden pots instead of vessels. It was a real breakthrough, and I've been making *pots* ever since.

Thin-walled hollow forms were a great challenge, but working with spalted and other distressed materials forced me to work at the upper limit of what the material would handle. *Chaco Pot* came from a piece of heavily spalted maple brought to me by a student, most likely as a challenge to see what I could do with it. The photo at far left shows the original condition plus my first attempt, which came flying off the glue block when I was working the interior, due to the heavy decomposition of the wood. The surface of the final form was then lightly sandblasted to give it a remarkably etched texture. The title comes from a similarly etched surface I once saw in the sandstone walls of the cliffs in Chaco Canyon in New Mexico.

David Ellsworth, *Pots*, 1991. White oak; tallest 10" high. This trio of pots
was the result of my desire to move away from the beauty of exotic burl
woods and to see if I could design beautiful forms using simple woods.

#5: Recessed openings

The surface of *Homage Pot* comes directly off the skew chisel. While the black spalted lines are floating wildly around the form, the startings and stoppings of the skew cuts leave a subtle striated surface that helps visually ground the form. The title refers to my homage to the art and architecture of the Native American cultures of the Southwest, where I was raised. The recessed opening was inspired by smoke holes in the horno ovens that southwestern Native Americans used for baking (see photos below). My goal while creating the opening was to give the observer the sense his or her psychic energy was being pulled into the interior of the pot.

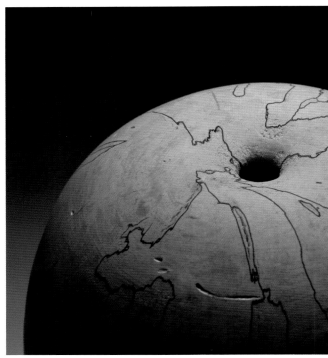

David Ellsworth, *Homage Pot*, 2002. Spalted sugar maple; 12" high x 9" wide x 9" deep. The vertically grained outside of this piece was cut with a skew rather than with my Signature gouge, because the wood was so punky I couldn't get a satisfactory surface using the gouge.

The smoke holes in the back of horno ovens inspired the opening in *Homage Pot*. These horno ovens are located in Taos, New Mexico.

David Ellsworth, *Tall Ovoid*, 2007. Spalted sugar maple; 13¼" high x 12" wide x 12½" deep. I utilized wood bleach and oil on this piece to highlight different conditions of the wood and create strong surface contrasts.

#6: Surface enhancements

The surface of *Tall Ovoid* shows a combination of finishes and textures (see photo at left). The lighter spalted areas are unsanded (straight off the gouge) and lightened with wood bleach. To establish more visual contrast in the surface, the areas of solid wood are also unsanded, but oiled. My intent in combining these surface effects was to provide dynamic visual excitement that becomes part of the design of the form.

Design elements

As your design style evolves, remember there are many types of design elements that you can utilize. I often use inlays, fire, and color as visual elements within my designs.

Inlays

One method of developing surface enhancement is working with inlays. It's common to develop cracks when working with green wood, naturally distressed areas, and burning techniques (see Chapter 16, "Finishing," on page 218). I've heard that many people, collectors in particular, think of distressed areas as flaws in the wood that are in need of repair. I do not. I think of them as design elements that celebrate the perfectly imperfect nature of wood. However, if you wish to use inlays, they can be a great way of enhancing the natural cracks in a form.

If I were blind, I would want to stroke inlaid forms and encounter an inlay as a surprise, to feel its shift in direction, to contemplate its reason for being. As a person with sight, I want to enjoy the beauty of the color, texture, and contrast each inlay presents to the overall composition. As a maker, I want to draw attention to these wonderful elements, to play with the designs, to create a sense of the known and the unknown, and to project them as being indispensable to the dynamics of the overall design.

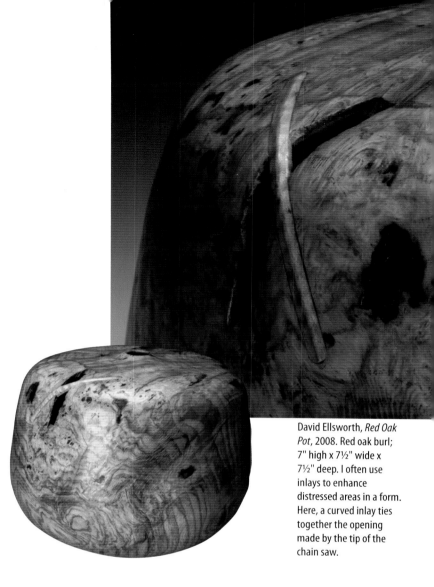

David Ellsworth, *Red Oak Pot*, 2008. Red oak burl; 7" high x 7½" wide x 7½" deep. I often use inlays to enhance distressed areas in a form. Here, a curved inlay ties together the opening made by the tip of the chain saw.

The block I cut to make *Red Oak Pot* (see photo at top) came from a larger burl. When removing it, I inadvertently crossed the area of the shoulder of the form with the tip of the chainsaw. Instead of cutting the piece down to eliminate the cut, I decided to turn it full size. It was the first time I positioned an inlay in such a strategic position in a form, but I couldn't resist the drama and the opportunity to unite the piece visually.

The inlay is cut from curly maple and is the full thickness of the wall of the piece so the underside matches the pot's inside surface. The inlay's exposed surface is raised slightly above the surface of the pot and unsanded, so it shows the marks of the knife I used to cut the excess down to the level seen here.

The pernambuco inlay in *Lunar Pot* (see photo at left) crosses a crack present in the pith when the tree was felled. It is matched by a second inlay on the opposite side of the form, again crossing the

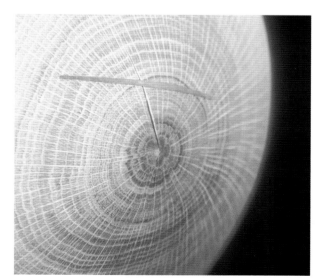

David Ellsworth, *Lunar Pot*, 1994. White oak with pernambuco inlay; 10" high x 9" wide x 10" deep. The inlay on this piece is raised above the surface and takes on its own character.

crack in the pith. All of my inlays are full thickness to match the wall of the form and are cut, shaped, and inset once the wood is fully dried. The surface of the inlay is slightly raised above the surface of the wood and shows tiny facets made from the edge of a thin-bladed knife. The inlay takes on its own texture, as distinct from the unsanded surface of the oak surrounding it.

Atlantic Pot (see photo at right) was made from a dry elm tree that washed up on Maryland's Eastern Shore. It had deep splits in the surface, so I wrapped it with tape so it wouldn't fly apart when turned. I carved the edges of the splits with a knife and cut each piece of inlay out of spalted sugar maple to give contrast to the lines of spalt in the elm. With the slight change in color and the discordant connections of the spalted lines, the surface picked up a visual shift I quite enjoy.

The fire-enhanced cracks in *Black Sphere* (see photo below) evoked this question: How many inlays should I use, and where should I place them on this dramatic and geologic surface? Remember, there are no design rules that shouldn't be broken. Designing should be total serendipity: If I like it *here*, it belongs *here*. Then, just do it…just don't overdo it. In this case, I crossed the crack with a series of interlocking pieces of curly maple. They are not structural; the wood is stable. Nor are the edges of the inlaid pieces meant to match perfectly to the sphere's surface. The fire pulled the edges away from the joints, lending a feeling of timelessness to their search for direction.

David Ellsworth, *Black Sphere*, 1989. Burned ash with curly maple inlays. 13" high x 13" wide x 13" deep. This burned piece exhibits open cracks next to inlays that are placed into solid wood; an interesting juxtaposition.

David Ellsworth, *Atlantic Pot*, 1997. Spalted elm with sugar maple inlay; 9½" high x 8" wide x 8" deep. Collection: Carnegie Art Institute. Gift of Ruth & David Waterbury. The inlays lend a visual shift to this vessel.

Charring

Woodworkers have always had a fascination with burned and charred surfaces because of the extreme contrast between the destructive force of fire and the creativity that can be loosed with blackened wood. I also believe that when we're considering the inherent beauty of the material of wood, blackened surfaces challenge our understanding of the term *beauty*. To me, this is another reason to explore and expand our design palette.

Using blackened surfaces in ceramic forms as a decorative motif has become a powerful influence on turned wooden forms. In the work of Michael Wisner, we see fired clay with an imprinted surface (see photo on page 93, top left), burnished with smooth stones before firing.

In my mind, the effects of burning wood are no different from those of burning clay. Each provides a textural surface that defines the volume and surface of the form, and each shows the material for what it is, be it wood, clay, or whatever. In some respects, burning is a way of transforming chaos into order. The process itself can become an integral part of the overall design.

Sharon Doughtie uses black as a foundation for her graphic designs, which are inspired by woven fabric patterns from her Gaelic roots. The strikingly consistent dimpled texture provides a perfect

Michael Wisner, *Vase*, 2002. Ceramic; 9" high x 8" wide x 8" deep. The texture of this piece is created by an imprinted and burnished surface.

Ciaran Forbes, *Bowl*, 2000. Bog oak; 6½" high x 8½" long x 7" wide. The grain in this piece continues to shift; there are some seasons when the bowl won't stand.

background palette through which she reveals the color of the wood (see photo at bottom right). She also incorporates a common characteristic of Norfolk Island pine—a single knot—as a carefully placed, sanded, and polished element, which I find exciting and essential to the overall surface motif. Every detail of this bowl is thoughtfully cared for, including the smoothly sanded area reserved for her signature in the base. Equally important, this is a straightforward, pure form that allows the surface treatment to reveal itself without competing with the bowl's shape.

The bowl at top right, created by Ciaran Forbes, demonstrates the natural gray-black coloring and extreme distortions of Irish bog oak. There are seasons when this marvelous bowl will not stand. It is a testament to Mother Nature's grand design, no doubt, and a reminder that wood moves, regardless of species or age. It could also have something to do with Forbes being a Benedictine monk.

There is no question of predicting movement in a wood notorious for change. The question is how much movement will occur. Of the thousands of bowls Forbes has turned, this one is possibly the closest to the line between predictability and hope. It asks whether a warped bowl is necessarily a good bowl. Must a bowl be functional to be a "good" design and, if not functional, can it be considered sculpture? And was it luck or a master's intent?

This is an intriguing situation where questions help define a bowl that defies definition. The answers are left to the observer. To me, serendipitous as it might be, there is a natural energy in this bowl that moves beyond labels or intent. It is one of those wonders I refer to as *pulse*. Possibly one of the strongest elements of the design is it inspires poetry as well as prose.

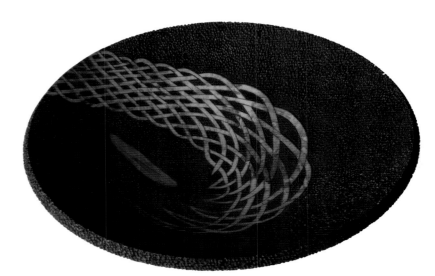

Sharon Doughtie, *From Seed to Seed*, 2005. Norfolk Island pine; 2¼" high x 8" wide x 8" deep. Black charred surfaces can be used as a foundation for graphic design. Even the knot (the amber streak) has been incorporated into Doughtie's careful design.

In my series titled *Black Pot–Dawn*, my wood of choice is ash. The density of grain in other materials like maple or birch is too consistent and would not give me the deeply etched effect I'm after. In the case of *#14* (right), I tried to develop a sense of transparency on the surface—not unlike a transparent ceramic glaze—by burning, polishing, sanding, and burnishing. With *Machel* (below), an intersphere from the *Solstice* series, I was looking for a matte surface to serve as a canvas, not a polished surface that would compete with the paint. To achieve this, I left the char from the torch as it was, then sprayed it with artist fixative to protect the surface and prevent smearing. The two objects came from the same tree, and it is interesting how the use of fire can yield two different design effects.

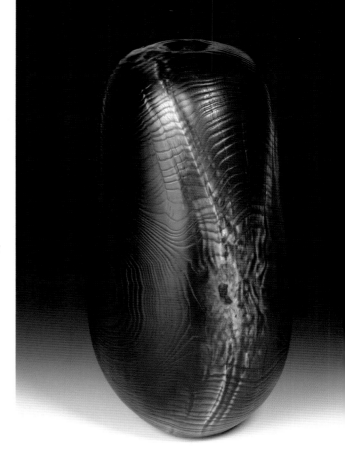

David Ellsworth, *Black Pot-Dawn #14*, 2004. Burned ash; 17" high x 8" wide x 8" deep. Collection: Jane and Arthur Mason. I used a variety of finishing techniques to give this surface a transparent glazed look.

Color

Color has been a part of woodturning and woodworking in all cultures and for as long as records exist. The works I'm showing here are as diverse in their use and application of color as I can find.

The O'Donnell bowl (Mick does the turning, Liz the painting) pictured on page 95 (top right) is from a theme they have been pursuing for many years—celebrating birds. During a trip to Australia, Mick and Liz were inspired by the wonderful color palette used by Aboriginal artists. Another interesting aspect of the design is Liz has used only a portion of the broad rim as her canvas.

My use of color in *Nelaq II* (page 95, bottom left) was meant to bring a visual uplifting to the otherwise emotionally dark surface of the sphere. The meandering blue and red lines are symbolic of life's interactions and the often random nature of our physical and emotional wanderings in search of...

Giles Gilson's skill in using transparent automotive

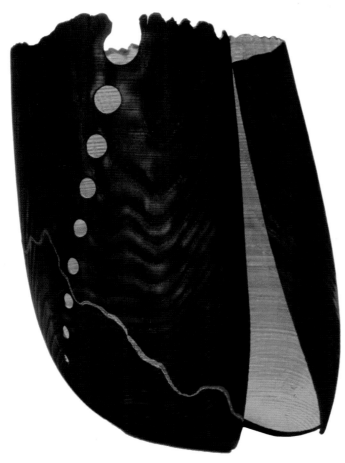

David Ellsworth, *Machel*, 1991. Burned ash and paint; 18" high x 13" wide x 14¾" deep. Collection: Museum of Fine Art, Boston. Gift of Anita & Ron Wornick. This matte surface accentuates the color used on the inside.

lacquers is shown in *Black Ribbon* (page 97, bottom left). The colors are between what they seem to be, including what might not even be there as they interact and flow into one another. Viewed from different angles, the surface shifts in different types of natural and artificial light. Gilson's inspirations come, in part, from his history with fast cars and airplanes, including one radio-controlled helicopter known to make an occasional pass inside his studio.

Steven Hogbin's *Walking Bowl* (page 96, bottom left) has an opaque dark blue interior that brings a sense of solidity to the bowl cavity, which is juxtaposed to its remarkably lithe and sensuous form. The design succeeds as sculpture on many levels. It is monumental and could be successful in any size from a few inches to many feet. It has no front or back side and is equally exciting from any angle, including from above and below.

The piece by Clay Foster on page 96 (top right) is an intriguing design because of the unusual way the artist has chosen to embellish the surface and redefine the form. The form is almost completely disguised by the strings and antler beads, so the viewer is challenged to consider the piece from an entirely new perspective. I see a conscious effort on Foster's part to both disguise and surprise. The

Mick and Liz O'Donnell, *Bird Bowl*, 1988. English sycamore and paint; 2" high x 5¼" wide x 5" deep. A large portion of the rim on this bowl remains undecorated.

David Ellsworth, *Nelaq II*, 1990. Burned ash and paint; 11" high x 10½" wide x 11" deep. The red and blue lines really pop on this otherwise dark piece.

piece begs to be held, and the final surprise is the wonderful sounds it makes when shaken: not swishy, but crisp, bright, and alive. It is an inverse rattle whose bead strikers create resonance over the surface of the hollow form. It is, in fact, an instrumental design that brings great pleasure to those who play it. What the casual observer wouldn't necessarily know is Foster is a feverish sketcher of his ideas and many of his influences come directly from African art, objects, and ceremony.

This just goes to show you doodling and sketching are wonderful ways of exploring ideas that happen to pop into your head. Sometimes, it isn't much of a stretch to take these ideas and translate them into something that might evolve into a turned object. Often, an idea going in one direction veers off and leads to a totally unrelated idea or direction. Dating your sketches is an excellent way of documenting a group of ideas or a train of thought, not unlike a diary. This allows you to look back and find out what you were thinking about at some point in time in the past.

Foster's piece helps to support my philosophy that design is an evolving process and a constant challenge to our senses. Each of us is influenced by our respective life experiences, and we understandably favor certain styles and types of designs as a result of these experiences. Culture also plays a huge role in how we view certain designs, especially when we throw in terms like *popular* or *fashionable*.

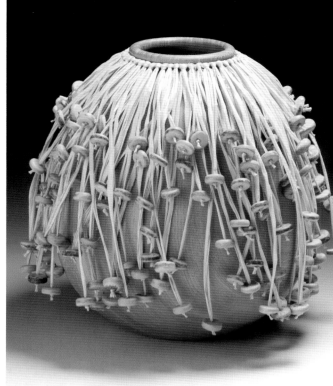

Clay Foster, *Untitled*, 1994. Pecan with sinew and deer antler; 7" high x 6" wide x 6" deep. The beads covering this piece lend an unusual dimension to the art—sound.

You might not think of translucence as a normal design component when working with wood, but Ron Kent's approach with his bowls confirms how easily this feature can become a vital part of his bowl designs (page 97, top). Norfolk Island pine is the perfect material for this application, as its light color and the crystallized oil in its fibers combine to transform the elegant line of the bowl's design into a fully illuminated and volumetric surface.

Stephen Hogbin, *Walking Bowl*, 1985. Elm and paint; 13" high x 13" wide x 7" deep. This sensuous form is grounded by the dark blue interior.

Ron Kent, *Bowl*, 1986. Norfolk Island pine, 5" high x 15½" wide x 15½" deep. Translucence can be used in wood as a decorative motif.

Closing thoughts on design

I have used this chapter to illustrate the differences in approaches to design, and how our personalities allow us to view objects from totally divergent yet equally valid perspectives. These differences continue to pump freshness and life into the designs of the objects we make. Design in any form is a continuous discovery process, with each element becoming a mirror of our own ideas and a direct reflection of ourselves.

Note: With the exception of Giles Gilson's *Black Ribbon*, all of the objects by other artists shown in this chapter are part of David Ellsworth's private collection.

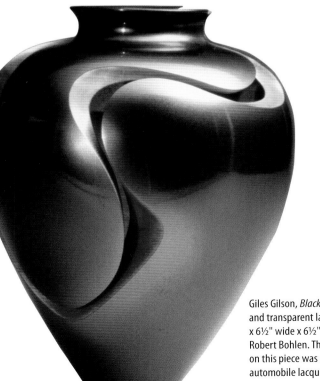

Giles Gilson, *Black Ribbon*, 1984. Birch and transparent lacquers; 10" high x 6½" wide x 6½" deep. Collection: Robert Bohlen. The shifting finish on this piece was created with automobile lacquers.

Chapter 8

The Body

It is quite likely that in all our decades of teaching technique, process, method, design, and intent, we have consistently overlooked one element: the importance of our own bodies as a resource for woodturning. As a young man, I couldn't have cared less. When I began developing my hollowing tools in 1975, I had no understanding of the importance of the relationship between the tools, my own body, and the process itself. I hacked away like most early-stage turners, and tried to control short-handled scraping tools with a death grip I'm sure nearly stopped the flow of blood. The result was I inadvertently focused all of my energy on muscle power to control the tools, especially the muscles of my hands and arms, and I began to feel I might end up looking like Popeye.

Morning exercises occur every day during the master classes I teach at the Anderson Ranch Arts Center in Snowmass Village, Colorado.

A change came in the early 1980s when I began watching the early-morning tai chi classes at craft schools like the Anderson Ranch (Snowmass Village, Colorado) and Penland School (Penland, North Carolina). I sat at some distance so I could observe the beauty of the bodies moving with a single energy, like the collective consciousness of a flock of birds or a school of fish. Then it hit me: Everything was in balance. I could see, especially in the instructor, that there was a mysterious line of connectedness between the head and the ground, and no element of the body extended in any direction beyond this line without another element projecting equally in the opposite direction. Toes appeared to be of equal value to fingers, as elbows were to knees. The head remained vertical above the shoulders, the eyes forward, looking but not seeing. Instead, each person sensed each element of the body without the need to look at the parts as they moved. Moreover, within the rhythms of this slow-motion dance, I could sense an immense amount of energy and power within each muscle at each stage of its movement. It was truly a kinetic experience.

I closed my eyes and began to mentally transpose the movements to my own body as if I were working on a form at the lathe, and it evolved into a short list of very important questions: How much energy is required to make an efficient cut, and where is the energy coming from? And secondly, if my feet are as important as my hands, what are my feet doing while my hands are turning white gripping tool handles and doing all of the work?

These questions lead to the big one: could I learn to consciously locate this energy in my body and could I shift it from areas where it isn't needed to areas where it is? I could then be more efficient with my cuts while at the same time reducing the fatigue factor, which is one of the greatest contributors to inefficient cutting and accidents. The answer is "yes." Consequently—for better or worse—I do not look a thing like Popeye.

The three classic body problems

There are three classic physical problems that occur when turning open bowls or hollow forms:

1 Dipping your head down to try to see inside the form.

2 Leaning over the bed of the lathe.

3 Pulling your back arm away from your body, especially with hollow forms.

It doesn't take long for your muscles to set their memory, so while each movement doesn't appear to be much of an issue, repeating them over time can cause muscle and joint pain, excess fatigue, and poor tool control. In many cases, closing your eyes and taking time to *feel* what you feel like, including discovering where tension is coming from, is all it takes to feel better and have your efforts rewarded.

Balance and support

Balance, both physical and emotional, is the most important factor in regulating your body's energy. As I've said, my own experience is that whether it's turning wood or splitting firewood, every physical technique requires a break-in period before the process becomes assimilated and you can begin to move *with* the process. Those early learning stages can be pretty ugly. The lesson is energy, force, and muscle are closely related, but not the same.

Consider for a moment the lathe itself and how much work you go through to make it stable: You triangulate a lathe's design to create rigidity. You add volumes of cast-iron parts and numerous bags of sand to weigh it down. As a last resort, you bolt the thing to the floor. RIGID is good. It seems fair to think the tool ought to be held rigidly too. Well, the body can never be truly rigid when turning wood. It works best as a shock absorber and support system for the tool being held. While rigid can be good, balance and support are the concepts to concentrate on while working with body movement.

Tension

Any time you have problems with support or are in an unstable situation when turning, tensing up the body—especially the hands and forearms—is a natural response. Unfortunately, in doing so, you lose the subtle responsiveness between the tool and the wood. Fatigue quickly sets in, making you even more inefficient, and the tool invariably begins to vibrate or even dig into the wood. The long-term result is the constant vibration transfers to your muscles and joints with the potential to create numerous physical aches and pains.

Your objective is to learn how to relax your entire body while providing the required amount of tool support. This can be a difficult concept in a culture where people spend so much of their day sitting instead of moving around. I believe if you spend as much attention on yourself as you do on the wood you're working with, good things are bound to happen. After 30 years of turning hollow forms, I am convinced that without an understanding of how the body works, I would not have been able to survive doing what I do, much less continue to enjoy doing it.

When I began to work on larger and larger forms in the mid-1980s, it became clear that if I didn't do something for my body, I would have to stop turning. Basically, everything hurt. Also, because I worked alone, I had no way of finding out where the pain problems were coming from.

Things began to change when I focused on how people moved. I observed my students. The first thing I learned was virtually 100% of the problems students were having with specific cuts were directly related to poor body positions, invariably beginning with the location of their feet. In extreme cases, people were so focused on what was happening between their shoulders and hands that the rest of the body didn't seem to exist at all.

It was interesting to observe how a lack of

Setting up the lathe

An important part of getting your body in the proper position to turn is making sure that your lathe is properly adjusted for you. The rule of thumb that the spindle should be at elbow height is correct for turning spindles, but not for turning hollow forms. Turning hollow forms involves using very long-handled tools. The only way to control them is to be on top of them (see photo at bottom). If the lathe spindle is at elbow height (see photo at top), the tool handle will be so high your shoulders will get jammed. Having the spindle around 3" to 4" below elbow height is a good starting point, but it may vary depending on how you feel and the type of work you like to do. When working on open bowls, I like the lathe around 2" below elbow height. One reason measurements can never be accurate for all people is some people are short and work their tools in shorter arcs, while taller people, like me—I'm over 6' tall—work their tools in broad arcs. As such, I need the lathe lower to complete the arcs. Part of the problem is most lathes are too high for the average turner and he or she can't extend the arcs in order to make the cuts effective. Another issue is that the spindle height is commonly measured with the turner's legs straight and knees locked. However, that is not the position the turner will be in to make a cut. His or her legs will be spread and the knees unlocked, making the spindle automatically too high. Part of the solution could be a platform to stand on, or a lathe with adjustable legs.

Positioning the spindle at elbow height is fine for spindle turning, but not for turning hollow forms.

The spindle should be approximately 3" to 4" below elbow height when using long tools for turning hollow forms.

movement affected the cuts people were making on their work. Suddenly, a huge light turned on for me: You just can't cut a curve if your body doesn't move. The steps to make the cuts work were to figure out how I was moving, the effects my movements were having on my cuts, and how I was focusing and directing my energy.

Tension is a big inhibitor to getting the proper body positioning. For example, I once worked with a student who was having problems with the most basic cuts using my gouge. He was wound up like a spring. So I suggested to him to "try to *relax*" when making the cuts and see if they didn't work a little better. The student continued to have problems. How stupid of me! It never dawned on me that I had asked him to do something he didn't know *how* to do. I should have asked, "Do you know how to relax?"

Most people starting out at the lathe are practicing awkward and even painful movements and procedures. They are focused on the tool, the edge, the bevel, and the shavings produced, and don't pay attention to the body that's supporting them. Every tutorial video I've watched, including my own, spends an incredible amount of time with super-close-up photography showing how the tool is supposed to look when cutting the wood: you want to know when you're doing it right. What also is needed is to show how the body is moving so the cuts can be made both safely and efficiently. Students have to be shown how to move while turning, in the same way you have to be shown how to swim and walk and pump your legs in a swing, especially if you've never had those experiences before. Sure enough, once the body begins to move as a unit, the cuts begin to move as well.

"I believe if you spend as much attention on yourself as you do on the wood you're working with, good things are bound to happen."

Muscle memory

I used to wonder how it was so easy for me to take a long break from turning, pick up a tool, and start at the same point where I'd left off. I used to attribute it to youth and clean living, but I knew that was only partially true, especially as I got older and retained the same instinct.

Then I thought about how a group of potters could all be throwing the same basic shape on the wheel, but the curves of their forms could be slightly different, yet consistent to their own respective design styles. More interesting is they were not consciously *thinking* about the forms as they made them. Instead, they had this wonderfully natural rhythm as their forms effortlessly emerged. Somehow, they had been able to remove the thinking process altogether. This is a perfect example of muscle memory in action. What a joy!

Exercises help you shift poor muscle memory habits back into positive ones. In most cases, these poor habits can start with something as simple as the feet being too close together, or placing one foot ahead of the other so your weight over your feet is unequal.

One easy way to correct muscle memory at the lathe is to pause just before you make a cut with a tool. Crinkle your toes, alternating back and forth from one foot to the other. You'll soon be able to feel which foot supports more weight from the body. Try to shift your feet or your stance just enough to equalize the pressure on both feet.

Next, select a cut that makes it easy for you to place both elbows near or against your sides. A few suggestions are a skew or gouge cut on a spindle or a gouge cut on the outside of a bowl. Don't turn the lathe on. Spread your feet to a comfortable distance slightly wider than shoulder-width. With your weight placed equally on both feet, unlock your knees so your legs act as shock absorbers. Now close your eyes and focus on breathing slowly and equally, in and out, with your diaphragm. You will soon realize you can move your body laterally back and forth in slow motion from over one leg to the other without discomfort. When doing so, you can feel the pressure on each foot, each calf, each thigh—practically everywhere.

Try extending this motion beyond vertically over either leg so you can sense what it feels like to be off balance (see photograph below). Hold the position for any length of time, and you'll soon feel pressure against the outside of your foot and the top of your thigh. It won't feel good. Return your weight over that leg and instantly feel the pain recede.

Every time you go to the lathe to make a cut—any cut—take ten seconds to crinkle your toes and take a few breaths from the abdomen. You'll soon train yourself to become in balance. Most importantly, you'll begin to sense the source of energy for the cuts coming from your feet, legs, and gut instead of your hands and arms. It will be a conscious shift at first, but with time, it will become second nature.

And lastly, you can practice relaxing the classic death handgrip by squeezing and relaxing your hands and fingers. By doing so, you'll discover how little muscle is needed to make a cut, and all of the extra muscle you've been using in that death grip is just wasted energy.

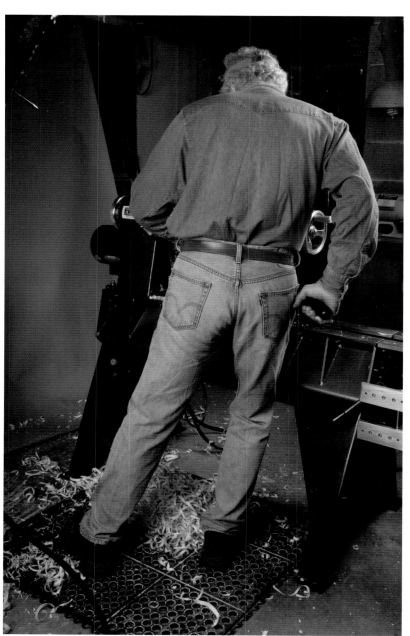

To help your body relax at the lathe, stand as if you were going to make a cut. Then, close your eyes, breathe deeply, and slowly transfer your weight from one unlocked knee to the other.

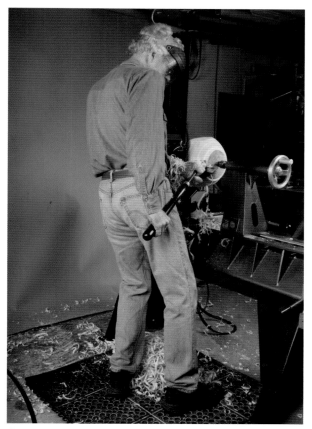

If you overextend beyond either knee, you will likely feel uncomfortably off-balance. Remember, you can always move your feet to readjust.

Flexion exercises

I use flexion exercises to help take the pressure off my lower back while turning. Each of us tends to favor one side of our bodies over the other, and these stretching exercises help to equalize the strength of the lower-back muscles and take the pressure off the spine and the sciatic nerve. As a result, I walk straighter, move better, turn better, and I no longer have that shooting sciatic pain from my waist down my legs.

These are standard exercises within both the medical and chiropractic fields, as well as in yoga. There is nothing mysterious about the exercises and they are proven to work. I also wish I could say I do them every day, but I don't. Instead, like most other people I know, I do them when my back hurts. I know my back wouldn't hurt if I did them every day.

Lie down on an exercise mat face up and place your arms at your sides. Stretch yourself out lengthwise by imagining that someone is pulling on your head while someone else is pulling on your feet. Scootch yourself around as if you were trying to melt yourself to the floor. Take several breaths very slowly and systematically to help you relax.

"Each of us tends to favor one side of our bodies over the other, and these stretching exercises help to equalize the strength of the lower-back muscles."

Next, pull one of your knees toward your chest, grab your shin just below your kneecap with interlocked fingers of both hands, and *slowly* pull toward your chest. Pull until it begins to hurt, back off a little, and hold for thirty seconds. Straighten the leg, shake your hips a bit, and try to relax both legs equally. Repeat with the other leg, holding for thirty seconds, then re-extend the legs and relax. Repeat the sequence five to ten times, alternating your legs and adding a slightly increased amount of pressure with each pull. Always straighten or extend the leg and try to relax between each movement.

Bring both legs up together. Grab both shins and repeat the pulling action toward your chest, followed by relaxing your legs. Repeat five to ten times. On your last series of pulls, grab your knees and rotate sideways to either side of your body. Try to touch your knees to the mat. If possible, also try to keep your shoulders flat on the mat. This can seem like a killer, as it won't happen the first few attempts. Stick with it. Rotate to the other side of the body and repeat the entire sequence five to ten times. Another method is to fold one bent knee over the other leg, trying to pull the knee down to the mat while keeping your shoulders square or flat to the mat. Try each method and see what you like. Try rolling to your side before standing up to avoid dizziness.

If you have any history of lower-back problems, doing these stretches two to three times a week is pretty good preventative maintenance. If you're really having trouble with your lower back, every day is best. One thing you can be guaranteed of is that if your back hurts and you only do these exercises once or twice, they won't do a bit of good.

Flexion exercises

I find that doing these stretches helps me to remain limber and pain-free while at the lathe.

Lie face up on an exercise mat with your arms by your sides.

Bring one knee to your chest by grabbing below the kneecap with both hands and pulling gently.

Bring the other knee to your chest in the same manner.

Bring both knees to your chest by grabbing below the kneecaps with both hands.

Rotate your knees to one side. Try to keep your shoulders flat on the mat.

Rotate your knees to the other side, again trying to keep you shoulders flat on the mat.

Instead of rotating your knees to the other side, you can try folding a bent knee over the other leg and pulling the knee down to the mat.

Muscle access exercises

If a tool is sharp and correctly placed, it will mostly likely cut. But if your body isn't relaxed, the tool might go in a direction you hadn't predicted.

Muscle access exercises are a way of finding out about the parts that make up your body. If you learn how to access the parts, you can learn to make them work as a unit. Take the connection from the toe to the knee, through the hip, up to the shoulder, and down to the fingers: If you remove any link from the chain of movement, the chain becomes weakened or breaks. When this happens, as it can for any number of reasons, you learn to compensate by shifting to another part of the body to provide support or using additional muscle power to perform a given task.

When turning wood—especially large pieces—compensating with muscle power can create problems. It can affect your ability to move fluidly, but it can also initiate early fatigue. For example, imagine a swimmer. Everything goes smoothly as long as all of the body parts are working together. With practice, muscle memory develops, and every movement the swimmer makes becomes fluid, synchronized, and efficient. Take away the movement of the swimmer's legs. The only way he can hope to swim is to use more muscles in his arms and shoulders. Even then, the process is less efficient than when the entire body was working as a whole.

Now think of a woodturner. If any links in the chain aren't moving, you compensate with extra muscle, usually from between the shoulders and the fingers. The problem comes if you turn while you're out of sync. As you work, muscle memory sets in, and you end up practicing how to become fatigued. If you access correct support muscles, you can take the pressure off your shoulders, arms, and hands. The question is, how do you find these muscles?

Muscle access exercises are the most efficient and direct way I know to learn *who* you are and *what* your body does. The most effective way I know to do these exercises is to put yourself in a position of great relaxation: on the floor. Here's my non-patentable ten-step program.

1 Lie down on an exercise mat face up and place your arms by your sides.

2 Stretch yourself lengthwise by imagining that someone is pulling on your head while someone is pulling on your feet. Scootch yourself around as if you were trying to melt yourself to the floor.

3 Take several breaths slowly to help you relax.

4 Select any muscle you wish and tense it up for a long count of five, then relax that muscle.

5 Select another muscle and do the same thing. Go through every muscle you can think of.

6 Constrict and relax muscles one at a time until you have covered your entire body.

7 Work in a wave from your head to your toes, constricting opposing pairs of muscles (like both biceps) simultaneously.

8 Constrict every muscle for ten seconds, then relax.

9 Relax the body through slow, systematic breathing.

10 Roll onto your side before you try to stand up.

What you seek is the ability to perform a cut while using your entire body as an energy source. The intent of the exercises is to help you do that. It takes about a week for the exercises to actually begin to work, because it takes time for the repetition to establish new muscle memory. Once your muscles begin to respond consistently to new patterns of movement, you can apply the various movements you use when working at the lathe.

The hanging bar

A hanging bar is a wonderful device. Like any form of instant gratification, it's easy to translate the experience as, "Boy, is that a rush!"

The best call I received about the bar was from a man who had to repeatedly go up and down two flights of stairs to take care of his elderly mother. He went happily on and on about how my exercises had made his trips enjoyable instead of a pain in the...back.

Set up the hanging bar at a height so that when you stand flat-footed beneath it and stretch your arms to their full extension, your fingertips will come to the bottom of the bar. Jump and grab it. Your heels will be about 3" off the ground. Hold that grip and imagine you're in a tub of water as someone pulls the plug. As the water level descends, let your body drop. Hold that grip until your heels are back on the floor.

Step away from the bar, walk around the room, and notice how liberated you feel. Your head will be erect, and you'll be walking in a straight line with equal pressure on both hips. The feeling only lasts a few minutes, but while your body was descending, it actually grew in length by that 3"!

When you're turning, your muscles are alternately in a state of relaxation and compression. When the muscles are under compression, the body's fluids that normally flow through the connective tissue become restricted. When you're hanging on the bar, the tissue expands, providing room for these fluids to move. You're allowing your muscles to breathe and be fed.

If it hurts...don't do it

There are many philosophies relating to body movement. I borrowed these methods from other people, including medical and chiropractic doctors, movement therapists, one Rolfer, two acupuncturists, and a few masters of yoga and tai chi. I've also added my own instincts that relate directly to turning wood.

I understand most woodturners are weekend warriors, and don't want to take the time to do a bunch of stretching exercises when they only have a few hours on a Saturday between mowing the lawn and their kid's soccer match. My point is, singers don't sing with a cold throat and dancers don't dance with cold muscles. That said—and this goes for any exercise you might be doing—if it hurts, don't do it.

Hanging bar

The hanging bar has helped to improve my posture and rejuvenate my body. I stretch on the hanging bar several times a session, and I genuinely recommend trying it.

Set up the bar at a height so that when you stand flat-footed beneath it and stretch your arms, your fingertips will come to the bottom of the bar.

Now, jump up a little and grab the bar. Your heels will now be off the ground about 3". Hold that grip until your heels are back on the floor.

Turning an Open Bowl with a Cut Rim

No other form is more universally identified with a turned wood object than the humble bowl. Many cultures have made wooden bowls for many millennia and in many different ways that it would be difficult to pinpoint any single method that stands out over the others. I expect most bowls made in Western cultures prior to the Victorian Era were turned green to a finished wall thickness, then let dry to an oval shape. They would then be used or abused and replaced by a newer model.

Note: Though this chapter describes how to turn a cut rim bowl, the procedures used are very similar to those needed for a natural-topped bowl. The techniques presented in this chapter can be used to turn any open form, regardless of size, shape, or rim type.

Bill Luce, *Bowl*, 2004. Madrone; 6¾" high x 14¾" wide x 14¼" deep. Collection: David Ellsworth. This classic design is an excellent example of "line as volume" rather than "line as shape."

"No form is more universally identified with a turned wood object than the humble bowl."

Most bowls turned today are double-turned—once to roughly shape the bowl and thick walls, and a second time to define final wall thickness after the form has dried—to ensure they end up perfectly round. Whether it's due to current fashion, a need for visual order, or the value of the objects themselves, I do not know. But it is rare to see lovely meandering rims on oval bowls in the marketplace today.

Some of the processes I describe for making bowls and vessels may seem unconventional, but I think the logic proves itself worthwhile. While there are many ways to make bowls and vessels, the methods I'm presenting will work for all open bowl forms, all hollow forms, and objects in all sizes from an inch to as large as your equipment will allow. Like most turners, I have succumbed to my own habits, but with this amount of versatility, there is certainly some merit to my madness.

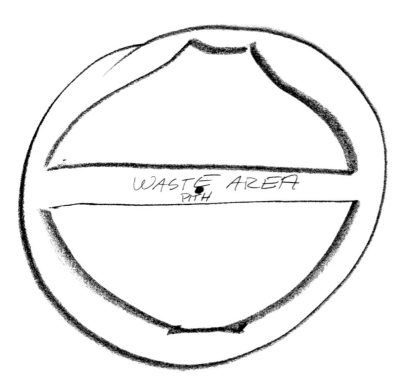

Open bowls are positioned bases out, brims roughly along the center, when viewed from the end grain of a log.

Preparing the block from a log

I prefer working directly from the log, because the fresh-cut end grain tells such a wonderful story about what forms might lie within. Studying a log is like reading a road map: a pith here, some spalted patterns there, a few bug holes, a bit of rot, a dip in the bark... anything influencing vessel shape, including areas I might wish to avoid. For instance, cracks through the pith don't work well in the rim of a bowl.

You can see in the sequence at right that I have marked out two open bowls in the spalted log, one with a cut rim and the other with a natural (bark edge) top, plus a tall vase and a low breast-shaped hollow form. All I need to do now is cut the shapes from the log and decide which one to turn first. I decided to cut the vase shape in half along with the small hollow form, so I ended up with two larger bowl forms and four smaller hollow forms.

There are many possibilities when working from a log. It takes experience in doing it before real confidence comes. If you're just starting out, don't be intimidated to cut open the log. You can't make a mistake. The next log you open up will be different. After many logs and bowls, you'll know more of what you're looking for before you begin. Your forms will evolve, and you will cut the log differently to accommodate design changes. It happened to me when I started turning hollow forms. Instead of cutting the log into smaller pieces, I got brave enough to leave the log whole so I could include the pith in the final shape. And, of course, the inevitable happens: sometimes you cut right through an area that might have yielded a beautiful form.

To make the block more manageable when turning, I trim off the corners, then cut a divot in the center of the bark using only the bottom surface of the tip of the chain saw bar. This is a safe cut if you don't make contact with the end or the top surface of the tip. This divot will receive either the spur or revolving center. If either center were placed directly against the bark, it would slip sideways or become clogged, possibly resulting in the block flying off the lathe.

From idea to lathe-ready block

I prefer working right from the log when deciding what forms to create. Here is the process I use to turn a log into a block ready for the lathe.

I design various shapes of bowls and vessels based on what I see on the end grain of the log. Then, I draw the outlines of those forms right on the end grain.

After sketching outlines on the end grain, I dissect the log with a chain saw.

Trimming the corners off the block makes the blank much more manageable when turning.

Cut a divot in the bark area to receive either a spur or revolving (live) center.

The final blocks are ready to be turned. All I have to do is decide which one to start with!

Mounting the block on the lathe. Notice the divot from the chain saw: It plays a key role in keeping the blank on the lathe.

Mounting the block on the lathe

When I mount the block on the lathe to make a cut-rim bowl, I position the bark surface facing the tailstock and the flat chain saw cut toward the headstock. The bark area will become the foot of the bowl when the bark is removed, and it's a lot easier to shape the base to receive a chuck, glue block, or faceplate from the tailstock side of the lathe than from the headstock side. The tailstock side affords much greater accessibility.

This method of mounting a block to the lathe is different from the more conventional method of attaching a faceplate to the flat surface of the block and turning a spigot on the foot to receive a chuck. I'm not actually designing the bowl at this point, because I don't yet have enough information

about the block itself. I know the relative height and diameter, but I don't know the exact layout of the grain patterns that will appear in my finished bowl.

To get the needed information, I have to trim off the excess stuff I don't want in the bowl to find out what I do want. The excess would include the bark and any strange or unusual grain patterns I might want to exclude from the final form. It's not unusual to find a stray bullet or a chunk of barbed wire buried in the wood that I didn't see when I initially cut open the log. As I begin to trim away the material, I also learn more about what I have, and can easily readjust the form until it's positioned the way I want it. It's at this point that I flatten out the base to receive a chuck, glue block, or faceplate.

Rough-turning the bowl using the roughing cut

I use the roughing cut when I begin trimming the form. This gives me the greatest control when cutting odd-shaped materials. It is particularly helpful when removing large amounts of bark, rough corners, and irregular surfaces on a fresh piece of wood. Roughing cuts are not pretty. Depending on your energy level, they can actually be quite aggressive in removing large quantities of wood.

This is the first departure from working with a conventional gouge. Don't use the bevel when making these roughing cuts. Instead, the tool rest supports the tool while simultaneously taking the force. I wouldn't use the bevel against the wood to make this roughing cut, because the bevel would bounce against the irregular surface and give me an uncomfortable ride.

Rotate the gouge axially so the line across the flutes is approximately 45° to the horizontal. Keeping this 45° angle throughout the cut will ensure the edge is in an efficient cutting position.

I position the tool rest at a 45° angle to the bed of the lathe and approximately ½" from the nearest corner of the block. If the gouge is properly positioned (horizontally to the floor and perpendicularly to the tool rest), the tool's edge will be cutting tangent to (across) the fibers. If I put the

Roughing cut: The Signature gouge versus the conventional gouge

The primary difference between using the Signature gouge and a conventional bowl gouge when making roughing cuts—both interior and exterior—is how I position the two tools in relation to the tool rest. Hold the conventional bowl gouge with the tip approximately 30° to 40° above horizontal. This positions the bevel of the gouge pointing upward so that when the tool engages the spinning wood, the edge cuts the wood. This is an efficient way of cutting, except it requires considerable energy to constantly push the tool up into the wood while making the cut. At the same time, the wood is also trying its best to push the tool down the slope of the tool rest and into the turner.

The Signature gouge, on the other hand, is used in a horizontal position so the force of the energy of the cut goes directly into the tool rest instead of the turner. Because the edge of this gouge is on the side of the shaft as well as the end, the area of the edge in contact with the wood is in an upward position. I am not a scientist, so I don't know how to measure force, but I do know what I feel like at the end of an eight-hour turning session when using these different tools. *Any* energy-saving measures are worth the effort.

A conventional gouge is held at 30° to 40° to make a roughing cut. It takes much effort to push the tool up into the wood.

The Signature gouge is held horizontally to make a roughing cut. The energy from the cut is diverted into the tool rest and not into the turner.

Rough-turning the bowl using the roughing cut

The exterior roughing cut can remove the majority of rough corners, bark, and irregular surfaces from the block.

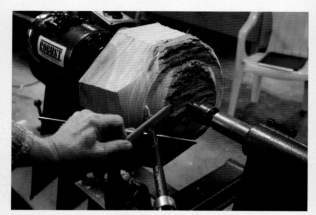

Placing a pencil across the flute when held at 45° shows the angle. Holding this angle throughout the roughing cut will ensure that the edge is always in an efficient cutting position.

To make a roughing cut, the tool rest is at 45° to the lathe bed and ½" from the nearest corner of the block. The Signature gouge is horizontal and perpendicular to the tool rest. The heel of your front hand will be against the tool rest, and your back hand will be holding the butt of the handle against your leg.

When you're beginning to trim a form, the roughing cut is extremely useful. It removes large amounts of bark, rough corners, and irregular surfaces.

The Roughing Cut

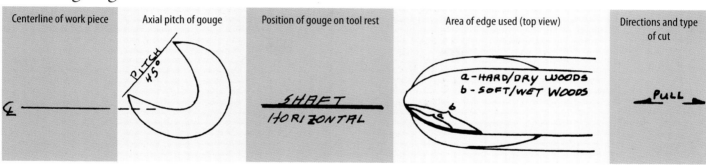

Centerline of work piece	Axial pitch of gouge	Position of gouge on tool rest	Area of edge used (top view)	Directions and type of cut

The exterior roughing cut with the Signature gouge removes excess stock in preparing to make a bowl or vessel form.

tool rest parallel with the bed of the lathe, there is no way to prevent the gouge edge from crashing into the end grain of the fibers and causing a huge mess to the surface of the wood.

Be sure to take a look at "Body position for the roughing cut" (right). With the heel of my left hand *always* against the tool rest and with the gouge in a horizontal position (perpendicular to the tool rest and parallel with the floor), I can make a roughing cut by drawing the gouge toward me, across the tool rest and the corner of the block, taking a cut between ¼" and ½" deep.

Because the roughing cut is very aggressive, it can leave an ugly surface on the wood. That's fine: It has done its job. But once the bulk of the rough material has been removed, I do all the remaining cutting with the slicing cut as I shape and design the form.

Comparing the tools

Using the Signature gouge challenges some of the traditional rules in woodturning, especially as they relate to how a bowl gouge is *supposed* to be used and when (or whether) to use the bevel. So it's always fun to outline how specific cuts are made, knowing full well many readers may simply shake their heads in wonder. It is for this reason that in describing how this tool works in this chapter, I will make many comparisons to conventional or traditional bowl gouges in an effort to explain the differences.

Body position for the roughing cut

Paying attention to body positions throughout the turning process will save you lots of pain and energy. Spread your feet slightly wider than your shoulders. Support the gouge with your back hand at the back of the handle. Position the fingers of your front hand over the shaft with your thumb underneath and the heel of your hand against the tool rest. This position will simulate an equilateral triangle so that you don't have to use more muscle in one hand than in the other. Contact with the tool rest is critical, as it ensures that you have control of the tool. It also helps to measure the depth of the cut by preventing the gouge from wandering too far off the tool rest. Without this contact, you have no control and danger lurks. Progress through the cut by pulling the gouge along the tool rest and through the wood while shifting your body's weight from vertical over one leg to vertical over the other leg.

Shaping the outside of the bowl with the slicing cut

Once the rough edges are removed, I switch to the slicing cut to continue removing waste material and begin shaping the form. The slicing cut, which could also be called a peeling cut, is similar to peeling an apple. It is one of the most beautiful cuts to make, or to watch someone else make, because of the long, continuous ribbons of wood shavings it produces.

Begin by positioning the gouge just as if you were making the roughing cut, that is, horizontal on the tool rest and with the line across the edges of the flute at 45°. Drop the handle approximately 20° to 30°, which raises the edge of the gouge to an equal angle above the centerline of the work piece. Doing so allows the edge to slice through fibers, instead of ripping through them, as it does with the roughing cut. Work with the front third or half of the edge rather than trying to use the entire length of the gouge's edge.

As with the roughing cut, no bevel is used in making slicing cuts. Consequently, you will not get a supersmooth contour on the resulting surface. That will come with the shear-scraping cut. What's most important about the slicing cut is you can remove a large amount of wood safely while shaping the form, and without tearing out the end-grain fibers.

The last step of the slicing cut is to begin flattening the base by removing the bulk material. I am ready to move on to the scraping cut when I am satisfied with the basic shape of the form and have found out everything I need to know from the wood.

Body position during the slicing cut

With your feet spread a bit farther than shoulder width and your knees unlocked, place your right hand on the bulb of the handle or just behind the junction of the handle to the shaft, being sure to keep the handle of the gouge against your leg. This reduces the original equilateral triangle used in the roughing cut, but it allows broader movement through the legs where you will generate energy for the cuts.

By starting the cut while your weight is vertically over one leg, you can then pull the gouge through the cut from the base to the rim of tall bowl and vessel forms. At the completion of the cut, you will have shifted your weight to vertical over your other leg, thus avoiding the problem of shuffling your feet during the cut.

The Slicing Cut

Centerline of work piece	Axial pitch of gouge	Position of gouge on tool rest	Area of edge used (top view)	Directions and type of cut

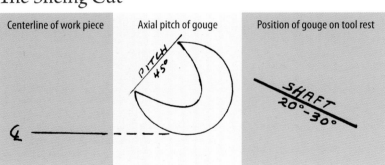
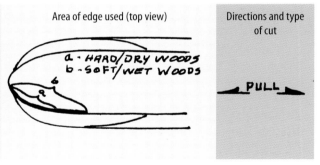

The slicing cut is an exterior cut used to shape the form and prepare the surface for the shear-scraping cut.

Shaping the outside of the bowl with the slicing cut

The slicing cut is efficient for removing a lot of material. The resulting surface isn't smooth, but the fibers are not torn or ripped on the surface as they would be from the roughing cut.

The slicing cut is the second step in removing waste material from the exterior of the bowl. I use this cut to shape the form.

Begin in the roughing position and then drop the handle between 20° and 30°. This action allows the gouge's edge to slice rather than rip the wood fibers.

When beginning to shape the form, pull the slicing cut up the side of the form from the base to the rim.

There's a time for design

I will do all of the final designing of the bowl after the base has been attached to the headstock, so there is no reason to continue to fiddle with the shape when I'm still working between centers. As well, lingering at this stage interrupts the flow of developing the entire piece.

Use the slicing cut to flatten the base of the bowl.

Flattening the base using the scraping cut

Once I have finished with the slicing cut, I waste no time in switching to the scraping cut to finish flattening the base, preparing it for mounting onto a chuck, glue block, or faceplate. The scraping cut is critical for flattening the base in order to prevent overcutting and ending up with a concave surface or, worse, a big dig. It is satisfying to be able to work down the bulk material in this area with the slicing cut, then rotate the gouge counterclockwise to drop the edge into the scraping position to smooth out the surface...and not worry about catching the gouge. If I went into this flat surface with the edge raised in the slicing position, I would definitely get a catch.

There is some controversy about a flat surface versus one that is slightly concave. Both will work, but my belief is using a concave surface in preparation for a faceplate puts an extra amount of pressure on the screws. If the wood is soft and wet, the extra pressure can cause the screws to loosen up when working with large chunks of wood. Conversely, uniform surface contact between the plate and the wood's surface provides extra traction and relieves the pressure on the screws. You can't use

a glue block on a concave surface. Don't worry...it's easy to learn to scrape the bottom flat with the side edge of the gouge. Regardless of where you fall on the flat versus concave issue, the important thing is to be sure not to make the surface convex, especially adjacent to the nub in the center, or the faceplate will rock on the surface.

A scraper is an edge that makes contact with the material at a 90° angle...like fingernails on a chalkboard. To position the Signature gouge as a scraper, lay the tool horizontally on the tool rest and rotate the shaft until the lower edge is 90° to the surface of the wood. In this position, the flute points almost directly at the wood's surface, and the upper edge is approximately 1/16" away from the surface of the wood and does not make contact with the wood. By lightly sliding the gouge forward and back over the surface, the edge scrapes the wood without grabbing it. If you were to raise the edge above the scraping position, it would cause the edge to overcut or even dig into the surface. Though a flat surface is important for any attachment method, it is absolutely critical when preparing it for a glue block.

The Scraping Cut

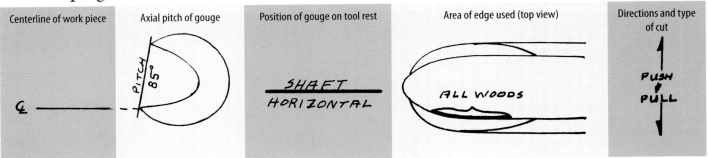

| Centerline of work piece | Axial pitch of gouge | Position of gouge on tool rest | Area of edge used (top view) | Directions and type of cut |

The scraping cut is an exterior cut used to flatten the base of the form in preparation for a chuck, glue block, or faceplate.

Flattening the base using the scraping cut

I like to use the scraping cut to flatten the base in preparation for a glue block, chuck, or faceplate.

Flattening the base of the form with the scraping cut requires positioning the Signature gouge like a scraper. The lower edge should be at 90° to the surface. The flute is pointing almost directly at the wood's surface. The upper edge is about 1/16" away from the wood.

Lightly slide the gouge back and forth over the surface, being careful not to raise the bottom cutting edge above scraping position.

Body position during the scraping cut

The scraping cut can be made from almost any position where your body feels comfortable. The important factor is to be sure your head is directly over the tip of the tool and in line with the surface being flattened. Without this view, you won't know whether the surface is concave, convex, or flat.

Preparing the base for attachment to the lathe

I use the scraping cut for flattening the base on all of my pieces, regardless of what attachment method I choose. After the base is flat, I prepare the base for either the chuck, glue block, or faceplate. For this bowl, I chose a chuck.

Creating a base cut

Regardless of the method I choose, I will first need to perform an important step I call the *base cut*. Quite likely the base cut is the most important cut in the developing bowl and vessel designs, and without question, the most neglected. The base cut leads to forming the object's base. If someone has already named it something else, I will gladly yield. Without this cut, it's almost 100% certain the design of the base of the bowl or vessel will be determined by the mechanical device holding it to the lathe, be it a chuck, glue block, or faceplate. The reason has to do with how your eyes interpret what you see.

When you use a base cut, the continuation of the outside line of the form—its silhouette—continues above and past the secondary step. There are now

The base cut is, without a doubt, one of the most important cuts for developing the design of any bowl or vessel form. It will help you to visualize the true location of the foot without running into the notch of the spigot.

an infinite number of choices in the shape, size, and diameter of the foot or base of an object being turned. In the case of a chuck, without the base cut, the continuation of the line of the form bangs right into the notch of the spigot, which forces the design of the foot to be the same diameter as the spigot itself. I call it an unforced error.

The same principle applies when using a faceplate with screws. Nothing is worse than getting to the final stages of turning a bowl and discovering a bunch of holes in the foot of the form—another unforced error.

The base cut also applies when using a glue block.

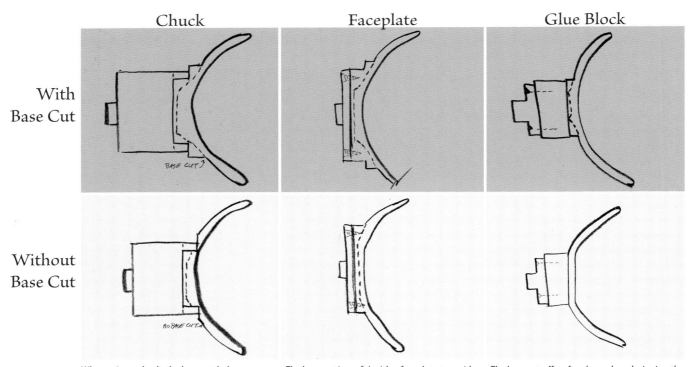

Chuck	Faceplate	Glue Block

With Base Cut

Without Base Cut

When using a chuck, the base cut helps you visualize the foot so that the walls are not cut.

The base cut is useful with a faceplate to avoid putting screws through the bowl walls.

The base cut offers freedom when designing the foot of a form with a glue block.

Without the base cut, we end up planning the design of the foot in relation to what we see, instead of what we might want it to look like.

The result in each of these cases is that without making the base cut, you confine the base of the form so closely to the chuck, the faceplate, or the glue block that you limit your freedom to design the foot. You also often end up with a wall thickness that is either too thick or too thin.

Another area where the eye is fooled is when you make the shape of this base cut into a nice pretty curve instead of a distinct angle. The curved surface looks good, almost as if it might become the finished base of the bowl. But what the curve really does is to slip the eye away from the direction of the line of the bowl, which prevents you from freely designing the foot.

Attaching the block to a chuck, glue block, or faceplate is covered in Chapter 6, "Chucks, Glue Blocks & Faceplates," on page 66.

Creating a base cut

The base cut is essentially a second notch, positioned above the notch that was made when forming the spigot. I use the tip of the gouge in the slicing position followed, if necessary, with any smaller-tipped tool that will ensure a 90° angle at the base of the notch. The base cut helps me to visualize the line of the form as it ascends toward the area of the foot. This gives me great freedom in designing the foot when I finish off this area in the jam chuck.

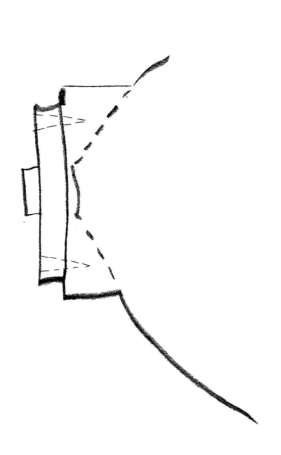

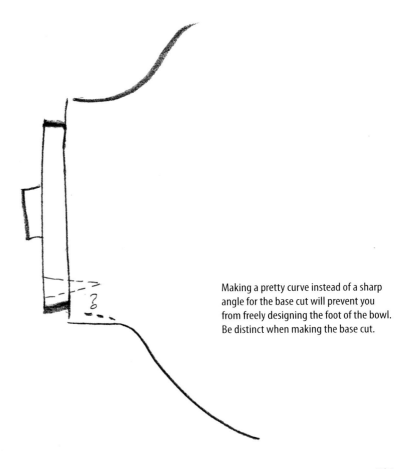

Making a pretty curve instead of a sharp angle for the base cut will prevent you from freely designing the foot of the bowl. Be distinct when making the base cut.

Shaping the bowl using the slicing cut

I like to use the slicing cut to create the final shape of the outside of the bowl. If you need to refresh yourself on the particulars of the slicing cut, visit page 116.

Use the slicing cut to shape the outside of the form exactly how you want it.

Oops! Look at the torn fibers on this dry, spalted ash bowl. No matter how slowly you go, these torn fibers are inevitable when you cut in the "correct" direction from the base to the rim of the bowl.

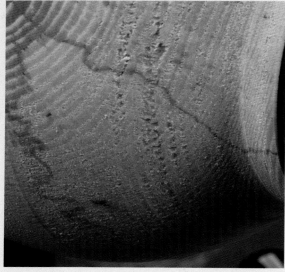

To cut out torn fibers, it is necessary to go the wrong way with the slicing cut. Riding the bevel, cut from the rim to the foot.

Shaping the final exterior using the slicing cut

Once the bowl blank has been installed on your chosen method of attachment and securely attached to the lathe, you are ready to use the slicing cut to do the form's final shaping. It is always an exciting moment for me, because I spend a lot of time working the form until I get it just right. It's impossible to get a catch in the slicing position, so it's very relaxing to simply draw the tool up the form from the base as I watch the upper silhouette take shape.

Just when I think I've got it where I want it, I turn off the lathe and discover the harsh reality of working with dry, spalted ash: The fibers tear like crazy. I'm doing everything right by cutting slowly and across the fibers of the grain, and still have problems. So it's time to break the rules.

To solve the problem, I make another slicing cut. In this case, I'm not only rubbing the bevel, but cutting in the wrong direction, that is, from the rim to the foot. I'll make this cut to what I believe is the depth of the torn fibers going down the side of the bowl and stopping near the base. My intent is to cut the torn area out in preparation for the final shear-scraping cut.

Finishing the exterior using the shear-scraping cut

Once the outside shape has been completed with the slicing cut, I make one or two final passes with the shear-scraping cut. This is one of those dream cuts that allows me to start sanding with 240- instead of 60-grit paper.

To position the gouge to make the shear-scraping cut, I elevate the tip so the lower edge that will do the work is approximately 45° across the surface of the wood. I then close the flute down by pointing it almost directly toward the wood, leaving only ¹⁄₁₆" of air space between the surface of the wood and the upper edge of the gouge that isn't being used. The gouge is in the same position as for the scraping cut, except the shaft has been raised to 45°.

Notice in the photo on page 125 (top) the position of my thumb and the first finger of my left hand. I also bring my right hand off the handle and move it way up on the shaft. Plus, I bring my wrists into my tummy and my elbows to my side. The thumb supplies downward pressure into the tool rest without you having to grip the gouge as you would do during a roughing cut. In this position, my entire body, from my belt line up, becomes a huge support system for the gouge. With my feet spread and my knees unlocked, the only movement I make when performing this cut is in the legs, not the upper torso.

Body position during the shear-scraping cut

In my opinion, this is the most intriguing cut of all those I describe in this book and certainly the most divergent from any other cut made with this gouge. The intent is to use your entire upper body as a supporting element to the gouge while allowing all the movement for the cut to take place in your legs. Some have equated it to golf putting. Spread your feet generously apart to allow full movement of the tool from rim to the base of the form, again, always moving from vertical over one leg to vertical over the other leg as you progress through the cut. Draw your right hand up to the shaft just behind your left hand (almost like a golf grip) and pull your wrists into your tummy. With the handle against your leg and the shaft of the gouge at 45° to the floor, you now have great support for the tool.

There are three key elements to successfully making this cut. First, keep the line of the edge 45° to the floor so that you don't drop the edge into the scraping position. Second, close the flute down to 85° so that the upper edge that does not touch the wood is approximately ¹⁄₁₆" from the wood. Lastly, unlock your knees so that your energy is down into the tool rest, not against the wood. This is very different from a traditional bevel cut where you're pushing against the wood. In this case, you only want the edge to glide across the surface as you shear the fibers. It definitely takes some getting used to, because it is so fundamentally different from traditional bevel cuts. However, the rewards are apparent when you are able to turn uneven grain patterns, knots, and wing-topped bowls without bouncing the bevel against the irregular surfaces.

The cut's direction is also unique and important in that I work against the grain by cutting from the rim down to the foot. It's worth cutting in both directions just to note the difference. Because the angle of the edge is at 45° to the wood, the edge has a high side and a low side. If I make a pull cut from the foot of the bowl to the rim, the last part of the edge to touch the wood will be the high side. Unfortunately, this high side will actually scoop the softer spring and summer fibers out of the surface as it passes by, resulting in a surface worthy of lots of 60-grit sandpaper. Conversely, if I make a push cut from the rim to the foot, the last part of the edge to touch the wood is the low side: In this case, the low edge leaves the surface of the wood as the cut progresses, *without* scooping the fibers.

What also distinguishes the cut is that instead of pushing the gouge against the wood as you might expect, about 90% of the force or pressure of the cut is *down* into the tool rest, and with only 10% up against the wood. The easiest way to envision how this works is to stand in position to make the cut and unlock your knees: You instantly feel the pressure of the tool going down into the tool rest. And that's exactly what you want when going through the cut.

As the edge cruises over the surface, you'll immediately notice there's no bouncing against the harder end-grain fibers and other obstructions like knots and voids. The edge slices through them. This will change, of course, the moment you accidentally start pushing against the wood instead of down into the tool rest. This shift in the direction of the force takes some getting used to; it is so totally different from the way you use a traditional gouge, where you must ride the bevel through the cut.

Notice also in the photo on page 125 (bottom right) the clarity of the surface of the knot as well as the grain around it. If I had had to make a very fine finishing cut with a traditional gouge while riding the bevel, the bevel would have bounced slightly on these dense fibers and interrupted the cut. When you are satisfied the surface is smooth, you are ready to cut the rim.

The Shear-scraping Cut

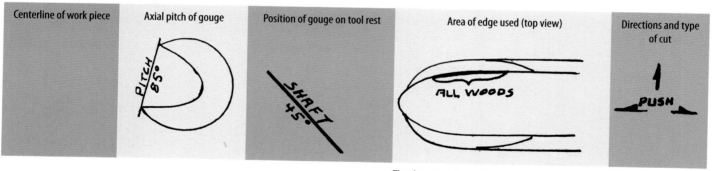

Centerline of work piece	Axial pitch of gouge	Position of gouge on tool rest	Area of edge used (top view)	Directions and type of cut
	PITCH 85°	SHAFT 45°	ALL WOODS	PUSH

The shear-scraping cut is used to put a smooth surface on the exterior of a form.

Finishing the exterior using the shear-scraping cut

I use the shear-scraping cut to put a smooth surface on the exterior of the bowl. When it's complete, you will be able to begin sanding at 240 grit.

Observe the position of my thumb and the first finger of my left hand. The lower edge of the gouge is doing the work.

When performing a shear-scraping cut, your body should be relaxed, your feet spread wide, and your knees unlocked. This cut is made by moving the legs, not the torso.

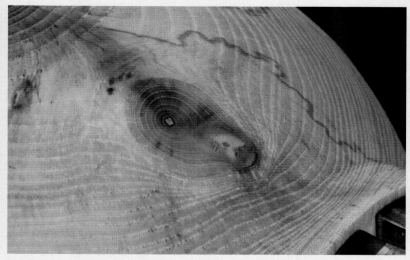

The final surface produced by the shear-scraping cut can skip 60-grit sandpaper and move right up to 240! Notice how smooth the surface looks—even around the knot.

Cutting the rim using the shear-scraping cut

The shear-scraping cut works well to form and smooth the top surface of the rim.

To form the rim of the bowl, use a shear-scraping cut. Remember to keep the gouge between 45° and 60° and to let the pressure of the cut go down into the tool rest.

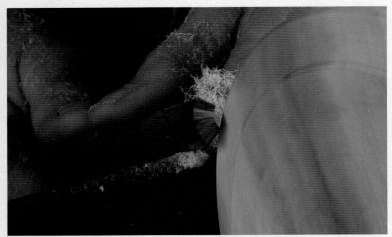

The shavings produced while shaping the rim of the bowl will be very fine. It is important to keep the upper edge of the gouge no more than 1/16" away from the surface of the wood.

Cutting the rim using the shear-scraping cut

Shaping and finishing the rim is easy when you use light strokes with the gouge in the shear-scraping position. To reduce the drag of the edge against the wood, I tend to raise the edge beyond 45° to even around 60°, especially on thin-walled bowls, which are inherently unstable. It is critical to keep the flute closed down so the distance between the top edge and the wood stays at no more than 1/16". The cuts can be made either by drawing or pushing the gouge around the surface of the rim.

Roughing-out the interior using the roughing cut

The interior roughing cut is the same as the exterior roughing cut, except I rotate the tool through an arc instead of pulling it. The hand on the tool rest provides the pivot, while the hand on the handle is the lever. The tip of the gouge begins the cut just to the left of the center of the bowl and progresses forward, stopping at the center of the bowl.

When making the cut, I place the gouge horizontally to the tool rest with the flute pointed right and the line across the edges of the flute at 45°.

The left hand can either be under the shaft (for lighter cuts) or over the shaft (for heavier cuts). This hand acts as support to allow the tip of the tool safe entrance into the wood. Once the cut begins, the left hand becomes a sliding fulcrum point. In both cases, the heel of this hand must be in contact with the rest to provide stability and guidance.

The right hand is positioned at the far end of the handle and provides power for the cut. By pulling the handle from right to left, the tip goes left to right through the fulcrum and cuts the wood.

Keep the shaft of the gouge horizontal and the line across the flute at 45°. If I rotate the gouge counterclockwise so the flute is pointing up, both sides of the tip will be touching the wood surface and will probably catch the tip. If I rotate it too far clockwise, so that the flute is pointing right, the edge will act like a scraper and plow into the wood.

It is not necessary to rub the bevel with this cut, because I'm not trying to produce a smooth finished surface. However, in very deep bowls, it's easier to stabilize the cut if I do ride the bevel. Every situation is different, so it's important to try both approaches.

Body movement is important for this cut. I start with the weight of my body vertically over my right leg. As I progress through the cut, I am sure to keep my knees unlocked so I end up vertically over my left leg. Through this sweep, the tip of the tool enters the cut on the left and finishes in the center of the bowl.

As I progress with the roughing cut, I'm mindful of the distance of the tool rest from the wood. It is important to stop the lathe and advance the tool rest so I'm cutting within a safe distance to the wood—within ½". Light cuts are always the way to start using any tool, but once in a while, it's fun to settle in with a long, slow roughing cut that makes 1"-wide shavings.

The Interior Roughing Cut

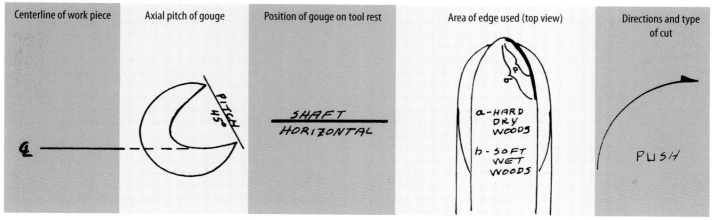

The interior roughing cut is used to clear mass from the interior in preparation for the finishing cut. The interior and exterior roughing cuts are very similar, the only difference between their executions being a pivoting action for the interior versus a pulling action for the exterior.

Roughing out the interior using the roughing cut

The roughing cut to rough out the inside of the bowl is basically the same as the roughing cut on the exterior, with a small difference: The interior roughing cut makes an arc through a fulcrum.

To move your body through the roughing cut, start with your body weight over your right leg. Keep your knees unlocked and transfer the weight to your left leg. The cut will have progressed from the left to the center of the bowl during that body movement.

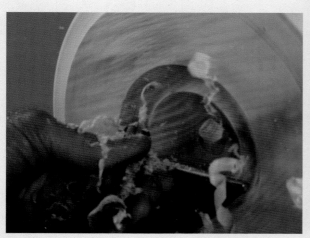

The direction of the roughing-out interior cut is from left of center to the center of the bowl.

Finishing the interior surface with the interior-finishing cut

The interior-finishing cut is one of the most elegant cuts in all of woodturning. The body makes a relaxing tai chi-like sweep of nearly a third of a circle, while using the tiniest portion of the tip of a very large tool that is moving fluidly from rim to base, coming to rest at an almost invisible point in the center of the bowl. It doesn't get much better than that. The cut is also a bit mysterious, because you not only use the wrong side of the tip to make the cut, but it is done in two stages.

The Interior-Finishing Cut

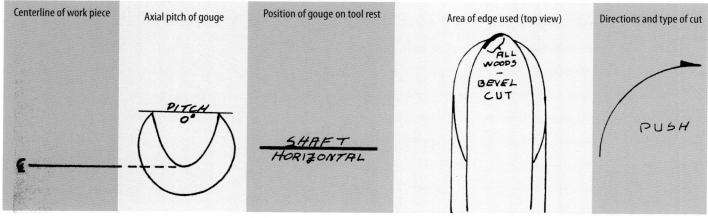

| Centerline of work piece | Axial pitch of gouge | Position of gouge on tool rest | Area of edge used (top view) | Directions and type of cut |

The finishing cut makes the final cut on the interior surface in preparation for sanding. The bevel must be in contact with the wood throughout the cut. To safely enter the rim, begin in the roughing position, then rotate the gouge counterclockwise to horizontal. The part of the tool that does the cutting is a small area to the left of the tip.

Body position during the interior-finishing cut

This cut is unusual in that it puts the body in an uncomfortable position. The lathe bed will be in the way of your legs. Keep your feet spread; this will allow the back of the handle to rotate fully through the third of a circle needed. The best way to practice this cut is to turn the lathe off, position the gouge tip in the center of the bowl base where the cut will end, and spread your legs so that you are balanced. Now look down and imagine a line between your feet intersected by another line that runs from your navel to the tip of the tool, forming a 90° angle. It helps to unlock your knees. Now, with the lathe still off, leave your feet in this position and reach out with your right hand. This will allow you to enter the cut without snagging the rim. Close your eyes and slowly pull the handle toward yourself, using your left hand as a floating pivot on the tool rest. Progress through the motion of the cut until the tip reaches the center of the bowl bottom. With the flute pointed straight up, rub the bevel on the left side of the tip as you rotate your body to the left. If you stop rotating, your torso will get in the way of the handle and the edge will go straight forward. When your body stops moving, you'll immediately feel the tip of the gouge get stuck in the wood. 95% or more of the problems that happen when making interior finish cuts occur because the turner gets nervous and forgets to rotate. The secret is to not focus on the edge cutting the wood, as it is quite capable of doing this all by itself. Instead, focus on the bevel stroking the curve.

Stage 1: Safely entering the rim

The following scenario has got to be one of the most maddening occurrences in bowl turning: The outside of the form is complete. The inside is 90% finished, and you're ready to make that final cut to shape the rim and thin out the wall. You bring the gouge to the rim and...Bingo! The tip of the gouge goes left instead of straight ahead, and you wipe out the rim.

The reason for this skip on the rim is the tip of the gouge has a U-shaped edge. If I turn the gouge 45° to the right to enter the rim, the right side of this U—the lower side—will be on the wood, and it works fine. But if I accidentally get even a smidge of the left side of the U on the wood—the upper side—it will feed the tip to the left just like the threads of a screw.

To correct this, always be sure the lower part of the edge touches the wood first. I have to enter the wood in the roughing position with the shaft horizontal and the flute facing 45° to the right. I make a cut approximately ¼" deep, which will leave me with a freshly cut surface so I can proceed with the finishing cut.

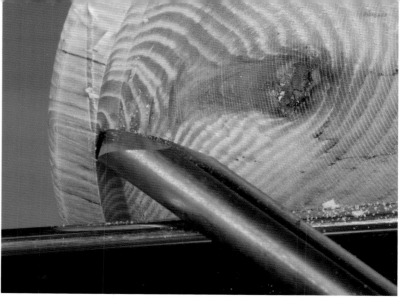

To correctly enter the rim, begin in the roughing position with the flute 45° to the right and the shaft horizontal. Make a ¼"-deep cut so you have a smooth surface to put the bevel on.

Stage 2: Finishing the interior of the bowl

This finishing cut is different from the shear-scraping cut used to finish the outside surface on a bowl or hollow form. It is very important to note the difference and not mix these cuts up. You do *not* want to attempt the exterior shear-scraping cut on the inside of an open bowl. There is too much edge at an elevated angle touching a surface that is predominantly end-grain fibers: Boom!

The interior-finishing cut is referred to as a "back cut" because, while the tip of the tool is moving forward through the wood with the bevel rubbing, it is the left, or back, side of the edge, that does the work. As with a traditional gouge, it is essential to use the bevel to support the edge throughout the cut.

As seen in the photo below, the position of the gouge is horizontal with the line across the flute at

To make a finishing cut, the gouge must be horizontal with the flute pointing straight up. Only ⅟₁₆" to ⅛" of the edge on the left of the tip engages the wood to make the cut.

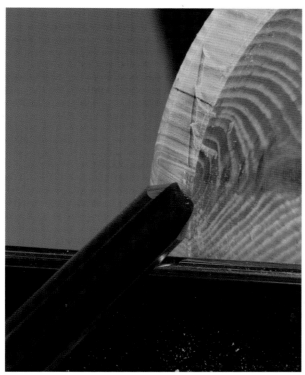

If you do not enter the rim properly when using the finishing cut, you will either scratch or wipe out the rim. This mishap occurs when any of the upper side of the gouge's U makes contact with the wood—the tip is fed to the left, just as if it had screw threads.

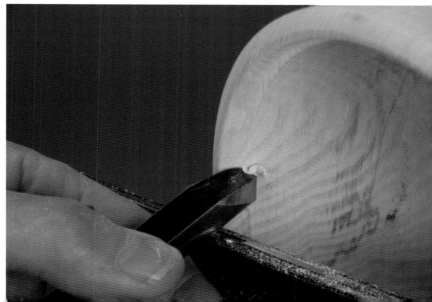

0°, or also horizontal. The area of the edge that does the work is a small region approximately ¹⁄₁₆" to ⅛" long, located just to the left of the tip (see illustration on page 128). In this position, the edge is pointing straight up while the wood is coming straight down. The result is an extremely efficient cut.

The angle of the bevel at the point of contact is broad enough that it can remain in contact with the wood while the gouge remains horizontal. If the angle were steeper (more vertical), I would have to rotate the gouge clockwise back to the roughing position to pick up contact with the bevel. In doing this, I would

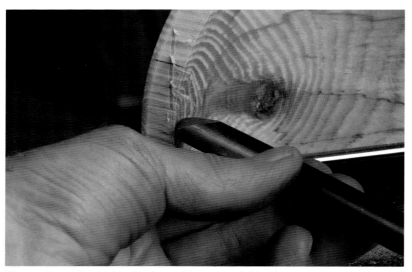

When you're entering the rim using the roughing cut, your left hand should be close to the tool tip for support. As soon as you create the ¼" area for the bevel, you can reposition this hand onto the top of the shaft and begin the finishing cut as seen below.

To perform the finishing cut, lift your left thumb up onto the top of the shaft, open your fingers, and use the heel of your hand to push the shaft down into the tool rest. Ride the bevel and push the tool with your right hand.

lose the acute vertical position of the edge that makes this such a remarkable cut.

Care must be taken not to rotate the gouge counterclockwise beyond horizontal. If it happens, too much of the edge will engage the wood, and a head-on collision will occur between the tool edge and the end-grain fibers of the bowl. WHAM! Time to start another bowl. Keep the gouge in the horizontal position, both axially and in plane, so *only* the ¹⁄₁₆" to ⅛" of the edge you need to make the cut makes contact.

The left hand is important when making this cut, as it progresses from the rim to the base. Besides being a pivot point for the shaft, it has only one function: to keep the gouge securely down on the tool rest.

To do it, I place my left hand close to the tip of the tool when I begin the cut in the roughing position. The moment I've cut that initial ¼" into the rim, I immediately retract this hand onto the shaft. I lift my thumb up onto the top of the shaft, I open my fingers, and using the heel of this hand to push the shaft down into the tool rest, I push the tool with my right hand and ride the bevel as I make the cut. Why? Four reasons.

1 I only need the support of my left hand to hold the shaft during the initial point of contact in the roughing position. This is the moment of truth, and I want to be sure the tip enters the wood correctly. Once I'm safely into the wood, the bevel takes over this support of the edge.

2 To make a fluid cut, I need to relax my body, unlock my knees, and swing the handle evenly throughout the arc as the cut progresses. With my thumb below the shaft and my fingers gripping it, there is an extreme amount of tension in this hand. By raising the thumb and unlocking my fingers, I release the tension and my knees automatically unlock. Try it…it's really quite amazing.

3 With the heel of my hand pressing the gouge down into the tool rest to support the shaft, I can pull my left hand away from the sharp edge of the spinning rim (or the wings on a natural-edge bowl) and release some more tension in my body.

4 All I have to do now is ride the bevel while I pull the handle toward me with my right hand. As I move forward with the cut, I can easily see the amount of wood I'm removing—usually about ⅟₁₆" to ⅛"—and I adjust the rotational movement of the handle accordingly.

I list these reasons because, at first, this cut was very tense for me. After I solved the problem, everything fell into place. The positions of the hands complement the cut and make it fluid. Tension is an awkward problem to recognize. But if you can find its source, you can learn how to release it. The way I discovered the tension problem in the left hand was to close my eyes and go through the motion of the cut with the lathe turned off. It soon became clear that the force of all the energy of the cut was at the junction of the tool and the tool rest, the same place it would be if I were lifting a rock with a lever on a fulcrum point.

I asked myself, "What is the job of this hand, anyway?" The answer was easy. "To create a pivot point and hold the gouge down on the rest so the tip won't bounce on the wood during the cut." The problem is creating downward pressure without also creating tension in the hand and body that would impede the flow of the cut. Shifting the thumb to the top of the shaft, opening the fingers, and moving the hand back away from the spinning rim solved the problems. Once again, tension discovered: problem solved.

Finishing the interior surface using the interior-finishing cut

The interior-finishing cut is beautiful to make. As you sweep from left to center, removing a ⅟₁₆"- to ⅛"-wide shaving, the interior of the bowl grows smoother with each pass.

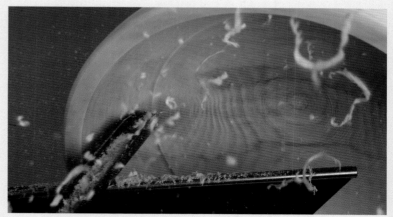

After entering the bowl using the roughing cut, ride the bevel toward the center.

Note that the area of the edge to the immediate left of the tip is doing the work. It is important to keep that part of the edge in contact with the wood at the same angle throughout the cut.

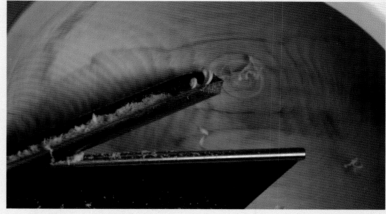

Note that the flute and the gouge itself remain horizontal throughout the cut from the rim to the center of the bottom of the bowl.

Removing the nib

You don't have to teach more than the first day of a bowl-turning class to realize how nerve-wracking that pesky little nib in the center of the bowl can be. All of your efforts at a nice relaxing finishing cut can come to an end when you overcut the nib and end up with a divot in the bottom of the bowl, forcing you to cut the entire surface again.

The difficulty comes from basically two directions: one procedural and one mental. The procedural part is you don't always know how to approach the nib. Should you push against it, pull across it, scrape it, or simply dig for it? The mental part occurs as a natural extension of the procedural: You simply get nervous. One begets the other.

One approach is to remember the nib is a single point on a continuous surface that starts at one area of the rim and continues through the curve to the rim on the other side. If you've already succeeded in making good cuts up to this point, what's the difference when you actually get to the nib? You ought to be able to continue the cut that started at the rim, take it right through the nib, and be done with it. Sounds good, doesn't it?

Unfortunately, something else happens when you arrive at the nib. You subconsciously shift your attention from the bevel stroking the curve of the bowl to the edge cutting the wood. When you make the shift, you drop your head so you can see the shavings being made, causing your shoulders to droop, your back to bend, your knees to lock up, your neck to crank, and the energy of the cut to shift from an even stroke balanced between both hands to an unequal stroke favoring your right hand and shoulder, which are now tense. Worse, you forget about the value of the bevel, and you begin to dig for the nib with the tip of the tool. The result is another divot.

The solution is to go back to basics. Forget about the edge cutting the wood. It's quite capable of doing its work all by itself, so why focus on it? Instead, *focus on the bevel stroking the curve of the bowl.* Do it and you can then develop the confidence that whatever is in front of the edge—a ridge, a lump, a bump, or the nib—will simply be cut away as the bevel progresses forward through the form's curve. When you do get to the nib, slow down the pace of the cut and focus again on the bevel. The edge will cut through the nib and leave you with a smooth surface that is a natural continuation of the cut that began at the rim of the bowl.

How do you make the mental shift from *watching* the edge to *feeling* the curve with the bevel? Easy. The answer is in the question: Shut your eyes. But before you do that, consider these steps of preparation.

1 Before you make the last few finish cuts with the gouge, turn the lathe off and watch yourself stroke the surface of the inside of the bowl with the meat of your fingers.

2 Close your eyes and continue stroking the surface with your fingers. Your fingertips will be much more sensitive to the surface with your eyes closed.

3 Now imagine the bevel of the gouge is the tips of your fingers and set yourself up to begin the cut. With the lathe turned off, close your eyes and stroke the surface of the bowl in slow motion with the gouge. You're only trying to feel the curvature of this surface. Repeat it several times. Wiggle your toes and squeeze some muscles in your legs, your butt, your abdomen...whatever it takes to reacquaint yourself with yourself. Always do it in slow motion. Observe while you're stroking the curve that when you do encounter a high spot on the surface, the edge of the gouge digs in and stops your forward progress.

4 Turn on the lathe. Repeat this same movement of stroking the curve with the bevel. Don't try to cut anything just yet; simply cruise across the surface on the bevel.

5 Finally, begin the cut and concentrate on the bevel stroking the moving surface. When you do finally encounter that high spot, the gouge will cut through it while the bevel continues to follow the bowl's curve.

When you build up your confidence that this method actually works, start with a 2"-thick bowl and practice the finish cut until you're sick of it. By the time you get to the final wall thickness, you'll have mastered both the interior-finishing cut and getting rid of the nib.

Along the way, or if you get bored from repetition, start the cut and then, about a third of the way to the bottom of the bowl, close your eyes and continue the cut to the center. It's amazing what you can feel within yourself when you gain the rhythm of the cut. And that little nib? Just stay on the bevel, slow down the pace of the cut, and slide right on through it.

Removing the nib

That pesky nib in the center of the bowl can be frustrating. This photo sequence shows my method for removing the nib.

Don't think about cutting the nib off...simply continue riding the bevel toward the center of the bowl.

As the tip approaches the center of the bowl, do not dig for the nib. Instead, slow the cut down, relax your hands, focus on the bevel stroking the curve of the bowl, and simply glide the tip through the nib.

When you have finished removing the nib, gently remove the gouge from the interior and congratulate yourself on remaining calm and unflustered by the nib. Not getting nervous and simply letting the gouge edge do its job are both vital to removing the nib.

Measuring the depth of the bowl

There is an old joke among woodturning teachers that you can almost tell what someone does for a living by watching him measure the depth of a bowl. Stereotypes aside, though, it's amazing how many gizmos—from rulers to lasers—there are out there today to accomplish this task. The good part is they all work.

I use a stick, or anything else lying around that's reasonably straight and longer than the depth of the bowl. It's not a very exotic tool, but wherever I go, there always seems to be one available.

My first step in measuring the depth of a bowl is to place the stick in the deepest part of the form, usually the center, and look across the face of the bowl from rim to rim with one eye. I then mark that point on the stick with my thumbnail.

Next, I transfer the stick to the bowl's outside, positioning my thumbnail on the rim's edge, marking the spot as I once again look across from rim to rim with one eye. It is absolutely critical to view this mark being on the line of the opposing rims.

Finally, I look down—again with only one eye—and mark a spot on the waste area of the form that is directly below the tip of the rod. This point represents the depth of the inside of the bowl brought outside where I can see it, so it's a good idea to turn on the lathe and mark a circle at this point to make it easy to see. Identifying the location of this line is critical, as it will help determine the location of the base of the bowl and prevent making a lampshade or a funnel.

Once this mark has been established, I can add a second line that represents the desired wall thickness in the base of the finished bowl, and a third line that will be the finished surface of the bottom of the bowl.

For a detailed description on using these lines to determine the foot of the bowl, refer to the section on centering open bowl forms in Chapter 14, "Jam Chucks & Vacuum Chucks," on page 200.

"There is an old joke among woodturning teachers that you can almost tell what someone does for a living by watching him measure the depth of a bowl."

Measuring the depth of the bowl

There are many ways to measure the depth of a bowl—rulers, lasers, calipers—but I prefer using a simple stick or rod.

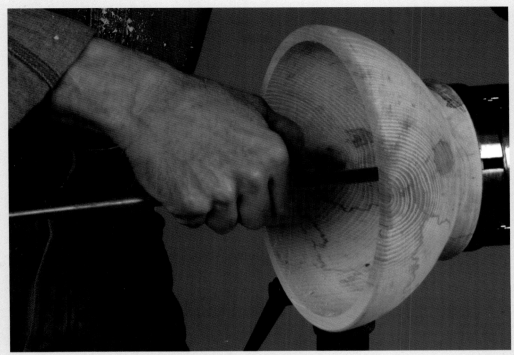

Place the rod in the deepest part of the bowl and look straight across the rim of the bowl to the other rim with one eye. Mark the point on the rod with your thumbnail.

Keeping your thumbnail in place on the rod, move the rod to the outside of the bowl and position your thumbnail at the rim. Look across the rim again with one eye and make sure that your thumbnail really is on the face of the opening.

Look straight down on the rod with one eye and mark the spot on the waste area that is directly under the end of the rod. Put the pencil lightly against this mark and turn on the lathe so that there is a line the whole way around the waste marking the bottom of the interior.

Chapter 10

Turning an Open Bowl with a Natural Edge

I believe the natural-topped, or natural-edge, bowl is the only true design illusion in woodturning. The shape of the rim comes directly unaltered from the log, and if you weren't a turner, you wouldn't have a clue as to how the form came about. Possibly, you might think it was stretched, molded, cut, carved, or, the one I like the best: "Is it wood?"

Note: The procedures described in Chapter 9, "Turning an Open Bowl with a Cut Rim," on page 108, are basically the same procedures you'll be using to create a natural-topped bowl. Because of the bark wings, there are a few critical differences in the cuts I use to make natural-topped forms, and I will detail the differences as they come up in the sequence of the text.

David Ellsworth, *Monument*, 1986. Redwood lace burl; 15" high x 10" wide x 10" deep. This is the only hollow form I ever made with no entrance hole. The natural bark inclusion divides this form into two halves, each with a natural edge.

I have seen pictures of Mayan bowls made of stone with a meandering rim, and wondered what possessed people to make bowls that didn't have round, flat rims. It could have originated from a wedge-shaped stone instead of a flat one. While I am sure there are many examples in objects from throughout history, my first exposure to this "unfinished" edge in woodturning was to Finnish spalted birch bowls made in the mid-1900s.

There always has been controversy about leaving bark on a finished bowl. I agree bark does add a good bit of visual drama to the form, but the truth is the cambium layer between the bark and the sapwood is actually a fluid, and acts as a natural separation layer. Some woods do hold their bark better than others, namely, holly, cherry burl, and pear. Also, cutting a tree in the winter when the sap is not running will minimize the separation. And, of course, you can always super-glue the bark as long as you don't mind stains in the end grain. Still, there's always the relative or neighbor who never gets invited back because he or she picked up your favorite natural-edge bowl by the rim and snapped the bark off. It's no wonder a lot of turners don't get repeat customers when selling bark-edge bowls. People love the beauty of the bowls when purchased, but they don't want to pay for more problems a week or a year down the road.

The choice to work with bark is a tough decision and one we all face. I don't claim to have the answer, because I don't believe there is a specific answer. But I also can't ignore the problem. In my own work, I've always tried to design for the beauty of the natural edge rather than the bark. I am particularly interested in the rhythm and harmony of the rim's movement, especially its orientation to the overall design of the form. I'll also note I've never seen a Stocksdale bowl with bark on it. However, working with bark can be a great adventure, and I recommend that you at least try it out. As long as you select a good species, cut the tree at the right time of year, and treat the edge delicately, your natural-topped bowl should turn out beautifully. Before you begin, I suggest you read the section on bark in "Parts of the Tree" on page 235.

Preparing the material

The natural-edge bowl is located in the log with the base near the center of the tree and the rim taking on the shape of the outside contour of the log. The procedure I use for making a natural-topped bowl is mostly the same as the procedure for the cut-rimmed bowl described in Chapter 9. Follow the directions for "Preparing the block from a log" on page 110 and for "Mounting the block on the lathe" on page 112, except reverse the direction of the blank when you mount it on the lathe. That is, the bark goes toward the headstock because I want the bottom of the bowl to be positioned in the tailstock. It's always easier to form the foot in preparation for mounting onto a chuck, glue block, or faceplate when the foot is positioned toward the tailstock rather than the headstock while being prepared.

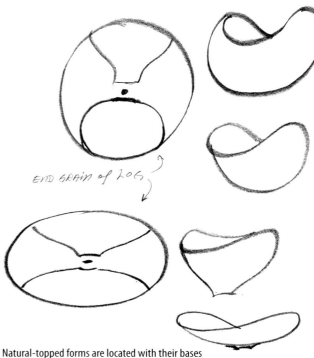

END GRAIN OF LOG

Natural-topped forms are located with their bases near the pith and the bark becoming the rim.

Roughing-out the form

After preparing the half log I've selected, I mount it on the lathe and begin to rough-out the shape. I cut from the base at the tailstock toward the rim at the headstock, using the roughing cut described on page 115 and then the slicing cut described on page 116. Don't cut all of the way to the top of the bark wing tips. The fibers located on the edges trailing the tips are unsupported, and as the edge of the gouge cuts through them, they fold back or rip out, making a terrible mess of the edge. The unsupported fibers in the areas of the bowl's edge can be either in the bark or the edge, itself, if there is no bark.

To solve the problem, I start at the tips of the wings and cut down toward the base of the bowl using the slicing cut. This is the same slicing cut I've used before. The only difference is it's going in the "wrong" direction. That is, the cut is directed into the fibers instead of off them, or, as some might note, cutting

"down hill" (rim to foot) instead of "up hill." The reason this cut works is the previously unsupported fibers actually pick up support from the high side of the tip of the gouge as it cuts through them. This differs from going the opposite direction, where this high part of the tip would pull the fibers away from the rim. To make this cut and prevent the wings from bouncing on the tip of the tool, I need to have a freshly sharpened gouge and a lathe running at approximately 750-plus rpm.

To set up this slicing cut, I place the gouge on the left side of my body so my head is directly above the tip of the gouge. This way, I can see the line of the bevel on the tip of the tool. I point the line in the direction I want to make the cut and ease the tool slowly into the wood. If the gouge were on the right side of my body, my head would be 90° to the line of the bevel, and I could only be hoping I knew where the cut was going. This is one of the few times left-handed turners have the advantage over right-handers. The most important part of making this cut is to NOT push the bevel against the wings. This would cause the tip to bounce away from the wood, and you'd never get a clean cut. Touch the bevel to the wings for reference, but focus on advancing the gouge forward by following the line of the bevel into the wood as the cut progresses.

To line up the slicing cut that will clean up frayed fibers, be sure your head is directly above the cut. This requires the gouge to be on your left side. Point the line of the bevel on the tip of the tool in the direction you want to go: in this case, from the rim to the base.

Torn fibers on the wings occur when you cut all the way to the top with the roughing or slicing cut. Because the fibers on the edge are not supported, they fold or rip when the gouge cuts through them.

Shear-scraping the outside surface

The final cut on the outside of the bowl is the shear-scraping cut. Because the wings are whipping around, it's critically important to focus on applying the downward pressure into the tool rest rather than into the wings. It is also very difficult to actually see the tips of the wings when they're spinning around, so it's hard to know where to start the cut.

I line up the tool rest parallel to, and no more than ³⁄₁₆" from, the surface of the bowl. Making sure the gouge remains on the tool rest, I begin the cut in the air slightly beyond the wing tips and feed the tip of the gouge slowly to the left until I feel it touching the wood. If you're just learning this cut, you'll most likely cut too deeply into the wings at first. If so, just back off a bit, go very slowly, and let the wings come to you instead of trying to overpower them.

It's subtle, but the rewards are worth the effort. It's also helpful to leave the bark on the bowl as long as possible when making this shear-scraping cut,

The final cut on the outside of a natural-edge bowl is done with the shear-scraping cut, just as with the cut-rimmed bowl.

even if you eventually want the rim to be barkless. Leaving the bark on helps to insulate the cut and prevent tearing of unsupported fibers in the bowl's rim. This was not possible with the piece of spalted ash shown in the photo below, but the cut still did a great job.

If executed properly, the shear-scraping cut will cleanly cut the unsupported fibers on the top of the bowl. Be sure the tool rest is parallel with the surface and ³⁄₁₆" away. Begin the cut above the wing tips and feed the gouge down slowly.

Roughing-out the interior

The procedure I use when cutting the interior of a natural-topped bowl is the same as for a cut-rimmed bowl. I obviously pay particular attention to the position of the tool rest and those whipping wings. But both the direction and the order of the cuts are the same. See "Roughing-out the interior using the roughing cut" on page 126.

Remember to keep the gouge horizontal and the flute at 45° when making the sweeping interior roughing cut.

The interior roughing cut is performed in the same way on a natural-edge bowl as it is on a cut-rimmed bowl. See page 126 for further information.

Bob Stocksdale bowls

The first natural-edge bowls I ever held were made by Lindquist back in 1978, and the first I purchased were made by Bob Stocksdale in 1979. Stocksdale's bowls were affectionately referred to as bird's mouth–shaped, the reference being to hungry chicks in the nest. The reference is more descriptive than complimentary, but that aside, he did refine and popularize this particular shape, and it has since been copied by probably every bowl turner I know...including myself. I make the bowls for demonstration and educational purposes only, and out of respect for Stocksdale, I do not sell them. Thank you for your inspiration, Bob Stocksdale.

(L-R) Bob Stocksdale, Untitled, 1981. Para kingwood; 3" high x 6½" wide x 5¼" deep. Bob Stocksdale, Untitled, 1980. Mesquite burl; 5" high x 7½" wide x 7½" deep. Bob Stocksdale, Untitled, 1979. Celon ebony; 3" high x 4¾" wide x 5¾" deep. Bob Stocksdale's bowl designs inspired a whole generation of turners.

Finishing the interior

Using the interior-finishing cut on the natural-topped bowl is similar to using this cut as described in Chapter 9 on page 128. However, it is not necessary to begin the cut in the roughing position as you would with a cut-rimmed bowl.

You will be able to begin the interior-finishing cut without fear of blowing out the irregular rim because it will not catch the gouge as it would in a cut-rimmed bowl. To begin the finishing cut, hold the gouge firmly with your thumb and fingers. Line up the left side of the bevel with the outside of the bowl by looking straight down on the tool.

When you're past the wing tips, shift your hand to a secure position with the thumb up to help relax your knees.

As you progress deeper into the bowl, shift your hand farther back on the tool to avoid the spinning wings. Relax your hand while applying downward pressure into the tool rest.

As you advance the cut toward the nib, remember to maintain downward pressure on the gouge and into the tool rest.

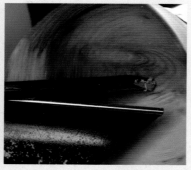

The finishing cut is complete after you have sliced through the nib. Do not think about anything beside sliding the bevel through the curve of the bowl.

Finishing the interior

The only difference in making the interior-finishing cut with a natural-edge bowl, compared with a cut-rimmed bowl, is I don't have to start the cut in the roughing position. Because the bowl has an interrupted surface instead of a continuous one, the gouge won't feed to the left when I enter in the finishing position with the flute pointed straight up.

In order to properly support the tip when I begin the finishing cut, I hold the gouge firmly with only my thumb and fingers. By positioning my head directly over the tip of the tool, I line up the left side of the bevel parallel with the outside surface of the form. It's like seeing two surfaces at the same time.

Once I'm safely past the tips of the wings, I shift my left hand back on the shaft toward the handle of the gouge so I can go deeper into the form without striking my hand on the spinning wing tips. Fear causes tension, which causes the body to stiffen up. This is a safe cut to make, as I am not muscling the tool, just supporting it. Equally important, to help relieve additional tension as I progress deeper into the bowl, notice I have brought my thumb onto the top of the shaft along with my fingers and palm. The simple act of moving the thumb helps relieve a huge amount of stress, not only in the hand, but also in my knees. With my hand open and my knees unlocked, I have dropped my entire body's energy downward and onto the tool rest. With this new-found mobility, I am able to relax the hand while putting downward pressure into the tool rest for good support of the edge in the wood. My entire body is able to rotate through the legs, resulting in smooth cuts with continuous curves.

To successfully make the final cuts when headed for the nib, it's critically important to maintain downward pressure with the left hand on the gouge and into the tool rest. The shaft of the gouge makes contact with the tool rest so far from the contact of the tip to the wood that the pressure is essential in maintaining a stable cut. Just like with all open bowls, slow down the cut and focus on the bevel stroking the curve of the form, not on the edge cutting the wood.

Measuring the depth of the bowl

Measuring the depth of a natural-edge bowl is a little different from measuring that of a cut-rimmed bowl because the wings are not necessarily on the same plane. I solve the problem by positioning the tool rest 90° to the bed of the lathe and touching the tip of one of the wings. I use a rod or stick to measure the depth of the bowl to the front edge of the tool rest, then from the tip of the wing to the base of the bowl on the outside of the form. Because the edge of the tool rest and the tip of the wing are in the same vertical plane, it makes the measurement quite easy. Mark the outside of the form to identify the locations of the interior depth, the desired wall thickness in the bottom of the bowl, and the foot. For a detailed description of using these lines to determine the foot of the bowl, see "Centering an open bowl form" on page 200.

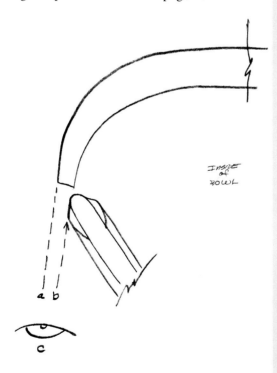

a - LINE of SIGHT, OUTSIDE SURFACE of BOWL
b - LINE of BEVEL, DIRECTION of CUT
c - POSITION of EYE

Entering the rim of a natural edge bowl to perform the interior-finishing cut is a delicate operation. Look along the outside of the wall, and make sure to keep lines a and b parallel.

Measuring the depth of the bowl

I like to use a slightly different technique to measure the depth of a natural-topped bowl than I would for a cut-rimmed bowl. Because the rim is not necessarily straight across, I can't look across the rim for reference. Instead, I utilize the tool rest.

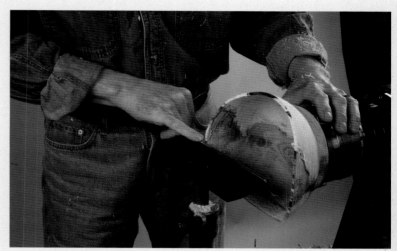

To measure the depth of a natural-topped bowl, put the tool rest at 90° to the bed of the lathe and touch it to the tip of one of the wings.

Use a stick or rod to measure from the tool rest to the deepest part of the form. Mark where the rod intersects with the tool rest using your fingertip.

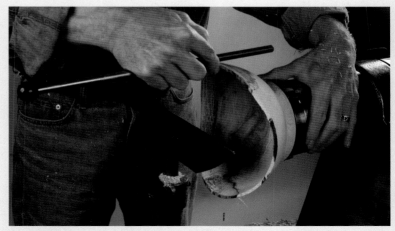

Hold the rod next to the wing tip that you lined the tool rest up to and mark where the end of the rod falls on the waste wood under the foot of the bowl.

143

Chapter 11

Turning the Exterior of a Hollow Form

As I reflect back on the thirty years that I've been turning hollow forms, I am happy to say the wonder and magic are still there for me. In fact, I may even be getting better at it. At least I don't blow the forms up much any more—meaning I don't lose control of the tool and break off a chunk—and the percentage of interesting and challenging design ideas that I think up continues to rise.

David Ellsworth, *Forest Artifacts*, 2008. Black ash burl; tallest 22" high x 11" wide x 10½" deep. A hollow object can take many shapes, from a pot (as described in the following chapters) to these tubular forms.

Part of the challenge of turning hollow forms is you can't see what you are doing when you turn the inside of a hollow form. When you take away the sense of vision, you become dependent on your other senses. Learning to trust these senses takes time, of course. But the rewards are everlasting. My pieces aren't as big as they were in the 1980s and 1990s—people seem to like big—but I'm not as young as I was then, either. I think my aesthetic has shifted from a sense of grandiosity that challenges the human scale to a more intimate relationship with that human scale.

I'm sure many of my students wonder when will that magic finally show up they have been looking for all along. It does come, although it might take more than a handful of attempts before they recognize it. One of the great satisfactions in making hollow forms is sharing the experience with others, either through the work itself, or in a classroom. In a teaching environment, it is satisfying to watch the struggles, tussles, and hidden aggressions come out until, one day, the classroom activity finally settles into a groove.

To turn the exterior of a hollow form, I suggest following these steps: mount the log, turn the log into a cylinder, flatten the ends of the log, create a sphere, rotate and remount the log, align the piths, flatten the base, and cut the final exterior surface.

POSITION OF Hollow FORMS in BURLS

Burls can yield hollow forms in nearly any position, and as large or as small as the burls themselves.

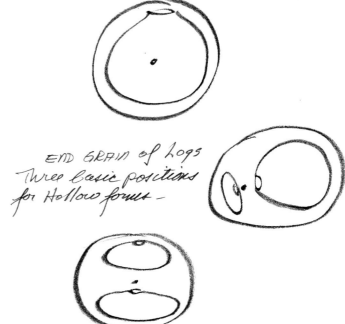

END GRAIN of Logs Three basic positions for Hollow forms —

A hollow form can include the pith from a log in its center, or if you want multiple forms from the log, you can cut them out from around the pith. Where you locate the opening in a hollow form is more a matter of personal taste than protocol. And while it may take time to gain the experience of extracting blocks so you get what you want, that's part of the fun of learning. My earliest hollow forms had piths all over the place. People kept saying, "I didn't know you could leave the pith in a bowl." Must have been one of those rules I forgot to learn.

Mounting the wood

Whether it's a burl or a plain old log, my method of mounting the wood on the lathe always begins by placing it between the driving spur at the headstock and tailstock revolving centers. I may have a general idea of what I wish to make based on the nature of the wood, its species, and its size, and on what I've learned in trimming it with the chain saw. To really get a sense of where I want to go with the piece—the refinements of the form and the layout of the grain—I need additional information. This comes from roughing-out the block. Each cut reveals more of what's hiding inside. Patterns of grain are revealed, moisture content felt, condition of the fibers unveiled, and color exposed. Soon, all of the things will be disclosed that will influence the decisions I'll make as to the final size and shape of the piece.

The first thing I need to do is get the wood mounted and balanced so it will spin without causing the lathe to start waltzing around the workshop.

Much more modest in scale than the method used for the 250-pound burl on page 148, this method is one I've been using for decades to make hollow forms. I begin by mounting a log between centers, with the grain running parallel to the bed of the lathe. Centering the log is very important to achieve balance. I could easily measure each end with a ruler to find the center point, but I like to place the log between centers and look directly at the end of the log from the tailstock end of the lathe.

It doesn't matter how the log sits. I just need to observe when there is more meat on one side of the revolving center then the other and shift the log until it looks centered left and right. Next, I hand-rotate the log 90° and use the same method to find the center on this axis. In two easy motions, the log has been centered on this end. I then repeat this two-axis process on the headstock end.

The block doesn't have to be perfectly centered, just well balanced. Still, I'm always surprised at how accurate this centering process is, easily within ⅛" to ¼". As I begin to trim off the bark, I'll check for any problems in centering and make further adjustments as I need them.

Mounting the wood

The first step I take when turning any hollow form is to mount the log between centers and ensure that the grain is running parallel to the bed of the lathe. You can use a ruler to find the center of the log, if you wish, but I prefer to place the log between the lathe centers and turn the log by hand, slowly adjusting until it is centered.

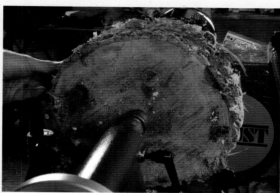

Mount the log between centers, getting it as close to being centered as you can.

Turn the log 90° and make sure it is centered on that axis. If it's not, loosen the tailstock and tap the log in the appropriate direction.

Check that the headstock end of the log is centered. Keep the pressure from the tailstock directed into the log so that you don't lose the centering you've just completed.

Turning the log into a cylinder

Turning the log into a cylinder is done using just the tool's tip in the roughing position. I don't go back and forth over the entire surface, as it would be a rough ride from the bumpy surface. I start near the right end and cut the rough stuff down until I end up with a smooth surface from that point to the right end of the log. I then take another cut to the left of the first, ending up on the previously cut smooth surface. Cut by cut, I end up with a smooth cylinder.

Mounting a large burl

Few turners will ever have the chance to work on a piece of wood this large, so I thought it would be exciting to put this in my book just to show what it looks like and share the experience.

I began by using a 1-ton chain hoist to bring this sugar maple burl up to the spindle. Once the burl was trapped between spur and tailstock centers, I was ready for the most exciting step: Just turning the lathe on. Who knows what mysteries await a 250-pound lump of wood at 800 rpm? With 4,000 pounds of steel and a 5-horse motor supporting the action, it was a truly awesome feeling of sound and sensuality.

The first step was using the 1-ton gantry to hoist the large burl up to the lathe.

A 250-pound burl moving at 300 rpm is something to behold!

Turning the log into a cylinder

One way to rough the log into a cylinder is to use the tip of the gouge to make numerous swathes on the log, starting on the right end and placing each successive cut to the left of the previous one.

Make the first roughing cut near the right end of the log. Continue to make short cuts from left to right, slowly working your way left.

The whole cylinder will be roughed-out when the bark and irregular surfaces have been removed. Do not try to cut all the bark off at once—progress in small chunks, or you will have a bumpy ride.

When the cylinder is smooth, begin shaping the form.

Flattening the ends of the log

The reason I flatten the ends of the log before going any further is the irregular surface from chain saw cuts can cause vibration from unequal weight distribution as I increase the speed to get a better-quality cut. In this case, that speed might go from around 400 rpm to possibly 700 rpm, depending on the size of the log and the size of the lathe. It is impossible to accurately pin down what rpm to use. Every situation is different, including the size of the object, its moisture content, species, shape, equipment, and so on. The best guide is to start at a very slow speed and work up. It's not the number of rpm that is important, but how you feel when turning the object. If you're uncomfortable, slow it down. Speed is never a substitute for efficiency.

This flattening cut is a great cut to learn because it comes in handy for so many situations, works beautifully, and is fun to do. I'm basically just cutting at 90° to the end grain, but with the 1" length of the edge on the side of the gouge, it's possible to remove 1" of material from the irregular edge if necessary. And that's quite a cut!

I begin the cut by feeding the tip of the gouge into the wood so that once the cut is begun, the bevel will rub against a continuously smooth surface. Put another way, if the amount of the irregularity is, say, ½" off from one side of the log to the other, I begin the cut ½" to the left of the greatest projection of this irregular surface. Then, with the bevel rubbing on a smooth surface, I point the bevel 90° to the line of the outside of the cylinder and push the gouge forward. In most cases, I can then flatten the end in one cut. I do this on both ends of the log.

Flattening the ends of the log

It is helpful to get rid of the irregular surface left by the chain saw on the ends of the log so that the unequal weight distribution doesn't cause vibration on the lathe. To flatten the end of the log, I use the gouge in the roughing position.

Flatten out the end of the log by creating a smooth spot with the tip of the gouge for the bevel to ride the rest of the way in.

Using the smooth surface created in the previous step, point the bevel straight in and push the gouge toward the center.

If the flat surface of the log is not on too severe of an angle, the whole end of a log can be flattened in one cut.

Creating a spherical shape

My next step is to shape the two ends of the log into hemispheres. This step can be done with the roughing cut, the slicing cut, or a combination of the two.

To perform the rounding process with the roughing cut, keep the Signature gouge horizontal and the flute at 45°. Push the gouge forward and ride the bevel.

To perform the slicing cut, begin in roughing position and elevate the tip by dropping the handle 20° to 30°. When using the slicing cut to round a log end, the gouge is actually pushed away. When you turn the log 90° and begin shaping the vessel, you'll be pulling. In both situations, the edge of the tool moves tangent to the grain, thus cutting smoothly.

To complete the rounding, use the tip of the tool in the slicing position.

Drop the tip into roughing position at the end of the cut near the tailstock center. If you don't, you'll only be able to cut above the center of the stem on the end of the log and you won't be able to remove it.

Creating a spherical shape

Once the ends are flat, I cut each end to a hemisphere so I end up with a round ball. Without rounding the ends and without removing these corners, I might not be able to turn the log 90° to make a cross-grain hollow form without the corners hitting the bed. In fact, this process allows me to turn hollow forms on a mini-lathe with a log that is only ½" in diameter smaller than the capacity of the machine.

Equally important, with a spherical shape, I'll have more information about the log than ever before, because I can see the entire surface of the form. There might be all sorts of things visible that I just couldn't see when the log was whole, like bug holes, lines of spalting, a bit of rot, or some #4 copper cable. All of this information will be helpful in designing the final form.

The rounding can be performed with a roughing cut, a slicing cut, or a combination of both. In general, I use the roughing cut to do the bulk of the hard work on irregular shapes, then switch to the slicing cut to do the final shaping of the piece. The combination of the two cuts allows me to move very quickly from a raw log or burl to a finished shape, but without feeling as if I'm rushing the process.

Remounting the log

The reason for turning the log 90° is that, with the exception of many vases, most hollow forms are done with the grain running cross-wise to the form. Turning the log after I've rounded it out gives me that orientation.

Once I have this spherical shape, I draw a pencil line around the equator of the form to divide the sphere in half. I place the pencil on the form and turn on the lathe. I use the line as a reference for remounting the log after it is rotated 90°.

Next, I remount the sphere with both spur and revolving center points on the pencil line. I generally will put the spot I have selected for the opening hole into the spur center, simply because it's easier to shape the base of the form if it's near the tailstock. However, there can be times when I don't want the spur center to chew up the area of the entrance hole, so I just mount it in reverse. The pencil line obviously divides the sphere in half on the vertical axis, but to get it centered on the horizontal axis I hand-rotate the sphere from one side to the other, comparing the distances from each side of the sphere to the tool rest.

Remounting the log

After the log has been turned into a near-sphere, it can be remounted in preparation for turning the outside profile of the hollow form.

Divide the sphere with a pencil line around the middle of the form. If the log is truly round in the middle, simply hold the pencil point against the form and turn the lathe on for a few seconds.

To remount the sphere, place both headstock and tailstock center points on the line. I usually put the spot I've selected for the opening into the drive center because it is easier to shape the base when it's near the tailstock.

To center the form on the second axis, compare the distance on each side of the tool rest using any handy stick or rod. Mark the distance with your thumbnail.

Hand-rotate the form 180° and see if the measurement matches up. In this photo, the form isn't quite centered.

Reposition the revolving center point on the pencil line until the distances are the same, at which point the sphere is centered and balanced.

Aligning the pith ends

The final step in orienting the grain in the sphere is to identify, mark, and align the pith. Turned green wood forms will distort from a circle to an oval along the line of the pith. If I know where the distortion is going to take place, I can design the shift into the finished piece. If I neglect the line of the pith, the distortion can easily compete with the shape of the form, and it might end up looking odd instead of interesting. This isn't to say odd isn't OK. It's just wise to learn the process so you have more control as you explore design ideas in your work.

The end grain of logs can often be pretty mucked up from exposure to the elements or cuts from the

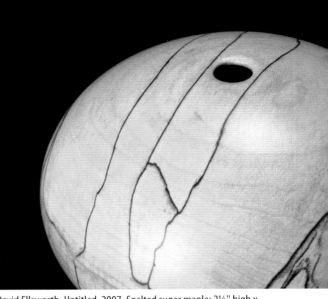

David Ellsworth, Untitled, 2007. Spalted sugar maple; 2½" high x 4" wide x 4" deep. Controlling the layout of the grain in the form may seem tedious, but it can have beautiful results. In this piece, I positioned the entrance hole in the exact center between the two lines of spalt.

Using the pith to alter design shape

The pieces shown in these photos illustrate several ways in which you can use the movement in the area of the pith to influence the design of your pieces. In *White Pot*, the spalted band of sapwood circumvents the form, while the pith falls horizontally through the center of the belly of the form. The effect is a sense of visual order, as the form has settled into a natural ellipse. With *Pot Dancing*, I positioned the pith diagonally through the form, which lends a very dramatic illusion of movement to the final design. In *Cloud Sphere*, the extent of the movement of the form is more subtle—a reflection of using spalted maple, which has considerably less tension in the grain than white oak (the wood used in both of the other pieces). Orienting the pith vertically through a form is the standard method of turning a vase; however, it can also cause some problems. Since the pith areas do project outward from the form as the face grain shrinks during drying, one can expect the base and the top of a vase to grow in height. Also, checking or outright cracking can occur in any location involving the pith, so this, too, would influence the overall design. Experiment with pith orientation in your designs—there are so many possibilities.

David Ellsworth, *White Pot*, 1993. Spalted white oak; 9" high x 10" wide x 9" deep. I've positioned the pith horizontally through the center of this piece. As a result, the wood has moved into an elliptical shape.

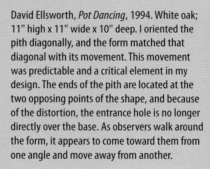

David Ellsworth, *Pot Dancing*, 1994. White oak; 11" high x 11" wide x 10" deep. I oriented the pith diagonally, and the form matched that diagonal with its movement. This movement was predictable and a critical element in my design. The ends of the pith are located at the two opposing points of the shape, and because of the distortion, the entrance hole is no longer directly over the base. As observers walk around the form, it appears to come toward them from one angle and move away from another.

David Ellsworth, *Cloud Sphere*, 2005. Spalted maple; 10" high x 10" wide x 9½" deep. The pith runs diagonally through this piece, but the movement is not as dramatic as in *Pot Dancing*, because the spalted wood had less tension. However, you can still see the two long points indicating the pith ends.

Aligning the pith ends

Since green wood distorts along the pith, take the pith location into account when designing your hollow form.

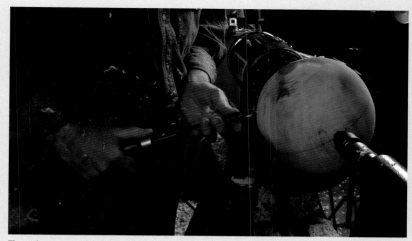

The pith is a powerful element in any vessel design, both visually and physically. But the pith can also be difficult to see. Because the wood is both weathered and rough from the chainsaw, trim off any excess material on the opposing ends of the log by cutting directly across the fibers with the tip of the gouge in the slicing position. This will clearly expose the pith.

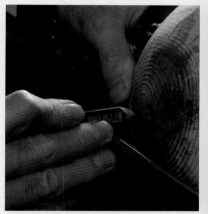

Put your pencil on one pith end and hand-rotate the form. If both ends of the pith come to the same spot, you know that the line of the pith running through the form is parallel with the foot. However, it is most likely that the pith runs obliquely through the form, out of alignment.

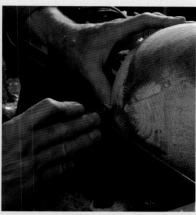

Measure the distance from the line you drew to the pith.

Draw a line from the first line to the pith. Move the points of *both* centers half of that distance in opposite directions to keep the sphere in balance. Continue testing and tweaking until the pith runs straight through the sphere.

chainsaw, so to get a clear view of where the ends of the pith fall on the sphere, I trim away the bad spots with the tip of the gouge in the roughing or slicing position—whichever works best for the object I'm working on.

Once the ends of the pith are cleanly exposed, I mark them with the pencil and hand-rotate the sphere from one side to the other to see if they happen to fall on the same line. If they do, I know the line of the pith running through the sphere will also be parallel to the foot of the final form. However, this rarely happens. In almost all cases, the pith ends up running obliquely through the sphere, anywhere from ⅛" to 2" out of alignment. Whatever the distance is,

I simply divide it in half and move the points of both centers off the pencil line half that distance and in opposite directions until the pith runs perpendicular to the lathe bed.

All of this fiddling with grain alignment might seem a bit tedious, but the rewards are evident in the final layout of the grain in the pieces I make. My intent is to compose the design of the entire piece. And part of my method is to put myself in control of the layout of the grain in order to affect the final design of the form. Unlike clay, wood comes with its own adornment, so it's important not to ignore the material as an element within the design.

Flattening the base

After you have decided upon the orientation of the grain, the next step is to flatten the base to receive a chuck, glue block, or faceplate. I will be preparing my piece for a chuck. To prepare for a glue block or faceplate, see Chapter 6, "Chucks, Glue Blocks & Faceplates" on page 66.

Flatten the bottom using slicing, then scraping cuts, so that the spigot is both flat and the correct height and diameter to fit into your chuck.

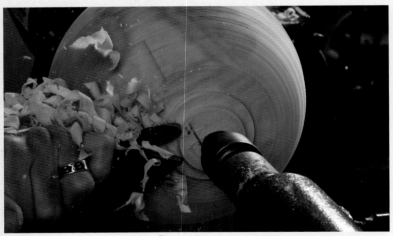

Make a slicing cut to create the edge of the spigot and a sharp notch in the base of the groove. Be sure this notch is crisp so the chuck jaws get a firm grip.

Create the base cut so you will have control over the design of the foot later.

Flattening the base

If I'm happy with the design, the final step in preparing the form for turning is flattening out the base to receive either a chuck, faceplate, or glue block. I do this first with slicing cuts to cut away the bulk, then switch to scraping cuts to finish flattening the surface. For this piece, I've chosen to form a spigot that will be inserted into a four-jaw chuck. If you'd rather use a glue block or faceplate, instructions can be found in Chapter 6, "Chucks, Glue Blocks & Faceplates," on page 66. I want the biggest chuck I can find and the largest-diameter spigot for the greatest amount of stability and the least amount of vibration. In this situation, the jaws of the chuck close fully at approximately 4¼" interior diameter, so I'll make the spigot 4½" diameter to get maximum grip from the jaws. And the reason I knock off the nib at the bottom is every once in a while, it will get in the way of the inner surface of the chuck's jaws and prevent the jaws from tightening fully against the spigot. Be sure to knock the nib off no matter which attachment method you choose—it will also prevent adequate contact with both a glue block and a faceplate. End grain nibs on vase forms will need to be cut off instead of knocked off. When I get rid of the nib, I lose the center mark for when I want to recenter it in the jam chuck to turn off the base, but that center point can be easily relocated. When you've knocked the nib off, apply the attachment of your choice.

Shape the form using a slicing cut by elevating the gouge 20° to 30° above horizontal, keeping a 45° angle on the flute.

Cutting the final exterior surface

The fun part, of course, is developing the final design using the slicing cut and then shear-scraping the surface in preparation for sanding and finishing. For more instruction on using these cuts to finish the exterior of the pot, see "Shaping the final exterior using the slicing cut" on page 122 and "Finishing the exterior using the shear-scraping cut" on page 123.

When you have completed the exterior of the hollow form to your satisfaction, you are ready to move on to the next chapter: "Turning the Interior of a Hollow Form."

Finish the surface with the shear-scraping cut. Be sure that the top edge of the gouge is only 1/16" from the surface.

Chapter 12

Turning the Interior of a Hollow Form

In the last chapter, I talked about working the outside surface of a hollow form. In this chapter, I'll discuss the procedures for hollowing it out. During this process, I'll excavate the interior through a small opening. I'll be working with scraping tools I designed in the mid-1970s that allow me to both core out the interior and refine the inner surface to a delicate wall thickness, thus giving the forms a wonderful lightness.

Turning the interior of a hollow form is a unique experience that you must do by feel, because you cannot see inside of the form while you cut it.

My original hollowing tools were created in 1975. I had many sizes and angles to reach the various areas of my hollow forms, all made of 0-1 drill rod.

I well remember my first ceramics class when I was trying desperately to center this huge lump of clay on the potter's wheel. The harder I worked, the more lopsided it became. My professor, George Downing, sauntered by and delivered his most casual "Aha," as if he were seeing something for the first time. He then bent down, leaned his upper arm and shoulder against the lump of spinning clay, and gently eased his body forward. One revolution later, it was perfect. That recollection continues to guide my methods and tool designs. Finesse, not force!

There is a powerful relationship between the maker and the material that manifests itself through the process. And, if you don't pay close attention to process, it is all too easy to focus on the finished object rather than on your methods for making it. What my professor showed me was that if I wanted to succeed in making a pot, I was going to have to learn how to let the material come to me through the process, rather than try to dominate the material using the process. The maker and the material need to learn how to shake hands.

Whether you're working with my tools or someone else's, making contact with the wood far from the tool rest is an awesome experience that tests you. So to go charging inside a hollow form with the same attitude you applied to shaping the exterior can be a teeth-rattling experience.

Preparing to turn the interior

To prepare for working with straight and bent hollowing tools, you might want to review the very basic principles described in Chapter 3, "Why Turning Tools Work," on page 22. Without this, you have no way of knowing whether the tools are working properly or, if not, how they can be improved.

Preparing your body

You might think that I've over-emphasized the importance of correct body positions. But if you get tired of reading about it, just remember: If, after turning your neck hurts, your legs ache, or your arms are in pain, you can prevent aches by following my advice on body positions. I'll cover hollow-turning body positions here, but be sure to read Chapter 8, "The Body," on page 98 for a full overview with exercises to prepare your body for turning.

Regardless of the types, styles, or designs of tools you use to make hollow forms, how you approach the lathe is critically important, not just for the safety of your body, but also for your success and enjoyment.

Prevent pith checking

Before I begin cutting very deeply into the form, I wrap the equator with 2"-wide plastic shipping tape. This helps prevent checking in the pith area caused by evaporation from spinning the wood and by the heat generated while hollowing the form.

The correct position for your body when turning the inside of a hollow form is directly in front of the form, with your head directly above the shaft of the tool and with your body squared up, that is, approximately 45° to the line of the shaft. If your shoulders and torso are parallel with the shaft, there's no way to support the back of the tool when cutting. Something will give, and it's invariably your shoulders and neck. With the handle against your body and your knees bent, the tool has excellent support, and the cutting energy will now come directly from your legs and torso rather than your arms and shoulders.

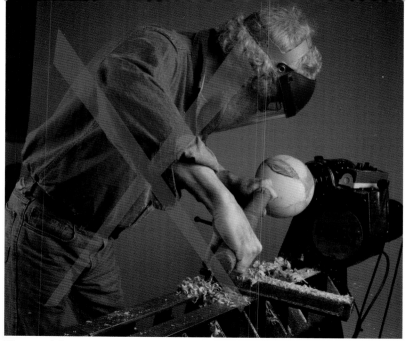

When people lean over the bed of the lathe with the right arm extended away from the body, the shoulder is totally vulnerable to vibration, and the arm remains too flexible to control the cut. As well, your line of sight is sideways to the tool instead of in line with it, so it's impossible to determine exactly where the tip is cutting.

The incorrect position for turning a hollow form would be leaning over the bed of the lathe with your rear arm hanging out, as shown in the photo at left. Not only will you be unable to support or control the cuts, but you also won't be able to determine exactly where you're cutting. Worse, once you pull your elbow away from contact with your torso, all the vibration will go directly into the shoulder, and you're heading for rotator cuff surgery sometime down the road.

Keeping the right forearm vertical allows the elbow to act as a shock-absorber and take vibration away from the shoulder joint. With the handle against my body, feet spread comfortably apart and knees unlocked, the tool now has excellent support. Also notice the various triangles formed between my hands and shoulders, feet and hips. Triangles are good.

Guidelines for hollow turning

The basic methods I use for working the interior of hollow forms are: cut for depth, clean for accessibility, measure the wall thickness.

You can remember these steps with the hollow turner's mantra: *cut, clean, and measure–cut, clean, and measure–cut, clean, and measure.*

In truth, I've experienced very few hollow-form blow-outs when it was the wood's fault. This includes all those wonderful pieces of rosewood and burl wood from the early days before I knew how to accurately measure the wall thickness, or when I was cutting in one location while imagining I was cutting elsewhere. Offering you these procedures is the best way I know to help you succeed in your attempts at turning hollow forms.

Triangulation of your body position is essential. Notice in the photo at right that I have established a triangle in my body between my shoulders and two hands. The closer this approaches an equilateral triangle, the more equally the forces are distributed, and the less strain there is on the individual muscles. My right forearm is vertical so that it acts as a pendulum. My elbow then absorbs the vibration, protecting the shoulder joint. If I were to move my right hand forward, I would break the strength of this equilateral triangle, and I would now have to use more muscles in my arms and shoulders to support the tool. If I were to use a tool in this position with my forearm forward, it would drive the vibration directly into my shoulder joint.

With recent lathes, you can work off the tailstock end or the outboard end, instead of from the side of the lathe. When using these lathes, I spread my feet and unlock my knees to form an additional triangle between my feet and my abdomen. This can't be an equilateral triangle, or I'd have to rope my feet together to keep from doing the splits. But it does give me great support and mobility when working inside a hollow form. Most beginning turners keep their feet too close together, thus constricting their movements. I think it comes from wanting to feel more secure in a situation that seems anything but secure, at least in the beginning.

Your head should be directly above the shaft. This helps you judge where you're cutting inside the form. Tilting your head down to look inside while you're cutting is counterintuitive. First, it's impossible to see anything. Second, your neck and shoulder will become fatigued. And finally, you'll probably cut right through a thin-walled form an inch or two away from where you thought you were working.

I triangulate my legs for additional support by spreading my feet to a comfortable distance apart. And with bent tools that require a lot of hand strength, I wrap the handles with foam rubber and duct tape to cushion vibration.

Your arms must be in the correct position to offer enough support. With your right forearm vertical, your elbow is the shock absorber. If the shoulder above the handle of the tool becomes fatigued, then either the lathe is too high, your arm is too far back or forward on the handle, or you're cutting too aggressively. Lighten up. The day is young.

Your knees must be kept unlocked. This balances your upper body, and allows you to maneuver. Any time there is rigidity or stiffness in the body, from the toes to the head, it increases tension and decreases your ability to make efficient and fluid cuts.

Straddling is a useful way to begin turning hollow forms. Straddling the bed of the lathe allows you to address the workpiece straight on instead of from the side. I position my weight over my left leg while I'm cutting in the center of the hollow form, then shift my position to the center of the bed to work to the left of center. All the while, I keep my head directly above the handle and shaft so that I can maintain directional focus on the tip of the tool even though I can't see it.

Most lathes today are simply too tall for turning hollow forms and shorter people may need riser blocks on both sides of the machine. A carpet remnant or rubber floor mat draped over the bed isn't a bad idea, either. I've often thought of making a saddle, but since I'm 30 years into it already, I'm not holding my breath.

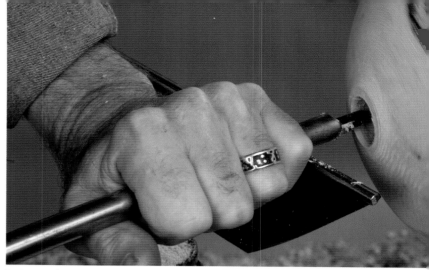

Positioning the tool rest at 60° to 70° to the lathe bed gives the heel of your hand the support needed while making internal cuts.

Preparing your lathe

Adjust the tool rest height so that when the shaft of the tool is horizontal, the edge of the tool tip is exactly on the centerline of the workpiece. Tool rests are all designed a little differently, but you can either cut a dowel to fit under the post or cut a ring to go around it, so that the tool rest always drops to the same height.

Position the tool rest about 60° to 70° to the line of the bed, not 90° as you might expect. This is because the heel of your left hand needs somewhere to rest. If the tool rest was set straight across the front of the form, your wrist would be pulled forward, pulling your left shoulder forward and pulling your upper torso out of position. Within a few minutes, this makes a huge difference in your fatigue factor and, of course, in your ability to make accurate cuts.

> ### Adjusting lathe height
> When multiple people are working on the same machine, you can build a U-shaped platform of plywood and 2 x 4s to help elevate shorter people.

Most long-bedded lathes will force you to straddle the bed while turning the interior of hollow forms. Keeping one leg on the floor will support your body while the other leg remains over the bed to help control the cuts.

Clearing the chips, in addition to following the directions in the right order and using the proper tools at the proper times, will help prevent dangerous catches. You must frequently stop the lathe and clear the shavings out of the form, so they don't build up inside and trap the tool tip. An air compressor is invaluable. With the tip of the nozzle placed just outside the entrance hole, shoot the air at a 45° angle into the hole. The air will circulate inside the form and blow the shavings and dust out of the hole. In addition, the cool air from the compressor relieves the heat produced by cutting. I could not make my Spirit forms without this cool air. If the entry hole is small, you'll have to use a bent rod to pull the long shavings out.

Using straight tools (boring bars)

The purpose of any straight boring tool is to clear out the bulk of the wood inside a hollow form, so you can make the more subtle finish cuts on the side walls. The primary direction of these cuts is the same as in an open bowl: from the left of center toward the center. If you cut from the center to the left, you immediately begin cutting into end grain, and the tip will instantly vibrate.

With the exception of the final finishing cuts across the bottom-center of a hollow form, there's nothing mysterious about making cuts with a straight boring tool. In truth, what the straight tool does best is clear out all the wood that's in the way of going in to do the refined cutting with the bent tool.

REMOVING CHIPS—AIR IN, AIR & CHIPS OUT

As you create a hollow form, it is very important to stop frequently to remove the chips inside. If you don't do this, the tool will become trapped in the shavings. Fortunately, most shavings can be removed with an air compressor blast at 45° to the entrance hole.

Drilling for depth

Drilling is a perfectly acceptable way to determine how deep you can go into a bowl without inadvertently creating a lampshade. It's commonly done when turning open bowls, because it establishes the interior depth before you begin cutting. The drilled hole also eliminates the troublesome nib in the bottom that can deflect the tip of the turning tool.

However, drilling a hole in hollow forms can cause problems, not the least of which is that as your skills increase, so does the height of your forms and you soon exceed the length of your drills. As well, you must constantly pull the bit out and remove the chips to prevent it from getting stuck in the hole from the swelling of the green fibers. This relates to the real problem, which is heat. Clean or not, the drill bit gets hot, and this heat transfers to the wood surrounding the entrance hole. With open bowls, you cut this area out. But when making hollow forms, especially those with small openings, a crack will develop across the opening shortly after you begin hollowing.

Alternatively, you can learn how to use a straight tool to drill this area, opening the cavity as you go and removing the nib all at the same time. There is no reason to drill to the bottom of a hollow form to guard against cutting too deep. It is easier to learn how to measure the depth as you go.

Practicing with a straight tool

Straight-tipped hollowing tools can be used to bore straight into a form to remove the column of wood directly underneath the opening and a little to the sides. Removing this central volume creates space for the bent tools to get in and remove the rest of the waste wood and refine the inner surface. The movement you will use most with a straight tool starts slightly to the left of center. Once you reach the exact center you will feel a dead spot where the tool seems to float on the surface. Here, you can delicately ease the tip forward and drill a hole the length of the tip. You can then make a second cut from left of center to the right until you reach the bottom of the hole. Repeating these cuts will systematically deepen the interior.

To practice this cut, try mounting a half log of some junk softwood on the lathe as if you were going to turn an open bowl, then back the tool rest away from the front face of the block about 6" to simulate the depth at which you would be working on a hollow form. Practice the cut first by watching, then by closing your eyes and feeling the movement of the tool in the wood.

Place the tip of a straight boring tool left of center.

Begin cutting toward the center.

Lean slightly forward with your whole torso and advance the tip into the wood...

...and advance the tool into the wood the full length of the tip.

Using bent tools

Once you have progressed about half-way into the form and have begun to open up the cavity with the straight tool, it's time to start with the bent tool. But before you begin, it's most important to be sure there is plenty of room for the bent tool to fit. The buildup of shavings in a confined area can grab the tip and twist it around.

The purpose of bent turning tools is making delicate cuts on thin-walled surfaces and in areas that can't be reached with straight tools. When I developed these tools, I discovered very quickly that the physical dynamics of using them were actually quite different from straight tools. And, of course, I made every possible mistake until I finally figured out

what was going on and how to solve the problems I was creating for myself.

The first problem relates to the rotation of the wood: The instant you touch the tip of a bent tool to a spinning piece of wood, the wood jerks the tip down. Next, if you don't have a good grip on the handle, this downward motion can pull the tool right out of your hand and might likely blow up the form. This doesn't happen that often, but it is exciting when it does happen.

So, how do you relax your hands so that you can make a cut without losing control of the tool and blowing up the form? The answer is twofold. First, just as with the straight tool, you use the entire body

Positioning the tip of the bent tool

To appreciate the subtleties of the bent tool, return to the practice log. The bent tool works best when the edge of the tip is on the exact centerline of the workpiece. Raise the tip above this centerline, and the edge will jam into the fibers and jerk downward. Drop the tip below this centerline, and it drags on the wood without cutting. However, when the tip is dropped slightly, it can touch the wood safely because the surface is actually turning *away* from the tip rather than into it.

To begin, rotate the shaft of the tool very slightly counterclockwise so that the tip is only around 5° below the horizontal. With the tip now safely touching

the wood, you can feel the inside surface to determine where to make a cut, then you can rotate the tip back to the horizontal position to make the cut. The shaft of the tool remains horizontal throughout this cut so the hand on the back of the tool handle controls the tip's rotational pitch.

Bent tools catch when you don't understand the location of the tip in relation to the surface of the wood. Rotating the shaft 5° downward means that the wood is actually traveling away from the edge of the tip rather than into it. Conversely, if the tool's edge does wander above the centerline, the catch is instant and often uncontrollable.

When the tip of a bent tool is on the centerline of the workpiece, it has the greatest efficiency and control.

When you rotate the shaft of the bent tool slightly downward, the wood travels away from the tip of the tool rather than into it. This allows you to feel the surface without fear of a catch.

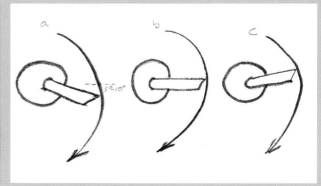

If the tip is raised above the centerline, the wood fibers will jerk the tip edge downward (c).

Once there is room to insert the bent tool, use it to remove the bulk of the wood to shape the thickness of the wall.

to support the tool so that your hands—important as they are—are no more important than your toes or any other part of the body. Second, and equally important, you don't go into the interior of a hollow form with the idea of *conquering* the wood the way you might when using a gouge on the outside. Using hollowing tools requires a mental shift.

To practice cutting the wood with a bent tool, return to your practice log and make slow, sweeping cuts across its face. If there are ridges left over from the straight tool, remove them. Using your left hand on the tool rest as both a depth gauge and a fulcrum point, think of this surface as a series of ridges and valleys and guide the tip from right to left, then left to right, across the ridges. Travel over air and wood until all the ridges have been removed and you end up with one continuous surface. Once again, make a few cuts, then close your eyes and do some more. Look occasionally to check your location, then close your eyes again to feel the progress of the cuts. The quality of the surface will be determined by the pace of the cuts and the relaxation of your body.

Practicing with a bent tool

To get the feel of what a bent tool can do, try removing the ridges created with the straight tool on your practice log.

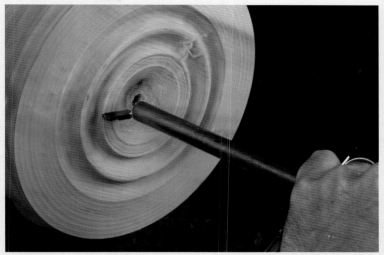

Slowly sweep the tool tip from right to left, passing evenly through both wood and air.

Reverse directions and sweep from left to right.

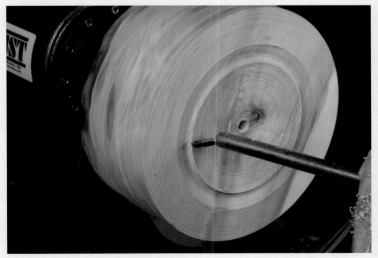

Repeat the motions until the surface is smooth.

Selecting tools

There are a number of differences among the various tools I use for cutting the interior side walls. Some are subtle and some are dramatic. To illustrate this, consider the three tools shown in the photo at right.

The bar on the bottom, at ⁹⁄₁₆" in diameter and with a ¾" extension of the cutting tip, is the most stable of the three. Not only is the shaft largest in diameter, but the tip is closest to the support of the shaft. The middle bar may seem unstable because of the bend, but it gains stability because the mass of the shaft is very close to the tip. The bar on the top, with its ³⁄₁₆" cutter positioned at a considerable distance from the shaft, provides the least support of the tip.

I use the ⁹⁄₁₆"-diameter bar to do the heavy roughing work in the area just before I begin to thin the wall. This is because, with only a ¾" extension, the tip is close to the shaft and provides good support. I then go to the ½"-diameter bent bar to finish thinning the wall. It is also good for reaching back into the upper areas of a high-shouldered form, especially when working through a small hole. I can also use the ½" bar with the extended ³⁄₁₆" cutter for the most delicate work of finishing off the interior.

Logic might say that for the final cuts, you would want the greatest support for the tip. The problem with this theory is that the tip on the larger bar is too well supported. On a thin-walled form where the wall is slightly flexible, this tip would rip through the wall.

Conversely, while the ³⁄₁₆" tip on the lighter ½" bar is less supported by the shaft, it is much more sensitive to the wood surface. This sensitivity allows me to subtly change the rotation of the tip—up or down—to put a quality surface on a thin wall.

Any bent tool will be pulled down by the surface of the wood if you enter the cut too aggressively. But this is actually a fail-safe by-product of the design, because if the tip didn't drop, it would rip through the wall. It is very easy to crash into the end-grain fibers when cutting the side wall inside a form without even realizing how aggressive you're being.

With practice, these cuts will become intuitive. When you eliminate the primary sense of vision, you

Different tool designs are used for different types of cutting. The bar on the bottom is used to remove most of the waste wood; the tool in the middle finishes thinning the wall; and the bar on the top is best for the most delicate cuts.

can understandably feel somewhat helpless. And yet, learning how to trust your senses of touch and hearing is very exciting. This includes breathing and using your entire body, from toes to fingertips. It simply takes practice to accomplish these cuts, for the same reason it takes practice to gain any skill.

When you understand this mind-body connection as it applies to hollow turning, each object you make becomes one more step in developing your skill. There is obviously a huge gulf between your first and fifth pieces. But by the sixth through the tenth, your sensibilities will become remarkably well-tuned to the process. Once you understand how the technical process works, there is no limit to the personal satisfaction you'll receive when making hollow forms.

I couldn't be more thrilled that there are, today, numerous types and styles of tools for hollow turning. We now have scrapers, cutters, stabilizers, hooks and loops, lasers...and who knows what's coming down the pike. They all work to a greater or lesser degree, depending on what you're trying to do and how much you practice. But what's common among every hollowing tool or system—including my own—is that each has limits. I continue to use my own tools instead of the others not only because they are more versatile, but also because the other tool systems all have shafts that are too large to go through the opening holes in my pieces.

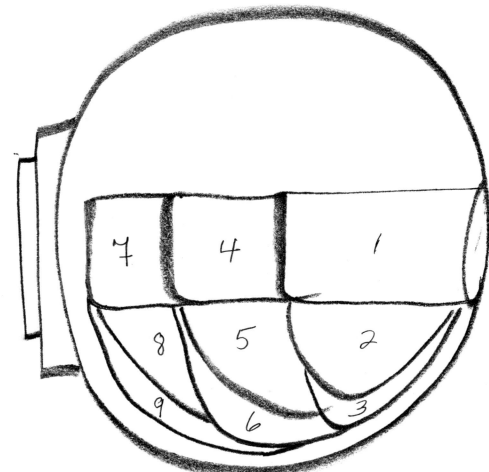

STRAIGHT TOOL	BENT TOOL
1, 2	2, 3
4, 5	5, 6
7, 8	8, 9

This illustration, which is one of the most important in the entire book, shows which tools to use in which region of the interior, and in what order, to organize the process of hollowing the form. Following the order of the cuts and using the suggested tool in each region will make the entire hollowing process more manageable.

Organizing the interior

Wading into a hollow form with sharp-edged harpoons can be intimidating, but also exciting. The excitement comes from discovering what these tools can actually do, even though you can't see them doing it.

Examine the illustration above closely. It is your guide to what tool to use where. When following the steps shown, it's important to complete each stage before progressing to the next. This way, you won't find yourself having to backtrack or redo areas you might have missed. Hollow forms take longer to complete than open bowls, green wood moves, and thin walls vibrate against the tool's edge while being cut. Combine these factors, and it's easy to see why it's so important to leave some mass in the lower regions of the form while you're thinning out the upper regions—the same as when making open bowls. Besides, by the time you finish the interior of a hollow form, it is quite likely to have stretched out of round, so trying to return to the undersurface in the upper regions, or trying to dress up the entrance hole, may not be possible. I've even had situations where the entrance hole was no longer centered, making it difficult to get the tool into the hole!

In my numbering system, there are overlaps in Areas #2, #5, and #8, where you can use either the bent or the straight tools. This is partly personal choice, but also, woods of different densities respond differently. Soft wet wood will cut easily with the bent tool, whereas hard, dense, or dry wood will probably require the straight tool, because it provides more support for the tip.

The regions I've illustrated are relative, meaning that you have plenty of personal choice in the matter. What's important is to use the straight tool to create room or clearance inside the form, before using the bent tool. There's nothing more disruptive than sticking the bent tool down inside a form when there's no room for it, and getting the tip caught. The caught tool will spin in your hands until you either figure out a way to turn the machine off, or you run for cover.

Areas #1 and #2

I begin cutting in Area #1 using the straight tool, working from left of center toward the center as I advance the tip. This cut will be in the same direction that a cut with a gouge would travel when cutting in the center of an open bowl. I could cut from the center to the left, but I'd be cutting directly into end-grain, and I'd surely pick up some unpleasant vibration. I repeat these cuts from left to center to widen and deepen the hole. I stop the lathe frequently to remove the shavings, generally after each cut.

Begin the interior cuts with the straight boring tool. Create a cylindrical area (Area #1) by moving the tip of the tool from slightly left of center to the center, just as you would when using a gouge in the interior of a bowl.

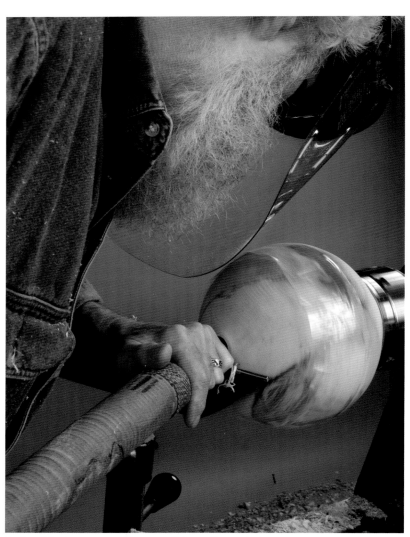

Cut from left of center toward the center. Make small, smooth plunge cuts.

Keeping the cavity cylindrical

As I continue to cut with the straight tool, the cavity may develop into a cone shape instead of a cylinder. I try to broaden this cone into a cylindrical shape by cutting more into Area #2, and then down to the center point in the bottom. Keeping the tool handle against my side will require that I shift my body from the left side of the lathe to the right side, either during or between the cuts. As long as I keep the tool handle against my side, the energy for the cuts will come from my torso regardless of what direction the tool approaches. If I take the handle away from my side for a couple of cuts, I'll instantly realize how vulnerable my shoulder is.

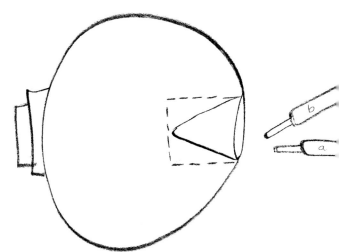

Forming a cone shape instead of a cylindrical shape is common when cutting Area #1. Be sure you widen it out into a cylinder by cutting from the direction of tool B before continuing.

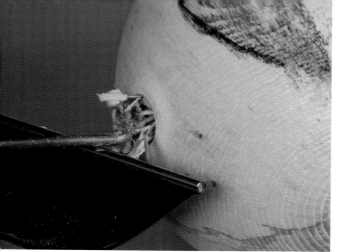

Stop frequently to pull the shavings from the interior with a bent rod. Even if you use an air compressor to blow out the finer shavings, there will be shavings too big to blow out.

Keeping the interior clean

I said this earlier, but it is so important that I will say it again: always take care when cutting inside a form to remove the shavings as they are produced. A buildup of shavings doesn't just get in the way, it can load up on top of the tip and cause it to jam and possibly break the workpiece, or worse, it could cause a bent tool to start spinning in your hand, and there's no way you can find the off switch fast enough. Any amount of shavings buildup can be a problem, but the larger the cavity, the more the shavings can build up. I use an air compressor to blow out the bulk of the short fibers from cutting the end-grain areas, but the long fibers off the face grain must be pulled out with a bent rod. And, of course, the smaller the hole, the more troublesome this becomes.

End-grain pieces

When beginning the cuts in an end-grain piece, such as a vase, I still cut from left to center, but because I'm going directly into the end grain, each cut is smaller and slower. Cutting from the center out will increase vibration, because these cuts would be moving away from the central axis of the lathe. Remember that these tools use scraping tips, not cutting tips as found on loop or hook tools, which always require cutting from the center to the left.

Removing the nib

When making cuts with the straight tool, a pointed nib will form in the very center inside the form. The reason this nib forms is that the tip of the tool is a round-nose fingernail shape, and the surface of the wood at the exact center point is spinning downward on the left side of the tip but upward on the right side. As you try to advance the tip directly into the center point, the tip can only cut on the left, or downward, side of the wood's rotation.

Do not, with either the straight or the bent tool, push against the nib or allow the tool tip to wander to the upward-rotating right side. The wood will grab the tip and rotate it up and over the center point to the left, or downward, side of rotation. This can cause the shaft of the tool to violently wipe out the rim of your hollow form. Worse, your little finger probably will be jammed between the shaft and the tool rest when the shaft slams back down!

Cutting the nib away is a simple process, but it takes practice with the straight tool...and a 180° shift in your approach.

To make the cut, I position the tool's shaft in the center of the entrance hole and parallel to the bed of the lathe. Since the tool rest is already at center height, I can now feel the nib with the tool tip. If I were trying to muscle my way through the nib, it would feel like bumping into a mountain. What I do instead is simply feel for the tip of the nib. I will know I've found it when I feel a dead spot where nothing is happening. Once I feel this dead spot, I do not try to cut it away. Instead, I slowly drop the tip below the nib and bring it up again to cut a little bit off. Then, using my left hand on the tool rest both as a depth gauge and a pivot point, I guide the tip horizontally to the *left* of the nib into the air, then back to the right to rediscover the center point.

What happens is that I'll cut a little bit away when I raise the tip up to the center point, and a little more when I guide the tip to the left. It doesn't matter if I cut any wood away when I move the tip back to the center, although it's fine if I do. What I'm doing is relocating the apex of the nib as a reference for repeating this down-up, left-right maneuver until

Removing the nib inside the hollow form

To learn how to remove the nib, return to your practice log and give this method a try.

Find the dead spot on the very center of the piece.

Drop the tip of the tool straight down.

Bring the tip back up and cut a little wood away.

Move the tip straight to the left into the air.

Bring the tip back to the right to cut a little wood away and relocate the center point.

I've removed the nib. Repeating this motion in *very slow motion* and with *paper-thin cuts* will reduce the nib to a smooth, flat surface. If I move too quickly through the cut, I won't be able to control its depth or, more importantly, feel the changes in the nib as I cut it away. It is critical to explore this surface with the tip of the tool as if shaking hands with the wood.

Work in slow motion, and remember that if you try to rush this process, you I will not *feel* what the tip of the tool is doing as it shapes and reshapes the interior. Working in slow motion helps you gain a full understanding of how these cuts work.

As a teacher, I've observed that most beginning students don't realize how aggressive they become in trying to remove that "stupid little nib." It's natural to think, "The tool is there to cut the wood, so let's do it!" But to watch these students, you'd think they were teasing a bear with a broomstick. In all fairness, trying to feel the difference between a precise cut and a muscle cut is not so easy. It requires thoughtfulness, shallow breathing, and the ability to relax your entire body. This cut really challenges this "body-as-the-energy-source" business I've been reflecting on. Anything over, say, 8" deep, and you simply won't be able to control the cut if you're holding the tool handle away from your body or trying to muscle it. The deepest I've gone is 37" off the tool rest with a 1½"-diameter, 8'-long tool. At this depth, or actually anything beyond 12" deep, the cuts are barely whispers. Practicing with your eyes closed will allow you to discover your own means of support at whatever depth you wish to go. This support includes a full engagement of toes, breath, and personal rhythm.

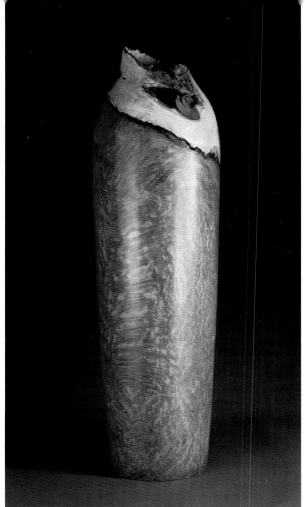

David Ellsworth, *Vase*, 1989. Redwood lace burl; 38" high x 11" wide x 11" deep. This piece was created by going 38" off the tool rest with an 8'-long tool—the longest distance I've turned free-hand off the tool rest.

Leave the lathe running

When working inside of a hollow form, always leave the lathe running when you insert or remove a tool. It is simply too much of a distraction trying to locate the off switch with one hand while holding the tool in the other, plus, if you're like me, you'll be off balance when reaching for the switch. Blowing up a piece because I lost my concentration is something I do not want to do. A foot switch would help, but it's just easier to form safe habits from the very beginning.

Continuing with Area #1

When you have gotten rid of the first nib, relax your entire body and allow the tip of the straight tool to settle into the exact center point of the spinning wood. In effect, you're trying to briefly freeze the tool tip in this location. Watch it to be sure that it doesn't wander around on the surface, and when you are sure you have found the center, take a shallow breath in the lower part of your abdomen and very slowly advance the tool. Watch the tip begin to drill a hole directly in the center of the workpiece. With this hole started, you can then lean slightly forward with your entire torso and push the tip farther into the center. You can go as deep as the length of the tip extending from the shaft. Now, you can continue to cut from left to center as you did in the beginning, deepening this region of the form. To review this process, see the sequence on "Practicing with a straight tool" on page 163.

Areas #2 and #3

When working in Areas #2 and #3 with the bent tool, there are three ways to begin the cut. You can push the tip straight to the left so that it penetrates directly into the end grain. You can pull the tip toward yourself so that it cuts across the fibers. Or you can push it straight ahead, where it will also be cutting across the fibers.

I work with all three cuts as I'm clearing out the wood in these areas, keeping in mind that plunging the tool straight to the left into the end-grain fibers will cause vibration and chattering. When this happens, I simply back off and lighten my touch. This is important, because everyone rattles the tool tip against the wood, including me. You have to. There's just no way to discover what each piece of wood can accept from which tool and in what area, unless you push the process. The important thing is to remain sensitive to the vibration and respond to it immediately in order to recover the cut. It helps if you always begin a cut with the tip of the tool dropped slightly below the centerline of the workpiece.

Once these cuts have been made, I stop the lathe, clean out the shavings, and check my progress with my finger and thumb. I also note the step that has been left over from the initial cut. This step now shows me where the next cut will be made. Each time I make a cut, I produce another little step. With the tool tip positioned slightly below the centerline, I first feel for this step, determine where I wish to make the next cut, and then go for it. Cut, clean, and measure.

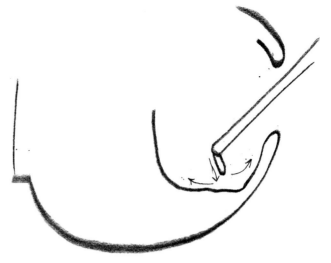

The bent tool will cut into the grain, as well as forward and backward. All three cuts are needed to hollow a form.

Check the interior after the first few cuts by turning the lathe off and feeling the inner surface with your fingers. Note the location of the step created by the first cut.

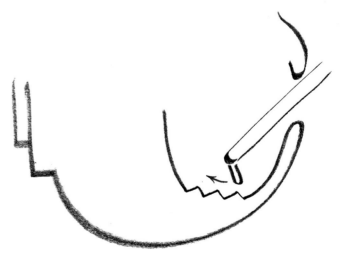

Every time you make a cut with the bent tool, it produces a step. You can use the steps as reference points in the interior—simply feel for the last step and continue cutting.

Measuring wall thickness

Once enough material has been removed in Area #3, I can measure the thickness of the walls with the wire caliper. Beyond the bent tools themselves, the wire thickness caliper is probably the most efficient and also the most mysterious tool I've developed. I say this because when I came up with the idea in the mid-1970s, it seemed so easy and logical that I couldn't understand why no one else had thought of it. What's mysterious is that I photographed the wire caliper for my first article on hollow turning in 1979 and then again for another article on hollow turning in 1986—but wherever I go today to teach, no one has ever seen it, including those who read the articles. I think it's because my caliper doesn't have a rosewood handle or a laser light, you can't find it in a catalog, and you have to make it yourself. And, oh yes, it costs less than a dollar, so it obviously can't be worth much.

Well, my entire career depends on this cheap wire tool because I couldn't turn hollow forms without it. So if you want one, go to the local hardware or lumber store and find zinc-plated rod, ³⁄₁₆" in diameter and 36" long. I cut it down to about 29" to 30", roll the tips on the grinder so they won't scratch the wood, and bend it into shape. It will work in any hollow form up to around 12" tall. ³⁄₁₆" seems to be the best because it has a good memory—it holds its shape once adjusted. I'm also free to adjust the caliper to accommodate different-shaped forms. I don't use brass, copper, or cold-rolled steel rods because they don't hold their shape once they've been bent.

The secret of this caliper is, unlike a typical caliper, the simplicity. Two tips do not come together at the same point. Instead, they are offset so that the leg of one end points to the tip of the other end. This offset allows me to measure the upper regions of a hollow form in one position, then flip it upside down to measure the wall in the lower regions (see photos at right). To measure in the middle, I just bend the wire so that it references that specific area. This tool also works great for any open bowl.

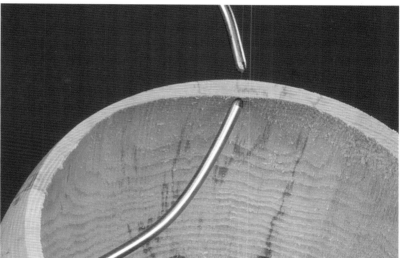

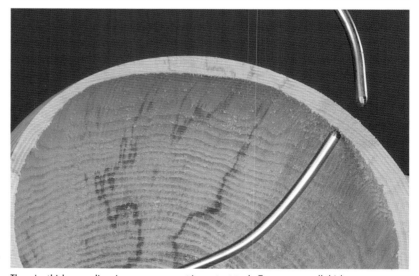

The wire thickness caliper is among my most important tools. To measure wall thickness, set the gap between the tips for a certain measurement and then note where the form is thicker or thinner. The caliper can be used to measure the upper (top), middle (center), and lower areas of the form (bottom). This bowl has been cut open to illustrate the method.

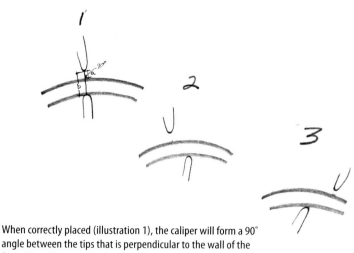

When correctly placed (illustration 1), the caliper will form a 90° angle between the tips that is perpendicular to the wall of the form. Placed incorrectly, the tips will not be 90° to the outside wall of the form (illustrations 2 and 3).

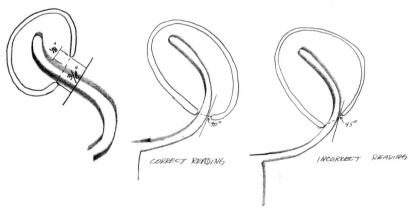

CORRECT READING   INCORRECT READING

To measure a wall that I want to be ¼" thick, I set the calipers to ⅜". If there is ⅛" of space between the outside tip and the wall, I know the thickness is ¼". Remember to keep the line between the tips perpendicular to the wall.

Using sound to determine wall thickness

Another way to determine wall thickness is to use sound. Place one hand over an area on the outside of the form and gently tap the tip of the tool against the inside wall. You'll be able to hear and feel the density of the wall. Thin areas will vibrate and sound a note, while thicker areas will make a thud.

This caliper works on the same principle as a normal caliper in that the line between the two tips is positioned 90° to the surface being measured. What makes this caliper different is that I don't set it to gauge the *exact* thickness of the wall. Instead, I use it *subtractively*. To illustrate: If I think the wall is ¼" thick, I set the tips of the caliper to ⅜" apart. I then place one leg of the caliper inside the workpiece so that the inside tip touches the wall and the line between the two tips is 90° to the outside surface.

If the tips of the caliper are ⅜" apart, and if there is a ⅛" gap to the outside of the form, the wall is ¼" thick. If I get a smaller reading than ⅛", such as ¹⁄₁₆", then I have a wall thickness of ⁵⁄₁₆". If the gap is larger, say ³⁄₁₆", then I have a wall thickness of ³⁄₁₆", and so on. If the tips of the caliper are not at 90° to the outside surface, either in the top, the middle, or the bottom areas of the workpiece, then I will not get an accurate reading.

In other words, I've learned to calibrate the actual wall thickness by subtracting the air gap visible on the outside of the form from how I originally set the caliper. Now, with the tip still in contact with the inside of the form, I slowly run the caliper back and forth along the surface and watch the outside tip. Thick and thin areas become pretty obvious, as do ridges and valleys.

If I'm uncertain as to how the tips will look once the wire is inside the form, I simply position the wire above the form and look down on it. I line it up so that the loop of the wire is positioned above the hole, and see if the line between the tips is 90° to the surface. If not, I bend the wire until it is correct.

Maneuvering the caliper

It's best to use only one hand to maneuver the caliper, because when using two hands, there is a natural tendency to expand the tips, which will give an inaccurate reading. Oops!

Determining inner location with calipers is the most common problem in learning where to cut on the interior of hollow forms. The inside wall can be very smooth, but since it is not parallel to the exterior wall, I have no reference for gauging the thickness of the wood, which makes it difficult to know where to cut. The answer is to use the wire calipers to find a thick area and mark that location with a pencil on the outside of the piece. With the machine turned off, I jockey the tip of the bent tool against the inner wall until I'm sure it's touching at or near the pencil mark.

Next, I grip the shaft of the tool with my hand on the tool rest, and hold that grip while I remove the tool from the form. I then turn on the lathe and reinsert the tool until my hand assumes the same position on the tool rest as before. Now I make a small cut directly to the left and into that thicker area…say, ⅛" deep. I turn the lathe off and measure with the caliper to see what I did, including where I made the cut and how much more I need to cut. I now have established a reference point for the next cuts.

If you are unable to picture what the calipers will look like inside the form, position the gauge above the form and look down on it. The line between the tips should be at 90° to the outer surface.

Measuring wall thickness with light

Sometimes, I use light to gauge wall thickness in a form, especially in green wood, because the moisture in the fibers helps transmit the light through the wood. I simply turn off the lathe and shine a light on the outside of the form while looking inside through the opening hole. This technique works better with lighter woods than darker woods, and sometimes, it does not work at all with darker woods. And you need to be careful to project the light through the face grain, not the end grain. This is because the end grain transmits light so easily that you're likely to think you're about to cut through the wall when there's still ½" of wood remaining.

J. Paul Fennell of Scottsdale, Arizona, has made a science of using light to measure turned vessels. He places a fiber-optic light on the shaft of the tool, then turns down the lights in his studio to marvel at the glow of the entire form, noting that the darker areas indicate thicker walls.

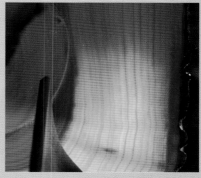

Light can be used to gauge the thickness of any form made of light-colored wood, such as this natural-top poplar bowl. Observe the quality of the light as it seeps through the wall.

Using a light while you turn will give instant feedback on the thickness of the bowl walls. Notice that light does not penetrate through the heartwood area at the base of the cut.

The final product has an equally thick wall the whole way around, as shown by the uniform penetration of the light.

Areas #4 and #5

Once Area #3 has been smoothed and thinned out, I return to the straight tool to clear out more material in Area #4, and also in Area #5 if I'm working dry or densely fibered wood. Use the skills you learned while cutting Areas #1 and #2 to cut these two regions.

Area #6

Area #6, just like Area #3, is reserved exclusively for the bent tools. In fact, Area #6 is generally a troublesome region to work in. It's almost entirely end grain, which causes the tool's tip to dance on the surface instead of cutting cleanly. It is also a difficult area to reach with a bent tool if you have a high-shouldered form, or when you get brave and make small entrance holes. Of course, all of this makes it a greater challenge.

Before I begin cutting in Area #6, I clear out some of the waste wood from Area #8, just below where I intend to cut. This creates enough room for the bent tool to cut without getting trapped by the buildup of shavings or by bumping into the uncut wood in Area #8. But I also want to retain enough wall thickness in this area so that the tip won't begin to vibrate when I thin the wall. Keep in mind that an unsupported wall will automatically cause vibration and that the drier the wood, the more vibration.

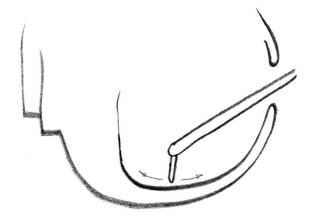

To make the cuts in Area #6, cut forward and backward with the bent tool. Cutting directly left into the end grain on a thin-walled form will cause vibration that could result in a catch.

Once this area has been prepared, I begin the cuts in Area #6 by dropping the tip of the bent tool slightly so that the wood will be moving away from the edge when it first makes contact. I then cruise over this area, moving the tip slowly back and forth to feel the surface. I do this by expanding and contracting my left hand while always keeping the heel of this hand against the tool rest. I'm not actually trying to cut any wood at this point. I'm simply familiarizing myself with what's there, including any noticeable changes in contour, and listening for the tones being emitted from the wall where the wood has already been thinned.

When the tip engages an area of thicker wood, the tone being radiated by the cutting action becomes quieter and dull. I can feel this increased thickness through the tip of the bent tool on the surface of the wood. It simply feels denser when the tip moves into these thicker areas. Now I rotate the shaft clockwise to bring the tip up to the horizontal position and begin the cut. Moving the tip in this forward direction is very important, because it allows me to cut across the fibers instead of directly into them...as would happen if I tried to cut to the left.

Once I have made a cut of, say, ½" to 1" along the surface, I cruise back over this region, feeling any changes in the contour that might need to be recut. I can then blend this newly cut area into the previously cut areas by listening to the emitted tones. Cut, clean, and measure.

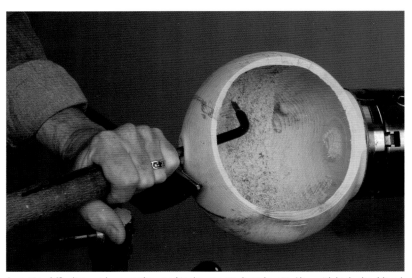

Area #6 is difficult to cut because the wood is almost entirely end grain. Also, with high-shouldered or narrow-mouthed forms, this area is hard to reach.

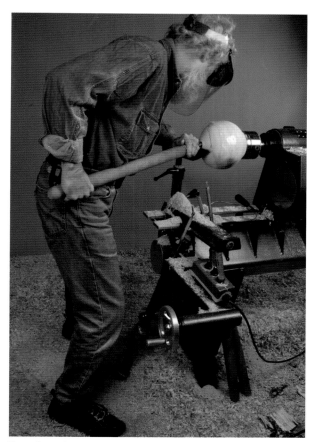

To cut Area #6, it is important to position your body correctly. Press the tool to the tool rest with your left hand, and hold the back of the handle with your right hand, keeping your forearm vertical. Balance over both legs if standing at the end of the lathe. Try bending your knees slightly and squaring your shoulders so that your head is directly over the tool shaft.

Working in Area #6 of the form is complicated by the tool being in an unstable position. The bent tool is cutting at an extreme angle to the central axis of the lathe, possibly through a small hole against a thin wall and in an area that is mostly end grain in what could be a dense, dry wood. This is where your understanding of body positions, plus the ability to correctly channel your energy, comes into play. This experience comes, of course, from making many pieces and not being afraid to blow up a few along the way. You never learn as much from a successful piece as the one that gives you trouble.

Preventing vibration

Here are some tips on how to help prevent the problem of vibration. First, sharpen the tool tip. Then, put yourself in position to make the cut, but do not turn on the lathe. Spread your hands out to the full length of the tool so that they form a broad triangle with respect to your upper torso, one hand on the tool rest and the other at the back of the handle and with the forearm vertical. Position your body so that your torso is directly above one leg if you're riding the lathe, or balanced over both legs with your feet spread to just beyond shoulder width if you're standing. Square your shoulders up so that your head is vertical and directly over the shaft of the tool, as if you were stroking with a pool cue. Bend your knees so you have a sense of movement and balance throughout your body.

Now…put a death grip on the tool with both hands so that you can feel what that's like. Relax your hands briefly, then give the tool another death grip, and relax again. Repeat this gripping/relaxing action, each time adding more areas of the body, beginning with the arms, then the shoulders, then the upper torso, and so on, until your entire body is involved—even your toes. Clench and relax…clench and relax. Each time you relax, use your diaphragm to push out a small amount of air from your lungs and imagine that your entire body is dropping an inch or two toward the floor. Take in a half breath, clench, relax, and exhale. Repeat this process a dozen times in slow motion.

Next, close your eyes and focus on selecting a variety of individual muscles in the body: first one calf, then the other; your left arm, right arm; the big toe on your left foot, little toe on your right foot. How about the forehead? And don't forget the jaw… you've got to learn to relax that jaw. I realize this may sound ridiculous, but what you're doing is training yourself to work as a unit by better understanding your individual parts. Keep your eyes closed so that you are forced to develop a mental picture of what each muscle feels like, and also so that you can learn to feel its importance in relation to the muscles that

Turning a pot with a natural-edge opening

Special care had to be taken during the turning of this broadleaf maple burl. The opening was defined only by the tips of the natural edge, and the tool had to go in and out of the form 100-plus times to cut the interior. The entire piece would have been ruined if the tool shaft hit the natural edge just one time.

Designing and roughing-out the form from the maple burl. At this point, I've only begun shaping the burl.

Note the irregularity of the natural edge. Much care was taken during the turning process not to accidentally hit the natural edge.

The bark openings allow me to see the tool working inside as I shape the interior of the form. Usually, I can't see inside the form at all.

David Ellsworth, *Broadleaf Maple Burl Vessel*, 1985. Broadleaf maple; 11" high x 19" wide x 19" deep. Collection: High Museum of Art, Atlanta, Georgia. Gift of Martha Connell.

surround it. For more help, check out the exercises in Chapter 8, "The Body," on page 106.

With the body in position to make the cut, open your eyes, turn on the lathe, and insert the tool with the tip rotated slightly below horizontal and the tool handle against your side. Relax your body and bring the tip into contact with Area #6 and sweep this surface to get a sense of where you are. If you encounter vibration, it will be the tip bouncing against the end-grain fibers twice with each revolution of the form. Select an area where the vibration is least prominent—usually where the wall is thicker—and drop the energy of your entire body so that you freeze the tool tip in a stationary position against the wood. You do not clench your body as practiced earlier, because this would cause your body to become rigid. Instead, you simply stop the cut in one position against the wood with the entire mass of your body as a support system for the tool.

At this point, the tip of the tool will be stabilized against the wood and will cut the prominent end-grain fibers—the high spots that caused the original vibration. The result will be a surface that is uniform and smooth. You can then use your diaphragm to breathe out a bit of air as you very slowly advance the tip forward. The pace of the cut—how fast you move the tool over the surface—will seem infinitely slow. This is a good thing, because you are discovering the character of this surface. If your body becomes rigid, the tool will instantly dig in or begin to vibrate. So it is important to learn to relax and enjoy the process.

And finally, there's nothing wrong with closing your eyes when making these cuts. It is a great way of removing any distractions so that you can focus on your body and the tool tip. Besides, you can't see down into the form anyway.

Areas #7, #8, and #9

Reference points are critical to finishing off the interior of the form—otherwise, you would not be able to tell where you wanted the surface to be. My first reference point is the center of the bottom, which I cut to final depth with the straight tool and measure with a straight rod. My other reference point is the thin wall of Area #9 that I finished earlier and measured with the wire calipers. Between these two reference points is the remaining amount of wood that I will now cut away using the bent tool to finish the interior of the form.

To remove the mass between these two reference points, I move the bent tool back and forth in a shallow figure eight, raising the tip axially slightly above center when working from left to right, and

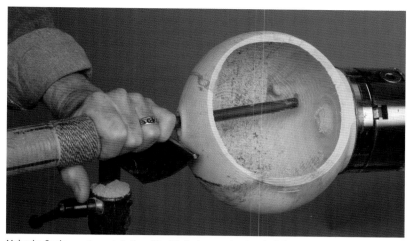

Make the final sweeping cuts in Area #9 with the bent tool, using the left hand as a fulcrum and removing only a paper-thickness of wood at a time.

dropping the tip slightly below center when working from right to left, making sure to never rotate more than 5° either way.

This figure-eight motion also produces a shearing cut on the wood that leaves a smooth finished surface. Ridges often form when working in this area, especially if it has been cut previously with the straight tool. The illustration at bottom left shows how I can remove these ridges until I have cut a continuously uninterrupted surface across the bottom of the form.

As I make the figure eight, I use my left hand (the one holding the shaft of the tool on the tool rest) as both a pivot point and a depth gauge. I can sweep the lower region of the form, allowing the tool tip to slowly move from air into wood and back again. Using my left hand as a depth gauge prevents the tool from advancing deeper than I wish and gives me excellent control over the actual amount of wood being cut. In these cases, that amount is generally around $\frac{1}{64}$"—basically, paper thickness or less.

During the sweep of these cuts, if the tip moves through a high spot and into the air, I know I have more of that high spot to remove. But as soon as the tip contacts one of the cut reference areas described above, I know that the high spot has been fully removed. I can now feel a continuous surface from one reference point to the other, free of any high spots or ridges. It's now most important to recognize

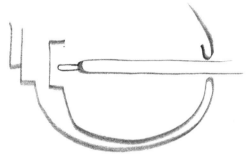

When removing the material from Area #7, you will create a well to the final depth.

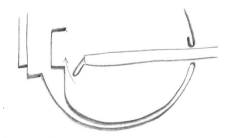

To cut Area #8, make sweeping cuts from the point you measured on the wall of Area #9 toward the bottom of Area #7.

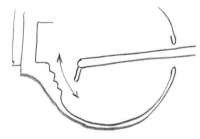

To remove the ridges that form when cutting Areas #7, #8, and #9, make a figure-eight movement by slightly raising the tip of the tool when cutting toward the right and lowering it when cutting toward the left.

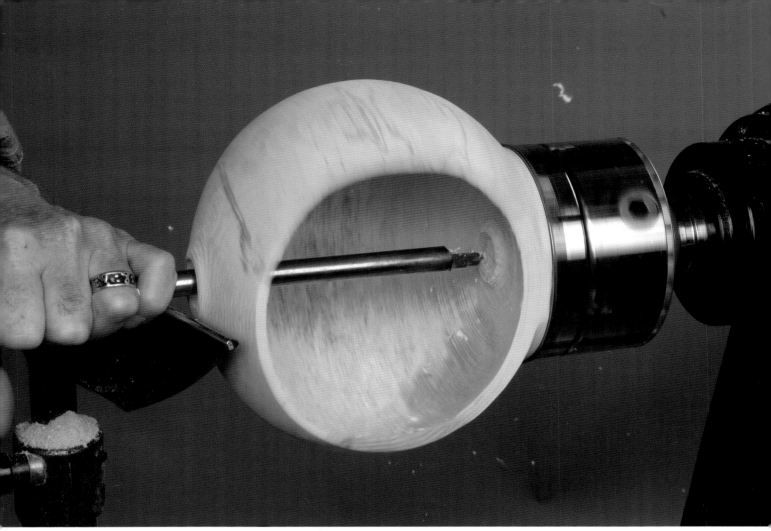

The last finishing step on the interior of the form is cutting off the nib in the center of the base with the straight tool.

that if I continue to cut into one or both of the reference areas, I am likely to go through the side wall or too deep into the center of the form.

These cuts are all done with the bent tool because the straight tool is simply too aggressive. On the other hand, be careful not to cut in the center of the form with the bent tool because this area is reserved for the straight tool.

The last cuts in the interior are in the center of the base, and these are reserved for the straight tool. A delicate down-up, left-right movement will remove the nib and allow me to blend this area into the surface that was just finished off with the bent tool.

The actual quality of these surfaces, or rather, how smooth they might look and feel, depends on the *sharpness* of the tool, the *rhythm* of my body movement, and the *pace* of the cut: The slower the pace, the more lines per inch and the smoother the surface. Making these finishing cuts is when hollow turning really feels good. I may not actually be able to see what this surface looks like, but I can certainly feel it. My experience in ceramics taught me to become both inspired by and satisfied with the finger marks on the inside of ceramic forms. It's not much of a stretch to appreciate that the internal marks I make with my tools become the true signature of my work. It is also true that with most of my wooden pots, no one can see these interior tool marks. So when people ask, "What's the difference?" I reply that I know the tool marks are there, and I know what they feel like...and *that* is the difference.

Turning off the base

Note: The information I provide here is to help you learn how I turned the base off this particular piece. Refer to Chapter 14, "Jam Chucks & Vacuum Chucks," on page 190, for full instruction on this procedure.

To finish off the outside, first I measure the depth of the interior and mark it on the outside. Then I add lines marking finished wall thickness and foot design. These procedures are the same as in Chapter 9, page 108.

I am using a large-diameter laminated-plywood chuck for this hollow form so that I can grab the top area just inside its maximum diameter. This gives me the greatest amount of support without having to crush the form under the pressure of the tailstock. This is critical when working with thin-walled objects, or, in this case, one with a window in the side.

Using a sheet of ½"-thick foam rubber, I center the body of the form inside the chuck by tapping it into place. Once centered, I check the base area and make adjustments with the point of the revolving center. Once everything is centered, I use my pencil lines as a guide and begin to trim off the base with the tip of the tool in the slicing position.

The final stage is to shear-scrape the wood surface with the Signature gouge and separate the nib with the ⅜" detail gouge. Taper down the nib with the ⅜" detail gouge. Then, with the lathe turned off, hand-rotate the form and advance the gouge forward to cut off the nib.

Measure the depth by inserting a rod the whole way into the pot and marking with your finger where the rod protrudes. Note the base of the interior of the form by removing the rod from the inside and placing it directly on top of the form. Make sure that your finger is right over the opening as it was when you made the measurement. Mark the interior depth, the exterior wall, and the foot.

Set up the jam chuck on the lathe. Use the foam as a cushion and tap the piece until it is centered. Begin to trim the base of the form by using the Signature gouge in the slicing position.

Shape the foot of the hollow form using the slicing cut.

Shear-scrape the surface of the pot, blending the surfaces together smoothly.

Turn the lathe off and hand-rotate the form as you slice through the nib with the ⅜" detail gouge.

Chapter 13

Turning Spirit Forms

I have always believed that well-designed forms should be monumental in their design regardless of their size. When I began photographing these small forms in groups of twos and threes, it struck me how remarkably powerful the forms were, including the negative spaces between them.

David Ellsworth, Spirit forms, 2007.
Various species; tallest 3½".

Origins

I started making small forms in the late 1970s, mostly just as an exercise to see how small and how thin I could go. A friend brought me some 3" x ½" round sticks of ivory from India and I made up a bunch of tools from concrete nails to do the interiors. They were basically small versions of my larger hollow forms, and people loved them. However, I couldn't sell them. I didn't know how much to ask, people thought they were "cute," and the small forms drew so much attention, people didn't look at the other work in my booth display.

I then began questioning the difference between "value" and "worth": value being the summation of an object's aesthetic characteristics; worth being the amount of money it would take to get it away from me. Still, I had difficulty evaluating what my small pots' actual prices should be.

Then one day in the mid-1980s, I was strolling through a show of Native American crafts at the Taos Pueblo in New Mexico, and I came upon a young couple making very tiny Zia pots—some as small as ¾" in diameter—each with the classic black-on-white

David Ellsworth, Spirit forms, 2006. Broadleaf maple burl; tallest 7" high x 3" wide x 3" deep. I often design my spirit forms as compositions of three forms.

geometric line paintings. They immediately reminded me of my own pots, as the forms and scale were very similar. Their prices started at $125 each.

I began talking with this couple and soon asked what their *connection* was to the pots. Well, it was a question they'd never been asked, and it really got them rolling. Most people, they said, just wanted to know why they were so expensive. Anyway, some of what I learned was while each artist works within his own tribal design style, the quality of the work—including the actual designs and technical skills—comes from within. You don't think about making, you simply make. The final result is a direct reflection of the personal energy put into the work during the making process. Positive energy produces positive pots.

I didn't have $125 that day, but the value of what I learned was I knew how to describe what I was feeling when I made my own little pots. That energy was the spirit within, hence, their name: spirit forms. I still had to learn how to price them, but once I recognized they were as important to me as my larger forms, I became a bit braver in pricing them for what I believed they were worth.

David Ellsworth, *Mesa Pot*, 1995. Silver maple, 6" high x 6" wide x 6" deep. Collection: Metropolitan Museum of Art. Gift of Alex Cook. The mesa pot design was inspired by the natural architecture of the American Southwest.

Preparing to turn a spirit form

I use glue blocks with a screw chuck to attach these forms to the lathe because it's the most efficient way of holding small objects. I also use a full-size lathe, as it's the right height and has more than enough mass to support the cutting process. (For instruction on how to use a glue block, see Chapter 6, "Chucks, Glue Blocks & Faceplates," on page 66.

The primary tool I use for exterior shaping is the same ⅝"-diameter Signature gouge I use on larger forms. The only difference is that it doesn't take many swipes with the long edge before the shape is complete.

To hollow the interior, I use tools I make from nails, screwdrivers, and Allen wrenches. When I first looked at the photo on page 187 (center), it occurred to me the reader would likely think I'm a little left of center. The wooden tray appears to be holding an assortment of tools from some nineteenth century wood shop. In fact, these are the most efficient little tools I've found for doing the interiors of little pieces. (For a detailed description of how I create the tools I use for making these tiny forms, see Chapter 4, "Making Tools & Tool Handles," on page 36).

Turning the exterior

Just like when I'm working with my larger forms, I begin by turning the initial shape into a cylinder. Then I shape the upper and lower regions with the slicing cut and finish the surface with the shear-scraping cut. To shape the base area near the glue joint, I use a thick ¼"-thick parting tool. By rotating the tool slightly clockwise toward the form, I can use the upper concave edge of the tool as a shear-scraper while the tip plunges forward to complete the shape.

Sanding is done with the Abranet mesh discs, starting at around 320 grit, depending on the quality of the material. Sometimes, I use the drill to drive the discs, but with the softer spalted woods, that approach may be too aggressive, and so I'll simply hold the disc directly on the wood.

Turning the exterior

Turning a spirit form is just like turning a normal-size hollow form, except you use smaller tools. I prefer to use a glue block to attach the object block to the lathe, as it works well on small chunks of wood.

Once the block is mounted on the lathe, turn the wood into a cylinder. Continue using the Signature gouge to shape the upper and lower regions with the slicing cut.

Finish the exterior surface with the shear-scraping cut.

Use a thick ¼"-thick parting tool to shape the base area near the glue joint.

Sand the exterior with an Abranet sanding disc. If the wood is spalted, like this piece of ash, you do not need a drill-mounted sanding disc; simply sand it by hand.

Turning the interior

You may find the hollowing chart on page 167 useful when removing the wood from the interior of the spirit form.

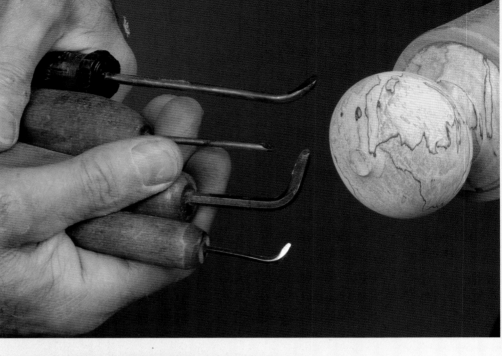

To hollow the interior, I'll use the four tools shown. Top to bottom: screw driver, Irish concrete nail, and two Allen wrenches. The concrete nail begins the process by opening up the cavity. The other tools are used as needed in various regions of the interior.

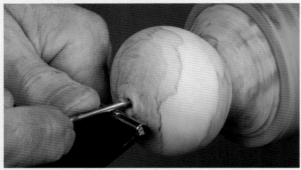

Use the concrete nail to create the cylindrical cavity underneath the mouth of the form. Use your left thumb and right forefinger to hold the tool horizontally.

Use the two Allen wrenches to work on Areas #2 and #3. Hold the tool with only your fingertips.

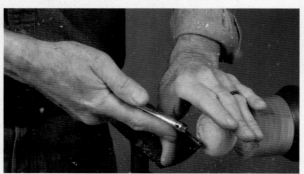

Use an air compressor at a 45° angle to the mouth of the piece to remove shavings. Make sure you do it frequently, or the piece stands a good chance of cracking from the heat generated from internal cutting.

Turning the interior

My methods of work are the same as when turning larger forms, including working in the same regions of the interior and in the same order. The four tools pictured on page 186 (top) allow me to do the interior. The one additional indispensable tool is the air compressor. Shooting air in from a 45˚ angle is the only effective way to get rid of the dust and shavings on the interior. The forced air also cools down the interior, which is critical when working dry, resinous wood. Otherwise, the heat generated by cutting the wood will crack the piece.

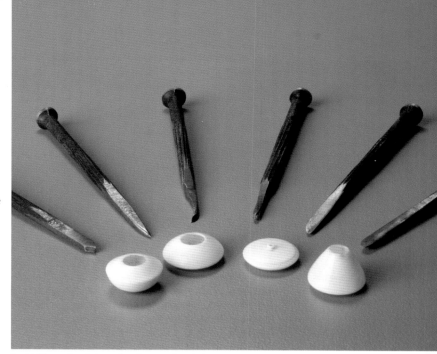

David Ellsworth, miniature bowls, 1977. East Indian ivory; ½" diameter. I created these tiny bowls with cement nail turning tools.

I create my own hollowing tools for small forms from nails, screwdrivers, and Allen wrenches. These are the most efficient tools I know of for completing the hollowing process on a small scale.

Finishing a spirit form

To illustrate a difference in finishing methods, I've drawn a pencil line down the middle of the piece. Spray lacquer was applied to the left side, and furniture oil to the right side. The sprayed side retains the natural color of the wood, while the oiled side looks muddy from the absorption of the oil. With denser or unspalted wood, I might have used the oil throughout. This is a good example of how to select an appropriate finish for the condition of the wood being used.

Furniture oil (right of the line) can cause a muddy color on spalted wood. I prefer to use an artist fixative (left of the line) as a finish.

Measuring wall thickness

This ¹⁄₁₆" spring-wire caliper is used in the same way as my larger ³⁄₁₆"-diameter wire caliper shown in Chapter 12, "Turning the Interior of a Hollow Form," on page 173. The photo at left top shows the correct way of using the wire in the upper and lower sections of this spirit form, with the line between the tips 90° to the outside surface in the area being measured. By setting the gap between the tips slightly larger than what I think the thickness is, I determine the wall thickness by subtracting the air space from the original distance between the tips. The photo at bottom left shows the incorrect way of using the calipers, because the tips of the wire are not 90° to the surface being measured.

Use a ¹⁄₁₆"-diameter spring-wire caliper to measure the thickness of the walls just as you would with the larger ³⁄₁₆" caliper. Be sure the tips create a 90° angle to the surface. Note that I've cut this form open so you can see inside.

If the caliper tips do not make a 90° angle to the surface of the form, the measurements you get will be incorrect.

David Ellsworth,
Spirit forms, 1990.
Various species;
tallest is 3½" high.

David Ellsworth, trio of spirit forms, 2007. Spalted sugar maple; tallest 4¾" high. Composing forms with subtleties of shape and size is a great challenge. Here I have one hole rising, one hole dipping inside, and one hole on an even plane. The surface is taken directly off the gouge, unsanded, and sprayed with an artist fixative for protection.

Turning the base

I finish the bases of all my spirit forms using a vacuum chuck. It's the only way I have of gaining 100% access to this tiny area of the form. It's possible to cut the base down when using the point of the tailstock for support, but the point is always in the way for finishing the base and for sanding.

Wooden vacuum chucks work quite well on the larger spirit forms.

I use a vacuum chuck with a PVC cup for the very small spirit forms.

Chapter 14

Jam Chucks & Vacuum Chucks

Turned bowls and vessels all have one thing in common: while the forms are being made, their bases are all hidden from view by the devices used to attach them to the lathe. Once a bowl or vessel has been shaped, we must deal with the problem of designing and shaping the base, commonly called the foot. Jam and vacuum chucks provide the opportunity to safely support the forms so we can finish turning the base. The two types of chucks are virtually the same, except a jam chuck needs the compression of the tailstock to keep the workpiece supported, while a vacuum chuck utilizes vacuum pressure and does not need the tailstock. You can use a jam chuck as a vacuum chuck, and vice versa, as long as you use the tailstock appropriately.

This cut-away shot shows how the compression from a jam chuck couples with that of the tailstock to keep a form mounted on the lathe to turn off the base.

Early jam chucks

I first used jam-chucks in the fall of 1979. I had seen Bob Stocksdale use the tailstock to compress a bowl against a leather-covered wooden dowel stuck in the headstock. It was a simple and effective solution for turning off the base. The only problem was it wouldn't work for the shapes I used. Instead, I stuck a wooden disc inside my vase-like shapes. The disc was supported by a V-pulley that slipped over a steel rod, which, in turn, was driven by a Jacobs chuck mounted in the headstock. This setup created a triangle of support from the edges of the disc inside the form to the point of the tailstock outside the form. I've also used a cardboard Sonotube as a jam chuck. To make the chuck, I screwed a faceplate into a ¾"-thick plywood disc the diameter of the inside of the Sonotube, then fit the tube over the disc and secure the tube by screwing drywall screws through the tube into the edge of the disc.

This early jam chuck design used a wooden disc mounted on a steel shaft and driven by a Jacobs chuck in the headstock.

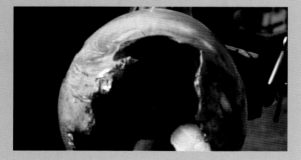

The wooden disc is placed firmly against the bottom of the interior of the piece, and the tailstock is brought against the exterior bottom to complete the compression.

Sonotubes can make great jam chucks for larger pieces. This 18"-diameter tube gives 56" of support.

Jam chucks

Jam chucks are used to mount a bowl or vessel on the lathe so you can shape the base and the foot once you have turned the inside and the rest of the outside. These chucks are simple compression devices that utilize the pressure between the tailstock and the chuck in the headstock to hold the piece. In other words, the workpiece is "jammed" between the two, hence the name. A yielding piece of foam is used in the jam chuck to cushion the workpiece and prevent scratches. The jam chucks I will describe are homemade and will work with a broad variety of shapes, from open bowls to hollow forms.

Today, I make my jam chucks in several ways, the first being stack-laminated scraps of ¾" plywood permanently attached to small-diameter faceplates I don't use for anything else. These simple chucks can be made to a variety of diameters and heights so they will accommodate any types and sizes of bowls and vessels.

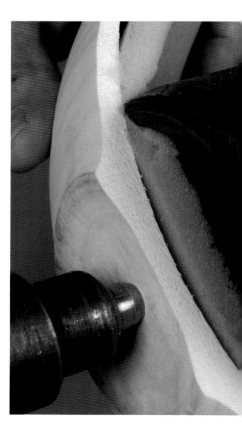

One style of jam chuck I use today is a cup-shaped hardwood block that threads onto the spindle. The tailstock provides pressure against the piece and a sheet of thin foam is inserted between the chuck and the piece to provide traction.

Jam chucks made from laminated ¾" plywood can be customized to fit any piece you may be working on.

The beauty of the jam chuck lies within its simplicity and versatility. It will support open bowls with cut rims and natural edges, while hollow forms can be placed inside the chuck (see photos at right). In addition to the chuck itself, you will need a piece of foam to increase traction between the chuck and the rim of the form. Use a soft, squishy foam instead of a thicker rubber. Thick rubber material, such as wet-suit material or computer mouse pads, remains slightly flexible under compression from the tailstock. This allows the object to shift slightly during cutting and cause the tool to vibrate or dig into the wood...not a good thing. With any thin-walled object, don't put a great amount of pressure against the form with the tailstock, just enough to support it. Soft foam is perfect. I stay away from the composite foam that looks like particleboard, as it has hard spots in it that can throw off the position of the object against the chuck.

Jam chucks work well on open bowls with cut rims. The jam chuck is inserted into bowls.

Bowls with natural edges can also be well-supported by a jam chuck.

Jam chucks are placed around hollow forms.

Vacuum chucks

Vacuum chucks are simply jam chucks with the added advantage of suction. The beauty of using vacuum is being able to hold an object to the headstock with no screws, glues, chucks, or tailstocks to get in the way. This then provides 100% access to the surface being turned. Using vacuum, you could turn and finish one side of a bowl or platter, then simply turn it around, recenter it, and finish the other side. A vacuum chuck is the only way to support my miniature spirit forms when I'm turning off the bases. My smallest vacuum chuck is only ¾" in diameter. Vacuum chucking is one of those processes you always thought you could do without until you tried it, and then you wonder how you ever got along without it. On the one hand, it is somewhat of a novelty. On the other hand, once you have it, you're likely to invent numerous ways of using it.

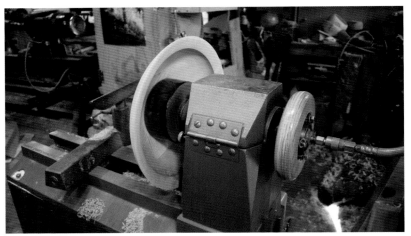

Vacuum chucks hold pieces securely without the use of a tailstock or any other parts to get in the way. Vacuum chucks work very well for securing bowls.

Platters can also be securely held by a vacuum chuck. The hose at right draws the vacuum through the lathe's hollow spindle.

Vacuum chucks work very well for turning off the base of hollow forms.

Commercial vacuum systems

In the United States, most turners use a closed vacuum system, meaning it's high-speed and low-volume, requiring an airtight seal throughout. This system uses a vacuum pump (the most expensive part of the setup). Milk pumps and surplus pumps also work and cost less. For those who view the whole vacuum business as a bit mysterious, the entire system can be purchased as a package through any of the woodturning catalogs.

Turners in other countries such as Australia and New Zealand often use a high-volume, low-speed vacuum system. This system is ingeniously simple to construct because it runs off a shop or household vacuum. The only problems you have to contend with are the noise level of the shop vacuum and that you must have some leakage in the system, or you'll either collapse your vacuum or burn out the motor... probably both.

Vacuum safety

The amount of suction vacuum systems produce is quite surprising. Care and common sense are required. Without getting too technical, let me just say that the amount of pull generated is directly related to the diameter of the opening of the chuck, 6" being far stronger than 2". Trying to hold a 20"-diameter platter on a 3"-diameter vacuum chuck is a good way to get hurt. Similarly, a 6"-diameter chuck has so much pulling power that it might cause a thin-walled object to implode. It's important to have a gauge and a release valve to control the pulling pressure, plus a filter in the line to be sure dust doesn't get into the pump.

Early vacuum chuck

I made my first vacuum chuck system in 1986. I had just picked up my big lathe, made by Jim Thompson, and I was trying to turn spherical forms using ash I cut from my property in Pennsylvania. I made up a 16"-diameter chuck with a cone-shaped interior out of plywood that I surfaced with commercial body filler (putty). I then fit a series of O-rings into the interior surface for an airtight fit. With all of the proper pipes and valves and gauges needed, it held the wood surprisingly well, until I got the first sphere turned down to around ½" thick in the base. That's when the pump started sucking air through the fibers in the ½"-thick walls, and I managed to back out of the way just in time to watch the sphere carom off the ceiling. Lesson: vacuum chucks won't hold woods with porous fibers on the lathe.

Vacuum chucks: (left) solid walnut with drilled and tapped hole; (center) metal hub with plate permanently attached to maple chuck with rubber O-ring; (right) 3" faceplate permanently attached to walnut chuck with rubber inner tube.

Making jam and vacuum chucks

Because we make shapes in many varieties and styles, it's a natural assumption that we would also need many chucks. Thankfully, it's not the case. Jam and vacuum chucks are extremely versatile and will work for a variety of both open bowls and hollow forms. I have found four or five chucks in different sizes and shapes are sufficient for most of my needs, and I can quickly make another if a new need arises. I'll present a number of options for making and using jam and vacuum chucks in this chapter, to explain the concept and define what style of chuck supports best different objects.

The multi-disc faceplate system, which can be used for jam and vacuum chucks, utilizes a hub and multiple metal discs that are screwed onto different wooden blocks.

Various sizes of PVC pipe are super-glued to the wooden blocks to hold different sizes of forms.

The multi-disc faceplate system works very well as a vacuum chuck. You can create whatever size chuck you need with this versatile system.

Multi-disc faceplate system

The multi-disc faceplate system is a very effective jam or vacuum chuck system when working with small- to medium-sized open bowls and small hollow forms. I buy a hub with five faceplates and modify them to create chucks. The system uses a hub you can thread onto the lathe spindle and a series of five metal discs that thread onto the hub. Each disc is permanently screwed to a piece of hard wood as a base. In some cases, I shape the base to receive a rubber O-ring. In other cases, I attach PVC pipe to the wooden base with epoxy or superglue. The PVC retains its shape while the wood might go through subtle changes depending on the climate. I trim the edge of the pipe to a soft, rolled shape with no hard edges that might mar the wood. PVC also comes in a variety of diameters from ¾" to 4". My choice of diameter for any jam chuck is something slightly less than the overall diameter of the object I'm trying to hold, something particularly important when using vacuum, as I describe later on. The hub and five discs cost around $100; the PVC is extra.

To get a tight seal, which is important whether you plan to use the chucks with a vacuum or not, you can cut a recess in the top of the chuck lip and glue in an O-ring or place a thin sheet of closed-cell foam over the lip. When using an O-ring for the edge of a PVC chuck, I find it very important to cut down the thickness of the O-ring with a gouge to no more than ¹⁄₁₆" thick. The O-ring is generally too thick and allows the object to flex. Put a tool to an object that's flexing and it will fly out of the chuck.

When using the multi-disc faceplate system as a vacuum chuck, I make gaskets from plastic coffee-can lids to prevent air leakage between all of the metal parts. I also use a thin layer of closed-cell foam instead of an O-ring. I use ¹⁄₁₆"-thick closed-cell foam used for packaging appliances. The thinner, the better, I have found. The thicker ⅛" and ³⁄₁₆" foams won't compress fully under vacuum pressure, which allows the form to remain slightly flexible in the chuck...not good.

Kiln-dried wooden chucks

Jam and vacuum chucks also can be cheaply made from kiln-dried lumber. I drill and tap a hole into the wood, then thread it onto the lathe and turn the chuck into whatever shape I need. Threaded taps are available through woodturning catalogs.

I seal the surfaces of the chucks with superglue so they don't change shape. This is critically important if using the chucks with a vacuum, because air can pull through the pores. To seal the surface, I set the lathe to a very slow speed (about 200 rpm) and use a sheet of closed-cell foam to apply medium-density superglue as you would with a rag. Superglue won't stick to the foam, so it is an ideal applicator. A quick spray with accelerator will ensure the glue sets firmly. To make sure I can remove the chuck, I drill a 1" deep by about ⁵⁄₁₆" diameter hole in the side of the chuck near the base. This way, I can stick an Allen wrench in the hole and use it as a handle to remove the chuck.

Making your own vacuum system

To make a vacuum system, I mounted a sealed headstock bearing on the hand wheel of the lathe, using four bolts drilled and tapped into the hand wheel and with an O-ring separating the outer race of the bearing from the surface of the wheel. I then turned a wooden cylinder (bushing), drilled and tapped the center hole to receive the ¼" pipe, and screwed in the pipe and the ¼" air nipple. When I want to use vacuum, I attach the air-hose coupling and turn on the pump. The plywood cover is there to protect my hand so I can still use the hand wheel.

A sealed headstock bearing is mounted on the hand wheel of the lathe with four drilled and tapped bolts. A wooden cylinder was turned, drilled, tapped, inserted into the center hole, and fitted with a ¼" air nipple. The hand wheel is covered with a protective plywood cover.

Making a kiln-dried wooden chuck

These wooden chucks work well as vacuum and jam chucks.

Drill and tap a hole into the wood, then thread the wood onto the lathe and turn it into the shape you need.

It is important to seal the surface of your wooden chucks with superglue. It will prevent wood movement due to humidity changes, and create a vacuum-tight seal. Turn the lathe on low and apply the glue with a piece of closed-cell foam.

After applying the glue, spray the chuck with accelerator.

Make sure you record the diameter of the chuck on its bottom for quick reference.

You may want to try a taller chuck for deeper forms, especially natural-edge bowls. The wings on these bowls can snap off if they hit the headstock.

Chuck diameter

The selection of chuck diameter depends on several factors. As shown in the illustration below, it's important to establish a triangle of support between the point of the tailstock and any two opposing points on the circle of chuck contact. The more the points resemble an equilateral triangle, the stronger the support for the form and the less pressure will be required from the tailstock. If you decrease the chuck's diameter, more pressure will be required from the tailstock to secure the form and keep it from slipping in the chuck. It's problematic, because the drag created by the tool cutting in the area of the base could easily cause the body of the form to slip.

In addition, care must always be taken when working with thin-walled forms to ensure that the pressure of the tailstock doesn't compress too much and distort the piece. The problem applies equally to open forms as well as hollow forms.

I will also use a tall jam chuck specifically for deep natural-edge open bowls, as shown in the photo at top left. This chuck helps prevent the delicate tips of the bowl from striking the front face of the headstock on lathes where the threaded spindle projects only slightly forward of this vertical face.

My experience is unless you're turning huge forms, you'll only need about four or five jam chucks to accommodate almost all of the forms you'll ever make. You make chucks to fit your needs, knowing that over time, they will change as your needs evolve.

A final note when using jam and vacuum chucks: *Always* check to be sure the chuck is running true (concentric) to the spindle. You can do this by attaching the chuck to the lathe, switching it on, and watching to see if it looks off-center. Even the slightest variation in the surface can throw off the object, so it's best to trim the rim of the chuck with your gouge if there's any question. Chucks can be a problem if the wood changes shape with seasons or humidity. Another concern is if you have two lathes with the same spindle size. A chuck may run true on one of the machines, but not the other. If the chuck isn't running true, trim off the excess material, or you'll never get the bowl centered.

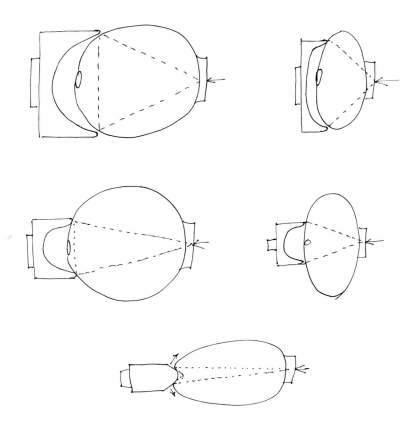

Forming a triangle of support between the chuck and the tailstock is extremely important. Equilateral triangles, which have three sides of the same length, provide the best support for the object (top). Isosceles triangles can cause forms to be crushed (center). Pressure from the tailstock can cause the form to spin on the cone end of the chuck, or worse, split the form at the hole (bottom).

Centering a hollow form is similar to centering an open bowl, with the exception you must center the form on both the tailstock and the chuck.

Centering a hollow form

Centering a hollow form can be difficult. I have to find the center point on the base and get the form itself centered in the chuck.

I place the tiny cup point of the revolving center as close to the center of the object's base as possible. I then place the form in the jam chuck and hand-rotate it to see how close to center it appears to be. It's usually not very close, so I tap the form in the chuck until it shows a minimum of wobbling when rotated. Without the foam in place, it would be nearly impossible to control the movement.

Once the pot is mounted on the chuck, my method of finding the center is to place the tool rest near the base hub of the workpiece and, with my thumb on the tool rest, rotate the workpiece until I feel the high spot on the hub. I let the high spot come to me rather than pushing against the hub. Next, I hand-rotate the workpiece so the high spot is at the top, and then I back the tailstock point away from the surface and gently tap the workpiece down. Next, I replace the tailstock point and check the piece again with my thumb to see if it is centered. I also push the workpiece against the chuck with my left hand so the piece won't slip out of place when I release pressure from the tailstock.

If I move the tailstock, I must re-check the position of the form in the chuck and tap it down accordingly. Next, I recheck the base's position, then in the chuck, repeating as necessary until the form is centered. It sounds like a lot of work, but with a little practice, it goes quite easily. This method will work on any type of hollow form, whether it's a cut rim or a natural-edge opening. My reward is the cuts I now make when trimming the base will match the outside surface as it was when originally attached to lathe.

Centering an open bowl form

Before the base can be turned off and the foot shaped, it is useful to know where to position the foot. Try this technique for centering.

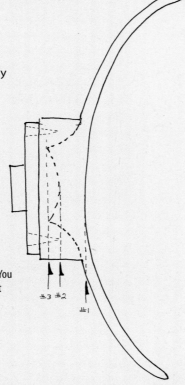

The three important reference lines for turning the foot of a form are: #1, the depth of the interior; #2, the desired wall thickness in the bottom; and #3, the plane of the finished foot. You will need the lines regardless of the attachment method you used when turning the form.

To find the base's center, put the tailstock close to where you think the center is. Bring the tool rest in close to the piece. Rest your thumb on the tool rest and hand-rotate the bowl. When a high spot hits your thumb, rotate the bowl so the spot is at the top.

When you've repositioned the bowl with the high spot at the top, loosen the tailstock and gently tap the top downward. Hold the bowl to the chuck with your other hand to prevent it from slipping on the chuck.

Centering an open bowl form

The first step in turning off the base of any form is to find the depth of the interior and transfer the location to the outside of the form. (For instruction on this, see Chapter 9, "Turning an Open Bowl with a Cut Rim," on page 134). I then add two additional pencil lines, the first representing the wall thickness I want in the bowl's base, and the second the location of the finished foot. Without the lines, I wouldn't know how much of the waste area to remove without fear of cutting through the bowl's bottom.

In most cases, I cut the depth of the interior of the bowl to the notch point of the base cut on the outside of the bowl. The extension of the line of the bowl going into the waste area will provide enough material for the wall thickness in the bottom of the bowl, plus enough additional room for a foot. Also notice the position and the shape of the foot itself will be inside the screws from a faceplate, or the jaws of a chuck, so I never have to worry about these elements getting in the way of the foot of the form.

Mounting bowls in any style of jam chuck is a simple matter of locating the center point you had marked earlier on the bowl's foot, centering the tailstock to this point, and positioning the bowl against the chuck with a thin layer of foam rubber between the two surfaces. The foam rubber keeps the bowl from slipping, and the chuck from leaving

I use a tiny-tipped cup center in a revolving center on my tailstock to center the workpiece. They do not make big holes in the bowl's base like a cone-shaped tip.

a ring mark on the bowl as a result of compressing the fibers. Because the chuck's rim is convex and the bowl's surface is concave, the bowl self-centers on the chuck when the center of the base is located and secured against the chuck by tailstock point.

However, locating the exact center with the tailstock can be a frustrating at times, because a tiny movement can throw the bowl off-center. The main problem is virtually all of the live centers made today have a lead point that is too long. You can't make subtle adjustments with a long point. A cone-shaped center is useless for this application because it puts a huge hole in the bowl's base and it's always in the wrong location. Use the tiny-tipped cup center in a revolving center. If all you have is a cone-shaped tip, place a thick steel washer over the tip to prevent it from protruding too far.

Next, I check the centering of the base (waste area) with my thumb in the same manner as described above for the hollow form.

Shaping the foot

When the form is centered, the first step in shaping the foot is to cut away the waste area so the new surface is dead flat and at the level of line #3. The bowl's finished foot will rest somewhere on this flat plane, even though I haven't shaped it yet.

Once the surface is flat at the level of line #3, I can now shape the bowl's base as it suits me. I don't have to worry about cutting away the other two lines. I only have to remember the distance between line #3 and line #2, as this will be the amount I undercut the base so the bowl sits on a ring instead of a flat surface. Flat-bottomed bowls rock and roll over time.

When the basic shape has been established with the slicing cut, I use the shear-scraping cut to finish the outside surface and prepare it for sanding. This shear-scraping cut is perfect for making fine, detailed cuts at the form's foot.

Shaping the foot

I like to use the slicing cut to shape the foot and the shear-scraping cut to put the final surface on the exterior of the form.

The first step is cutting the wood down to the level of line #3. Notice the leftover holes from the faceplate screws. These will be removed in the next step as I shape the foot of the bowl.

The next step is shaping the foot as you choose. Remember the distance between lines #2 and #3, as you will need to undercut the foot later to this level.

Continue to shape the foot with the slicing cut.

Finally, shear-scrape the finished surface.

Smoothing the transition

Hollow forms and many open bowl forms made of green materials will generally distort a bit when being made, in most cases becoming slightly oval. When positioned in the chuck, you'll notice high spots on opposing sides near the form's base, making it impossible to have a smooth transition between the fresh-cut base and the original surface when it was attached to the headstock. To smooth out this transition, I turn the lathe speed to 100 rpm. If your lathe won't go that low, you can rotate it by hand.

Hold the gouge in the shear-scraping position with your right hand on the gouge handle and the base of the handle against your leg. With the gouge's edge on the original (upper) surface, turn the lathe on and watch the gouge rise up and down as it follows the irregular surface of the form. Now, using the burr edge in the shearing position, slowly advance the gouge forward across the transition point and onto the freshly cut surface near the base. This process allows you to take the hard steps of the transition areas and draw them out or blend them into a uniform surface. You can now sand out the extra material, and you'll be left with an almost invisible transition in the surface.

Turn the lathe to 100 rpm or hand-rotate it. Use the Signature gouge to shear-scrape the surface, integrating the new surface with the old.

Avoiding transition lines

The finished surfaces of most of my spalted pieces are unsanded and straight off the gouge. When I reverse the form to turn off the base in the jam chuck, the edge of the tool is actually going through the wood in the opposite direction as when the form was attached to the lathe. The result is, to my eye, a very offensive transition line where these old and new surfaces meet. To solve the problem, I move the tool rest to the opposite side of the lathe, put the lathe in reverse, and turn the foot off while standing on the opposite side of the machine. The edge of the tool is now going through the wood in the same direction and there is no transition line.

Undercutting the base

Undercutting the base allows the bowl to sit on a ring instead of a flat bottom, which would rock over time.

Use the Signature gouge to remove the wood from the center to near the edge of the foot.

Use a ⅜"-diameter spindle gouge and ride the bevel to give the concave surface a smooth finish.

Cutting off the nib

The smaller I can make the base's nib, which connects the workpiece to the tailstock, the less handwork is required to complete the area. It's an irresistible challenge to see how small I can make the nib before something exciting happens. I ride the gouge's bevel as I cut down the surface, then taper the stem to minimize its diameter at the point of contact to the form's base. The final step is to turn the lathe off and hand-rotate the bowl as I advance the gouge forward and cut off the little stem.

Undercutting the base

To undercut the base, I use my Signature gouge in the slicing position to remove the bulk, cutting to a depth from the foot's surface (line #3, see illustration on page 200) to what I remember as the distance from that surface to line #2. I then switch to a ⅜"-diameter spindle gouge to cut the final surface, riding the bevel all the way to give a smooth, polished surface.

Cutting off the nib

The last step in turning off the base is removing the nib of wood connecting the workpiece to the tailstock. The smaller I make the nib now, the less handwork I need to do after it is removed.

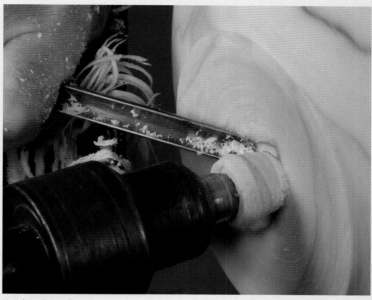

Use the ⅜" spindle gouge to cut down the nib's size.

Really thin the nib to reduce the surface area that has contact with the base.

Get the nib's base as small as you can. The smaller the nib, the less handwork you will have to do after breaking it off.

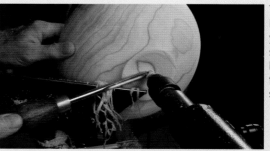

Turn off the lathe and hand-rotate the bowl as you cut through the nib, separating it from the base. Be sure to have a firm grip on the piece so you don't drop it!

Chapter 15

Sanding

I remember in 1975, when I first discovered there were other woodturners on the planet. It was the same time I discovered the battle between gougers and scrapers. Gougers were pretty sanctimonious about their ability to cut fibers instead of scraping them, but scrapers held their ground on the theory it was the way their fathers always have done it. Also, scrapers tended to have broad shoulders and huge forearms, so regardless of their methods, not too many people were going to argue with them. Anyway, what both groups had in common was once they were done with their gouging and scraping, they'd all turn the lathe up to around 1,000 rpm, grab the strips of paper covered with 36-grit rocks, and proceed to scratch the hell out of the wood while they nearly disappeared from view in a cloud of dust. I soon realized high-speed, heavy-grit sanding is a tallyho approach equivalent to a head-on collision and a third-degree burn. I can just hear those wood fibers screaming, "Oh, my God, you beast! How can you treat me to such callous abuse?"

A smooth surface isn't far away when you use one of my cool sanding methods, like this PSA disc mounted on flexible 1"-thick foam.

Sanding traditions

I wonder what other people think about while sanding a piece of wood. Every woodworker sands at some point in his work, but unlike with cutting and carving, no one I know actually enjoys it. If people spend a lot of time doing something they don't like doing, they must compensate by thinking of interesting topics to carry them through the task—in this case, to the point when they begin to put the finish on and can finally say, "Wow! Now all my efforts have been rewarded."

I have talked to a number of woodworkers about it and received a range of interesting answers. For instance, some people do simple mathematical problems in their head, like addition and subtraction. Several furniture makers have told me they envision the details of assembling the individual parts that will make up the finished desk or chair. One man said he practices birdcalls while he's sanding. Another said he thinks through the unpleasant episodes that occurred with his first wife.

Here, I am stationary sanding a natural-edge bowl with an Abranet disc.

When are you done?

I suppose we all think about an endless number of ideas or topics while sanding—anything, that is, except the sanding process itself, which is why we let our minds drift. Whatever you do to get through this stage, at some point you must ask this question: when is enough enough? That is, when do you stop sanding? Most people respond to this question by saying, "I sand up to, say, 220 grit," or "600 grit," or "12,000 grit" and so on. To me, this is another way of saying they have formed a habit of sanding to a point of acceptability, or maybe to whatever they think perfection is, and then they stop. I see nothing wrong with that approach, because it increases the number of choices people have for the different effects they are trying to express in wood. It also means two people can use the same piece of wood and come up with a totally different look with their objects. It does make me wonder if the purpose of going to mega-thousandths in grits relates to the needs of the wood or to those of the maker. I suspect the latter. What if I'm sanding a rosewood box in the morning and a spalted-maple hollow form in the afternoon? Do the materials ask for the same degree of sanding? Should I stop at the same grit?

3" snap-on rotary sanding discs with Velcro or bonded surfaces are a useful alternative to sanding with a folded piece of sandpaper.

Where do you begin?

Equally important to where you stop sanding is where you begin. When I was young, I would line up neat little stacks of sandpaper in all the grits and go through them all, one after the other. It was a way of bringing order to the task, but it presumed I *should* always begin sanding with the heaviest grit. That would be a problem if I were sanding woods of various species that have different densities... like rosewood and spalted wood. When it comes to selecting sanding materials, I am careful not to form a method of sanding so fixed it doesn't allow for variations in the materials I'm sanding. Here, the old saying still applies: When in doubt, ask the wood.

I remember both James Prestini, who turned thin-walled forms from 1933 to 1953, and Bob Stocksdale, who was one of the fathers of art turning, saying they, too, both sanded through the grits, as I'm sure most everyone else did prior to the late 1970s. I call it the Depression approach, because if you could afford all the grits during the Great Depression, you knew you were a rich man. Of course, no one threw sandpaper away, because over time, your 120-grit paper became your 150 grit, then your 220 grit, and on and on until you pretended it was 600 grit, even if you knew nothing was happening. Eventually, they'd all end up in a box on the floor, but you never threw the box away, either.

Developments relating to sanding

Think of the enormous changes that have occurred in woodturning since the early 1970s, many of which relate directly to sanding. First, there was the shift in the function of objects made, from industrial-based spindle turnings to decorative objects. Then, there was the addition of rotary and orbital sanding discs.

A lot of advancements occurred during the next decade, including aluminum-oxide paper, which was introduced as an alternative to garnet paper. The real breakthroughs came with the sticky-backed discs (pressure sensitive adhesives or PSA) and Velcro-backed discs. By the mid-1970s the idea of holding a folded-up piece of sandpaper against a spinning piece of wood became a thing of the past. It created excessive heat against the wood, and the dust that didn't end up in the room clogged the paper. You couldn't sand irregular or bark-edge bowls without crushing the oncoming edges, and sanding green wood was virtually impossible. Rotating discs opened the door for the latest innovation: a polyamide fabric mesh with resin-over-resin bonding of aluminum-oxide grit and hook-and-loop backing. Wow!

The variety of finishes grew from traditional oils to French polish and spray lacquers, water-based lacquers, plastic sprays, paint, and even superglue. Finally, there was a shift in the kinds of wood being used. Mark and Melvin Lindquist's pioneering use of spalted wood in the early 1970s challenged the sanding process. My early work in sanding green wood in the late 1970s was, as well, an attempt to get a smooth surface from another distinctly uncooperative material.

It's easy to forget that in that era, there were few woodturners actively showing their work compared with today, and that the communication system between us was so minimal, there was no one around to tell us we were *not* supposed to sand spalted or green wood. In fact, many traditions in woodturning are still so strong I can expect a good ribbing whenever I sand green wood in a demonstration.

My thoughts about sanding

So, why do I love sanding? Because I work with efficient methods, I don't have to do a lot of it. I think of sanding as a *learned skill*, no more or less important than any of the other processes I go through to make an object. I learn as I use it and the process yields a sense of satisfaction. Also, I cheat sometimes, because some of my pieces don't require sanding at all. But that's a matter of circumstance and personal choice.

Good sanding requires good surface preparation. Whatever type of woodworking you do, you can ruin a good piece of wood with sanding, and probably a portion of your physical and mental health in the process if you don't prepare the surface properly. Torn fibers *always* show, regardless of how much finish you use to try to cover them up. Whether you use a scraper, a gouge, or a skew chisel, your sanding results will improve the moment your tool skills improve.

When I look at a piece of wood and ask myself, "OK, what would I like this piece to look like?" sometimes the answer is obvious. There are other times when I never know the answer until I get involved in making the piece—cutting away the bark or observing how the gouge feels as it slices through the fibers. Or, maybe it doesn't cut well at all, or there is solid wood in one area of the form and spalted wood in another. Do I want the entire object to look the same, or does my experience with the material cause me to consider other options? Do I want it to appear shiny or matte, porous or smooth? How do I want the surface to perform...as a functional or as a decorative surface? And maybe most important is how I feel that day...about the material, the form, or maybe even about life itself.

Sanding is involved in *all* of these decisions. Once I've made the final tool cuts, sanding is the stage that leads to finishing. In almost all cases, once you've begun the sanding process, you don't turn back.

I've learned we all have our own answers to these questions, especially when it comes to how far you go with sanding. My answer is I sand until I'm finished. Once I have brought the surface to a point where I like

Velcro-surfaced soft rubber and foam-backed discs are another innovation in sanding. Simply press Velcro-backed sandpaper discs on the pad to attach, and pull to remove.

what I see, I'm finished. That might mean there's no sanding on the surface at all, as with a heavily spalted piece of wood, or a piece of white oak I want to have a coarse, sandpapery look like that on a raku pot. The most important aspect of my work is I try not to oversand if the effect I am trying to achieve doesn't warrant it. Once I have brought an object's surface to a state of completion, I stop sanding. And what that state is, I can never be sure of until I get there.

That brings me to an odd question: Why do we sand? If that seems a bit too obvious, think a little harder. Do we sand to make the wood more beautiful? No doubt. This leads us into the old trap regarding the fashion of the times: "What is beauty, anyway?" Do we sand to bring out the wood's lustrous color and chatoyant depth? Most likely. Do we sand to preserve and protect the wood in some way? Probably. Many would say, "I sand because it sells the piece." For better or worse, sanding is an issue that leads back to your perception of the terms *fashion, beauty,* and, equally important, *intent.*

I believe it is the differences–rather than the similarities–in how we deal with the surfaces of our objects that bring such a wonderful breadth and richness to them. And as with any other creative expression, it is the differences, the opportunities for personal choice, that make the topic interesting. Maybe the question of "To sand or not to sand?" is not such an obvious one after all.

Scratching the scratches

Regardless of how you feel about sanding, another given truth is that what you're actually doing to the surface of the wood through sanding is transforming it from what it is to what you want it to be. It is for all the reasons mentioned above that I often refer to sanding as one of the more mysterious processes we use in making objects on the lathe. I also believe it is somewhat evil. I don't just mean the considerable amount of consumable dust we produce while trying to create magical surfaces. I'm referring to the many contradictions and the vast amount of misinformation about sanding we all grew up with. No wonder our minds wander when sanding...maybe we just don't want to think about it.

From a purely mechanical standpoint, consider all of the heat generated by friction between the spinning sanding disc and the spinning wood, and how that heat produces those annoying little checks on the end grain of our bowls. On one hand, we talk openly about how we so revere the beauty of our material. On the other hand, we turn the lathe up to 1,000 rpm and chew up the surface with all those hot little rocks. And what about the uneven surfaces we produce on our bowls and platters simply because we're sanding both the face and end grains with every revolution?

Every furniture maker is taught to sand with the grain so as not to drag those little rocks diagonal to or across the fibers. Yet spindle and bowl turners alike sand in *every* direction, as if it were required because we created the piece on a rotating lathe. At least a spindle turner will usually stop the lathe and sand with the grain once in a while. Bowl turners generally just go on to finer and finer grits.

Sanding is a skill that can be learned as easily as other woodturning skills. The real problem is most people consider sanding to be a necessary burden. They ignore the skill required and end up oversanding everything.

Wouldn't it be better if you could develop the beautiful surfaces you want without ripping the fibers? Or without producing the end-grain checks that come from overheating the surface? And all without reducing the wood's natural luster? It is all possible, but requires a shift in your approach to preparing the surfaces of your bowls and vessels, and a *lot* of practice using your turning tools—regardless of whether you prefer gouges or scrapers.

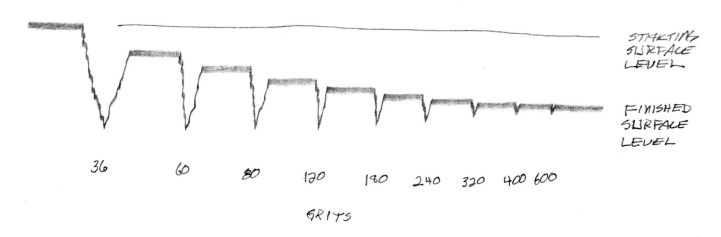

Beginning sanding with heavy grits not only reduces the level of an object's surface, but the side wall of each groove created by the aggregate damages the fibers and reduces the wood's chatoyant glow.

David Ellsworth, *Koa Pot*, 2008. Figured koa; 7" high x 8" wide x 8" deep. Koa is prized by turners and instrument and furniture makers for its wonderfully lustrous chatoyant glow.

Chatoyance

Wood lovers constantly talk about "the beauty of the wood," and no doubt everyone has personal preferences when it comes to species, color, tone, or grain pattern. Beauty is subjective, and it is equally difficult to define whether referring to wood, people, or life in general. When it comes to wood, most people do agree on this: the beauty of the natural glow that occurs in some woods, or what is commonly referred to as *chatoyance*.

Chatoyance refers to the luster you see in the wood's surface that is similar to the cat's-eye effect in a glass marble. The chatoyant effect is created by light rays entering the surface of the wood and bouncing back to your eye in what is referred to as "the angle of incidence to the angle of reflection." Curly and quilted wood surfaces maximize this lustrous effect more than straight-grained surfaces because the fibers undulate through the material like a serpent. The radiance you experience is the culmination of light rays bouncing off all the rising and falling fibers at the same time. In resinous woods like African blackwood and Hawaiian koa, this effect is maximized and can make the surface appear almost three-dimensional.

Furniture makers have long known a cut surface

yields a greater luster than one that is scraped, and that whether planing or sanding, always try to go *with* the grain, rather than across it. Woodturners don't have that option. If you're making a bowl, you turn the lathe on and the grit from the sandpaper instantly scrapes across the face-grain fibers and then slams into the end-grain fibers, twice in each revolution. If you're sanding the surface of a spindle or an end-grain vase, you're *always* sanding across the fibers.

When you drag a pointed object crosswise to the grain of wood, like a 60-grit rock for instance, you interrupt the flow of light emitted from the surface, and because the opposing surfaces of the groove itself are torn and jagged, the light rays are broken up further (see illustration at 209). The result is you can have a perfectly beautiful bowl, but when the surface is viewed from different angles, there is virtually no radiation of light coming from *within* the surface. Its chatoyant potential has been interrupted due to the damage done to the wood fibers. With a little practice, you can learn to spot an oversanded bowl from across a room.

What happens during sanding

Before I get into the nuts and bolts of how this sanding method works, I need to outline what happens when you sand wood fibers, and how easily oversanding happens. Oversanding is starting with too coarse of a grit, spending too much time using each successive grit of paper, or putting too much pressure against the wood.

With every piece of sandpaper, you cut grooves into the wood to a depth the size of the grit being used. Your intent in using successively finer grits of sandpaper is to remove the grooves produced from each of the previous grits. At some point, the human eye will no longer be able to see any of the grooves produced, and that is when you usually stop sanding. What you don't see is that the side walls of each of these grooves are being torn or ripped by the sandpaper, especially when you're sanding across the fibers. If you were to begin sanding with a grit as coarse as, say, 36, you'd probably never be able to sand below the level of the original fiber tearing without sanding right through the bowl's wall. The result of the ripping action is the finished surface of the wood appears visually flat. The grain patterns and color will be there, but the wood loses its original luster and chatoyant glow. The same effect occurs in spalted wood because the fibers' cells have been decomposed. A similar result occurs when wood is boiled or frozen to neutralize tensions in the wood by exploding bound cells. In all of these cases, the raw edges of the damaged cells reduce the glow in the wood.

Cool sanding

How can you sand your turned objects without damaging the wood's fibers? Part of the answer is good tool preparation will lead to a quality surface by minimizing the amount of sanding required. If you can get that quality surface, you can begin to sand in the range of 220 grit instead of 60 grit, and it will greatly reduce fiber damage. Heat is one of the primary enemies of wood. Part of the skill of sanding is recognizing that ramming a 3"-diameter P-O-W-E-R sanding disc into the wood at 1,000 rpm creates enough heat to melt the Velcro disc's glue and dry out the wood fibers. That's the source of all of those mysterious little end-grain checks.

Cool sanding means you soften the foam backing that supports the sandpaper, use a thin-bodied pliable paper, and slow down the speed of the lathe to reduce friction and, therefore, heat. I developed the term *cool sanding* because it aptly describes the process. It is also an effective means of distinguishing the process from the heat-producing power-sanding process described above.

The methods for cool sanding came to me as a gift from my good friend Giles Gilson of Schenectady, New York, who stole the idea from his good friend and furniture maker Robert Whitley of New Hope, Pennsylvania. Whitley, I am told, discovered it from a traveling sandpaper salesman sometime back in the late 1970s, or so the story goes.

I use two methods of sanding that satisfy this cooler approach to the process. I am sure the reason so few turners know about cool-sanding is the soft rubber backing discs are not available in turning catalogs. You need to make them up yourself, and the ingredients are available most anywhere.

A PSA system is composed of a hard rubber disc, a 1"-layer of soft foam, and a self-adhesive aluminum-oxide sanding disc.

Pressure sensitive adhesive (PSA) discs

I use self-adhering aluminum-oxide sanding discs on both hollow form and open bowl surfaces. Because they provide such a soft contact with the wood's surface, they are extremely efficient compared with any disc with a firm rubber backing, such as a Velcro or snap-on disc. I can use 220-grit sanding discs to do the same work of 80- to 120-grit papers in a harder-backed style of sanding disc. I was once amazed at being able to sand the entire exterior surface of a 10"-diameter, 10"-high hollow form in Ponderosa pine with just one 6" disc in 220 grit and one in 320 grit. The number of discs you use varies depending on many factors, including the density of the species, its moisture and resin content, the pressure applied against the wood, and, as always, the quality of the surface as cut from the tool.

Self-adhering aluminum-oxide sanding discs are available through most tool catalogs, any auto paint supply store, most syndicated auto stores, and metal supply catalogs. My preference is Norton or 3M, in part because both are readily available. Other brands can cost less, but, they are sometimes of lesser quality, both in the cutting action of the grit and the quality of the adhesive.

What distinguishes these discs from other forms of sanding is the softness the 1" foam backing provides. In effect, the paper rolls smoothly over the wood, conforming 100% to its surface and making the sanding extremely efficient. In contrast, hard-backed discs bounce off the end-grain fibers and dig into the face-grain fibers with each revolution of the lathe.

What makes this process so cool is you rotate the lathe at a maximum of 200 rpm. When sanding green wood, I don't even turn the lathe on. Instead, I hand-rotate the object and sand where I need to—more on the end grain than the softer face grain. In all cases, the advantages are you're not throwing moisture into the sandpaper, there is little or no heat produced, and the paper becomes more efficient in its cutting action because it is not being abraded or worn down by high-speed rotational friction of the wood.

Aggression versus efficiency is a distinction I'd like to talk about. Velcro-backed P-O-W-E-R sanding discs are very aggressive. You can remove a multitude of sinful tool marks and even change the shape of your bowl. But you can't sand green wood, and you wouldn't want to hand-rotate an object while sanding because you would grind flat spots on the surface.

The soft foam discs are efficient, but they are *not* aggressive. You can sand without creating flat spots, but they will not remove large tool marks unless you go to heavier grits. They also will not help you reshape a bowl. However, due to their efficiency, you can generally begin sanding with 180- to 220-grit paper. The result is you don't damage the fibers and the final surface of your form looks alive and healthy.

Non-recommended uses for the PSA system are worth considering. The PSA system does not work well on objects that are very small or have sharp edges in their designs. The foam backing material is simply too soft and will roll over these crisp edges.

A second area where these discs don't work well is on the insides of open bowls. At 6" in diameter, the discs won't fit very well inside most bowls. If they do fit, they generally cut only on the outer edge of the disc, rather than the face. You can cut the diameter of the hard rubber discs down to 3" so they do fit inside a bowl, but my experience is the foam is so soft it causes the PSA discs to pop off the foam's surface.

In these cases, I switch to the 3" Velcro discs, but I take extra care to slow the speed of the lathe down to 150 to 200 rpm so the paper cuts more efficiently. Again, I also avoid the temptation to press the discs firmly into the wood.

Setting up a PSA sanding system will require these items: a 5"- or 6"-diameter hard rubber disc, a Jacobs chuck, a sharp pointed tool, contact cement, 1"-thick foam, a PSA disc, and artist fixative. The process is relatively simple and quick.

First, I place a hard rubber disc, which is available at most hardware stores, in a Jacobs chuck mounted in the lathe. Using the point of a sharp tool, I scuff up the smooth surface of the rubber disc so the contact cement will have something to grab hold of.

Next, I cut out a 1"-thick layer of soft foam to fit the rubber disc. The foam can be purchased at most fabric stores. I do not use the composite foam made up of chopped foam pieces, because it contains a mixture of hard and soft elements that will cause the thin-bodied sandpaper to streak the wood.

I then apply the contact cement liberally to both the rubber disc and the foam, let them stand for a few minutes until dry, and then press them together. One caution: If the finished surface of the foam rubber is slightly domed after being glued to the rubber disc, turn on the lathe and sand the center high spot down with another disc of coarse-grit paper mounted in a drill until you have a flat surface. Otherwise, the self-adhesive sanding disc will crinkle against the domed surface and fly off when in use.

Spray the surface of the foam with a couple of coats of any spray acrylic lacquer (artist fixative), letting the surface dry between coats. The invisible coating will help prevent the glue of the sanding disc from damaging the foam when the disc is stripped off. Also, the discs will stick better if you blow out the surface of the foam frequently with compressed air to prevent the accumulation of dust. Finally, attach the self-adhesive aluminum-oxide sanding disc to the foam.

PSA sanding system

Here is the process I follow for creating a PSA sanding system. Give it a try and see if the PSA becomes your favorite sanding method.

Mount a 5" or 6" rubber disc on a Jacobs chuck in your lathe. Scuff up the surface of the disc with a sharp tool so when you glue the foam on, the adhesive will have grooves to hold onto.

Cut out a foam disc to fit the rubber disk and use contact cement to attach them.

If the surface of the foam rubber is convex after it has been glued to the rubber disc, use a drill-mounted disc of coarse-grit sandpaper to remove the high spot.

213

Abranet sanding discs

The second approach to cool-sanding—Abranet sanding discs—came to me from Elmer Adams of Hilo, Hawaii, in 2006, and it has seen wide exposure since. KWH Mirka Ltd. of Finland developed Abranet discs. The discs feature aluminum-oxide grit with resin-over-resin bonding (whatever that is), which is attached to a polyamide fabric (whatever that is) and has a hook-and-loop attachment design (I know what that is). The discs come in a range from 80 grit to 1,000 grit, which ought to cover just about every problem a woodturner will encounter.

The primary advantage of these discs is dust can pass *through* the woven fabric. When I'm sanding green wood and the disc gets clogged, I strip it off the hook-and-loop pad and either shake the debris out or blow it out with the nozzle from my air compressor. You can also use a vacuum hose on the backing disc to suck the dust right through the disc.

One of the oddities of this new sanding approach was brought up to me by one of my students. He said, "You don't use the Abranet discs like sandpaper discs." The reason he was correct is most of us who grew up using hard-backed sanding discs, myself included, always *pushed* the paper into the wood. We did it unconsciously, probably because we thought it would hurry the process up. With Abranet discs, you must reduce the pressure against the wood and reduce the object's rotation speed to an absolute minimum. Otherwise, you wear down the sprayed aggregate and the disc becomes useless. The lesson is to take it easy and let the tool do its job.

Dust passes into Abranet sanding discs. When the disc gets clogged, blow the dust out with an air compressor or vacuum, or shake the disc.

PSA versus Abranet

What's the difference between PSA and Abranet discs? The result on the surface of the wood is pretty much the same. You do have to purchase quite a number of each grit (box of 50) of Abranet discs to get the cost down, or a roll of 100 of the PSA discs (and the cost doesn't come down). Either approach could be cost-prohibitive for hobbyists, but the long-term view favors Abranet, as the discs are reusable until fully worn. The foam-backed Abranet disc is not as soft as the 1" foam used with the PSA discs, but that is overshadowed by the higher efficiency. I still begin sanding at 240 grit and finish with, say, 400 or 600 grit, but the process goes faster, and because the discs can be cleaned, they last *many* times longer than PSA discs.

Sanding a form

Here are some methods to use to begin sanding a form. First, drop the speed of the lathe to around 150 to 200 rpm. Then, position a drill with the 220-grit sanding disc of your choice so that the disc's contact point rotates in an upward direction while the wood is coming down, and go slowly over the form's entire surface. At this slow speed, the 220-grit paper will work at full capacity, smoothing out most of the face-grain areas on the surface so you can see remaining problem areas. These areas will almost always be on the end grain rather than the face grain. If there is moisture or resin in the wood, the disc will fill up with debris. But that's fine. You're only evening out the surface to find problem areas requiring more sanding.

Turn the lathe *off* and hand-rotate the object. Using another 220-grit disc mounted in the drill, lightly sand out problem areas. If the 220 grit isn't efficient enough, try 180 or even 120 grit. Try not to force the paper into the wood or linger on one area for a prolonged period. Let the grit of the paper do its job. If you find the surface area between the face grain and the end grain is still a problem, it's probably because the surface wasn't properly cut with the tool. You may have to go back and re-cut it. (For more on this, see "Finishing the exterior using the shear-scraping cut" on page 123).

Once you have sanded the entire surface with 220 grit, move up to a 320-grit disc and go back over the surface again at slow speed. Inspect the surface for more problem areas and, again, with the lathe turned off, hand-rotate the form as you sand these areas with a fresh 320-grit disc.

The process can be repeated until the surface is as smooth as you wish. If there are distressed areas in the wood, or natural-edge bark areas, leave the lathe turned off and hand-rotate the form as you sand. Because this soft sanding method is so efficient, a 320-grit surface can often give the appearance of a 500- to 600-grit surface.

Green wood and sanding

I started sanding green wood the first time I put a green piece on the lathe. I didn't know I wasn't supposed to do that. All of my methods of sanding, to date, have evolved from that first oversight. What I've learned is that conventional wisdom suggests you cut green wood, let it dry, re-cut it, sand it, and put the finish on...all of which works fine if you're making conventional objects like furniture, bowls, platters, and boxes.

Hollow forms, especially those made from green wood, offer new opportunities in surface treatments that go beyond traditional objects and methods. Prominent among these are the more tactile crinkled, or what I call "transitional," surfaces, or even objects where the entire forms become distorted.

The primary reason I get so charged by these moving or textured surfaces is they are a direct reflection of the inherent nature of each species being used. They help present wood as distinct from all other materials used in making vessels and bowls.

David Ellsworth, *Ash Pot*, 2007. Black ash burl; 8" high x 6½" wide x 6½" deep. Sanded while green, then dried and oiled, the surface of this piece developed a natural crinkle that is inherent to the species.

The subtle elements in an object's surface bring it great visual power, including the ability to reveal and disguise the energy in all vessel forms. An object's surface also can help project a sense of mystery about the form and, for each of us, a relationship to the form's identity. What you get with wood is more than what you see– it is also what you feel.

Personal preferences aside, and given the choice of available surface effects, how do you prepare green wood so that once it dries and crinkles, you can get what you want? If you seek a smooth and evenly sanded surface, the answer is you need to sand the wood while it's still green and *before* the crinkling occurs.

David Ellsworth, *Oak Pot*, 2007. Red oak burl; 10" high x 8" wide x 8" deep. The wonderful distortion of this form gives a sense of internal energy released.

Sanding green wood

My method of sanding green wood begins after I have shaped the form and made the final finishing surface cuts, but *before* I begin hollowing the form. I begin in the same way I described on page 215, "Sanding a form." That is, I use slow rpm rotation with a 220-grit paper, and one even pass over the entire surface so I can discover problem areas in the surface.

If the wood is too wet to sand, which is often the case with freshcut burls or spalted woods, the sandpaper will clog immediately. If that happens, I begin to hollow the form, and wait to sand until enough surface moisture has evaporated. In many cases, the wood is so wet I complete the piece before starting to sand. Every wood is different, so I evaluate each situation as it arises.

In either case, following that initial pass with the 6"-diameter foam disc, I finish sanding by hand-rotating the piece while sanding only in areas that require attention. In most cases, it will be the areas of end-grain fibers, because they are much denser than the face-grain fibers. The bark inclusions of a natural-edge vessel may require additional attention, because this is where the gouge might have skipped over the surface or caused a tiny groove. Another reason for sanding while hand-rotating is so I don't roll over or crush the crisp bark edges of these natural-topped bowls. If I find an area with particularly deep torn fibers, I'll either step down to 180-grit paper or, more likely, re-cut the surface with the shear-scraping cut of the gouge. Remember, soft foam discs don't grind down the surface like the harder rubber discs with Velcro backing. Even if I do lower an area slightly, it's easy to blend it into adjacent areas with no distinguishable surface variation.

I realize this method of sanding may seem a bit unorthodox. I believe sanding is a process where common sense wins out over convention. The more I observe what my methods of work are actually doing, the more I connect with the completed object *through* those methods and processes. I might be working on ebony in the morning and pine in the afternoon, and it's rare when any method or process works equally well on such divergent materials.

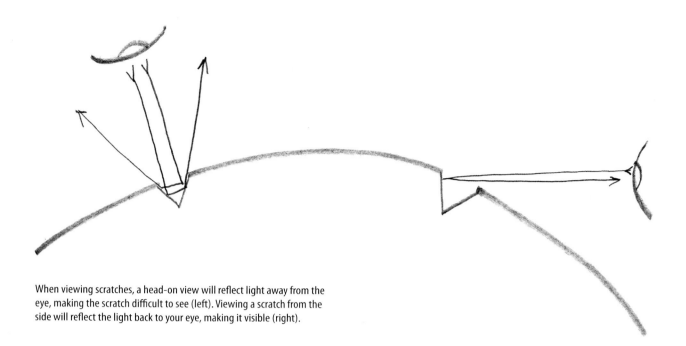

When viewing scratches, a head-on view will reflect light away from the eye, making the scratch difficult to see (left). Viewing a scratch from the side will reflect the light back to your eye, making it visible (right).

Looking for problem spots

One of the primary difficulties when sanding wood is locating where problem areas are on the wood's surface. I don't mean obvious areas such as ridges, torn end-grain fibers, and tool digs, but rather, more subtle things such as very light sanding marks in the end grain created by the initial use of heavier-grit sandpapers. Getting them out is not much of a problem, but seeing them is because they seem to hide until after you've put on the first coat of finish. Going back and re-sanding through the finish to get them out is a pain for you and the wood.

One way to locate light scratches is to position a 75-watt (or higher) incandescent or halogen light about 15" directly above the object while it's on the lathe. Then, hand-rotate the form while you look in the areas of the surface near the upper and lower silhouettes.

Once you locate some of these scratches (below), try rotating the form so they move directly into the middle, and watch them suddenly disappear. This is a good example of the chatoyant effect and how light can play tricks with your eyes. If a scratch is in line with your eye, or at a reduced angle to incoming light, the angle of incidence and refraction will be so slight the scratch will not be visible. But place the scratch either above or below this line, and it becomes an interruption to the reflection of the light...and the scratch suddenly pops out at you.

Another way of locating these problem areas is to take the object to a sunlit window or, better, outside. Here, the light will be coming from many directions at once, so you can more easily see the scratches as you rotate the piece in your hands. Of course, this is not always convenient, which is why I use a lightbulb.

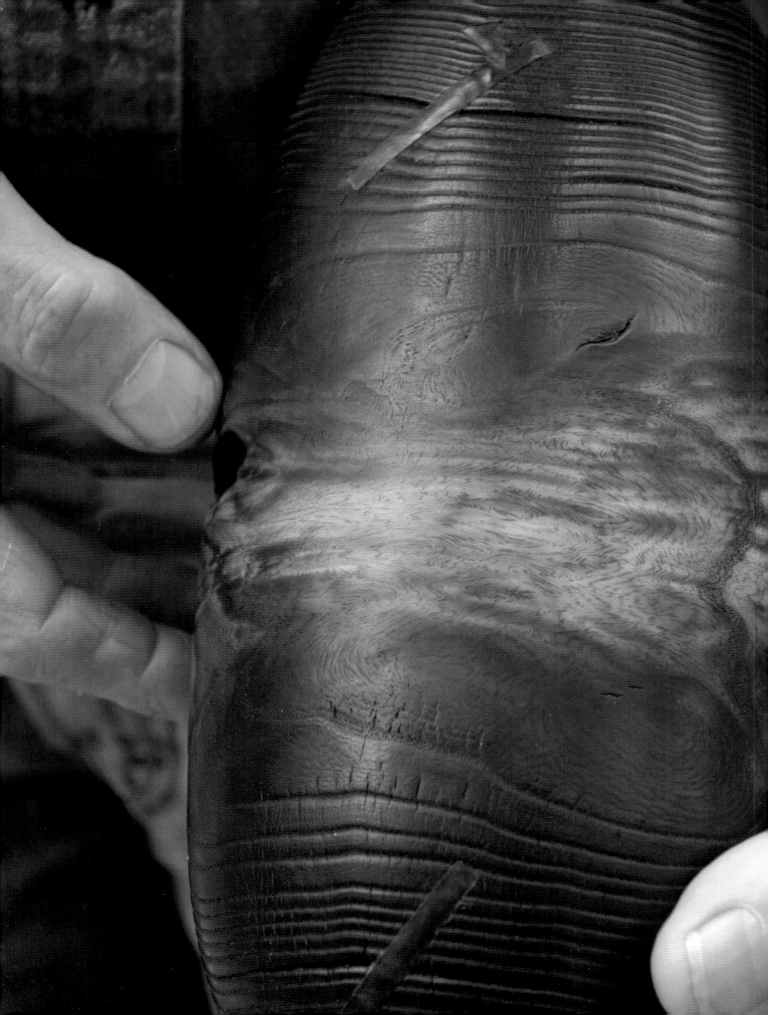

Chapter 16

Finishing

I made mention in Chapter 15, "Sanding," that sanding leads to finishing, and this brings me to an intriguing question. It relates to the type of finishes we use, but specifically, it's this: *when* is a piece finished? I'd like to explore this idea in the chapter.

I am always in a quandary when someone asks me what the "right" finish is to use on an object. There is no right finish. In a field so broadly based and fully expressive with so many ideas in so many dimensions, I believe the right finish is simply the one that satisfies the maker's intent. Over time and with experience, that intent can change. So the finish I use today may be different from the finish I used ten years ago. Both approaches are equally valid.

If I know what I want my object to look like, I will find the finish that will provide the look for which I'm searching. The finishing techniques used today are often executed with such extraordinary precision that I sometimes worry the wood doesn't really have much of a vote in the matter. Maybe that's a little harsh. Selecting a finish for a piece of wood is such a personal matter that it's...well...let's just leave it that it's a very personal matter. I've seen finishes that ranged from pig's blood to pine pitch to char to superglue.

Your piece is finished when you say it is. In this case, I was done after I'd charred, burnished, and inlaid this pot.

Trends in finishing

There are, however, two very common trends when it comes to the types of finishes turners use. The first is that while most turners will spend a good deal of time experimenting with various finishes, once they find one they like, they tend to apply it to just about every species of wood they use.

And the second trend is a reaction to the old days, when most turned objects were meant to function in some way: Turners tended to finish their work to look presentable, but especially to stand up over time and use. Today, with increased attention given to decorative objects, turners tend to use finishes that expand on the beauty of the wood, or an image or an impression they wish the object to convey. In either respect, I believe wood has always been considered a very sensuous material.

You could easily make the comparison that the older-style finishes were more muted, while today's finishes lean a bit toward the bright or even flashy side. And that would make sense, considering the variety of chemical finishes that weren't available fifty years ago. These would include water-based lacquers, urethanes, acrylics, various types of epoxy, and, yes, even superglue. Who's to say the older generation of turners wouldn't have used these new products if they had been available? I suspect many would have, as we see in the use of epoxies by such pioneers as Ed Moulthrop and Harry Nohr.

> "The finishing techniques used today are often executed with such extraordinary precision that I sometimes worry the wood doesn't really have much of a vote in the matter."

Influence of other media

My experience with people working in other media within the decorative arts seems to indicate the finishes used in wood, ceramic, and glass have always evolved as a reflection of current technology, cultural styles, and the ever-changing statements of fashion. Every generation challenges and redefines the term *beauty*, whether it is in front of a mirror or on the surface of a wooden bowl.

We can see how much of an influence other media have had on contemporary woodturning by looking at the finishes of the work of the late twentieth and early twenty-first centuries. Some of the early pioneers who fall into this category have had a profound influence on turning. Ed Moulthrop, of Atlanta, Georgia, developed a reflective, glass-like finish that has been adopted by many turners. Frank Sudol, of Saskatoon, Saskatchewan, Canada, pierced his pieces and painted them with an airbrush, which is an idea that evolved from fabric, paper, and stamped metalworking. Mark Lindquist, from Quincy, Florida, developed heavily textured surfaces that were inspired directly by clay, stone, and bronze sculptures. Michael Peterson, of Lopez Island, Washington, created patina surfaces that came from the influence of metal and stone. Giles Gilson, of Schenectady, New York, called on his experiences with hot cars and hotter airplanes when creating his lacquered surfaces. And there's yours truly, whose spalted and burned/burnished surfaces were inspired from clay, most notably Native American ceramics.

Historical influences

Painted wood surfaces date back thousands of years to the Japanese, the Celts, the Maya, and probably most indigenous cultures. All of us who have burned wood for one reason or another have been looking at old wooden structures, be they buildings, boats, bridges, or whatever. Most historical wooden objects have either rotted or been burned.

Choosing a finish

Considering the variations in finishes, it might be difficult to pinpoint which one you want to use. All you have to do is fill in the statement "I would like my finishes to look like...," and somehow, you will find a product or a style of finish that satisfies your needs.

Creating a singularly expressive finish

In the case of my own work, I like my finishes to be singularly expressive and born from the material being used. The term *singularly expressive* is critical to my finishing approach. Basically, it refers to the fact that ebony doesn't look like spalted maple, so I don't try to put the same finish on both materials. My finishes attempt to develop a surface that expresses the energy and the force of each object I make. I believe it can only be accomplished if the finish I use is compatible with and generated from the character of the species used in each object.

Compatibility is a very complex term when it comes to woodworking because it means different things to different people. One person might consider the chemical compatibility as it relates to how a certain finishing product sticks to various materials. Someone else might think of how some finishing products might react to a material in terms of a change in color or texture. Another element of compatibility involves selecting a finish in relation to

David Ellsworth, *Sapah*, 1991. Burned and painted ash; 23" high x 5" wide x 5" deep. Collection: Gordon Mayer. I used a charred and painted finish on pieces from my *Solstice* series, which offended many people and inspired others.

David Ellsworth, Untitled, 1996. Cocobolo rosewood; 2½" high x 2½" wide x 2½" deep. I chose a polished acrylic finish for these salt and pepper shakers.

how an object is to function or not function. When it comes to finishes, my use of the term *compatibility* pertains to how a certain finish—whether it be a product, a process, or an application—relates to the object's entire essence.

The pieces from my *Solstice* series had charred and painted finishes that offended many people when introduced in 1989. They also inspired many others, although I admit these were mostly my artist friends and a few loyal collectors. My point is the finish I chose was *as* compatible with those forms as a polished acrylic finish was for my salt and pepper shakers: The *Solstice* pieces were meant to be artistic, while my salt and pepper shakers were meant to be functional.

When is an object finished?

Before I get into the finishing specifics, let me back up to my original question: when is an object finished? I've had numerous people comment that my spalted pieces and especially my white oak pieces weren't finished, which means they don't have a sanded and polished surface. My response is that with each object I make, I work the surface to a point when I decide it has reached its optimum impact for what I want the object to represent...then I stop. It's a very subjective process, because I might be working with two pieces of the same species but have a different feeling about each and choose a variation of my finishing approach to match that feeling. The net effect is one object might have a certain look, while the second one will have a very different look, but both are finished.

Does this make one object more successful? The only way to determine that would be to observe the object over time—sometimes years—and see if my feelings about the piece remained strong. My experience is that—over time—if the piece continues to inspire me, or if it leads me into new ideas with other objects and thus becomes my teacher, then it can be considered a success. Part of that success will be the way in which I finished it. But if over time it just sits there without giving me any feedback, inspiration, or direction, then it is probably just another dog; well made, I would assume (and hope), but without any "woof."

Finishing products

I use a limited number of commercial finishing products with my work, and yet, I try to use them in as versatile a way as possible to explore the many visual effects I seek. The finishes I use are Waterlox, a tung oil–based sealer, for when I want an oil finish; Krylon UV-resistant matte finish, a spray acrylic lacquer (artist fixative), for when I want an invisible coating on textured woods; Wood Bleach, a bleaching compound, for when I want to lighten the wood color; and brown Tripoli, which is a buffing compound I use to cut back the surface buildup from oil finishes and when burnishing the surfaces of my blackened pieces.

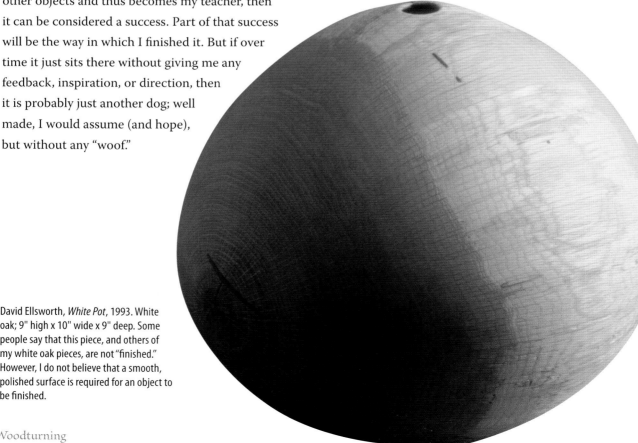

David Ellsworth, *White Pot*, 1993. White oak; 9" high x 10" wide x 9" deep. Some people say that this piece, and others of my white oak pieces, are not "finished." However, I do not believe that a smooth, polished surface is required for an object to be finished.

Oil finishes

Oil finishes are extremely versatile because they can be rubbed to a low luster or polished to a high gloss. I lean toward an oil finish when I am working with a wood that asks for a warm, evenly distributed lustrous glow. This would include the denser woods such as rosewood, ebony, maple, and beech, particularly when the wood displays strong grain patterns such as fiddleback, quilted, curly, burl, or crotch figure.

I don't use an oil finish on spalted woods, because the porous fibers tend to drink the oil like a sponge and turn the surface color to mud. Similarly, I don't use oil on textured surfaces, especially bark, because there's no way of cutting back the shine of the dried oil without damaging the natural texture of the bark. Shiny bark surfaces give me the impression of Christmas wrapping paper, and my aesthetic just can't handle it.

Oil finishes can also darken many woods, especially over time. An example would be all of the maple pieces I did twenty years ago that all look exactly alike today, including those made in silver maple, which were originally quite light in tone. I believe they are even more beautiful in the darker tonal range, but that wasn't my intent when I made them.

My belief is the oil should enhance the fibers' optical qualities, so the wood's natural radiance can be viewed and enjoyed, and the integrity of each species is preserved.

Oil finishes on resinous species like rosewood and lignum vitae don't always work, in part because there is so much resin in these materials that the oil always seems to remain tacky on their surfaces. The woods obviously have beautiful grain patterns, but also face shallow depth of optical radiance. They appear almost matte with an oil finish, which is one reason people often use wax or a glossy finish on these woods—to raise their optical qualities.

On the other hand, African blackwood, which is also a resinous rosewood, projects a very deep luster, but only in the areas of quarter-sawn grain. In fact, blackwood isn't actually black, but rather, a purplish brown with creamy pearl-colored streaks that can only be seen on the quarter-sawn grain. An oil finish enhances this effect, but only if polished to a medium-bright luster.

For my purposes, I use an oil finish to draw the viewer into the surface of the wood in the same way the surface captures the light from its surroundings. I don't use highly polished or reflective surfaces on my pieces, because while these are very hot and seductive surfaces, they also reflect the light away from the object and thus repel the viewer. For my aesthetic, my primary interest is to establish a dialogue between the viewer and the object, and I find a calmer surface allows for that dialogue.

Another advantage in working with oil finishes comes when working with burled woods that develop a crinkled surface when the wood dries. Oils are penetrating finishes, so they can be rubbed into the grain and buffed evenly in the low areas of a textured surface. Acrylic, urethane, and other poly-type products are basically surface treatments, and they tend to build up in the valleys of these crinkled areas. The result is you can't polish them evenly and the finished surface looks spotty.

"Oil finishes are extremely versatile because they can be rubbed to a low luster or polished to a high gloss."

Applying an oil finish

An oil finish can function not only as a final finish, but also as a protective coating while turning. Especially on hollow forms, I find that applying a coat of oil helps to keep the walls from drying out and cracking while turning the interior.

I dry my oiled pieces by hanging them on a hook in my workshop.

When the wood and the oil dry, a residue will form on the piece's surface.

To remove hardened oil residue, buff the piece with a stitched muslin buffing wheel and brown Tripoli.

The final step is to buff the piece with an unstitched wheel to remove any Tripoli residue.

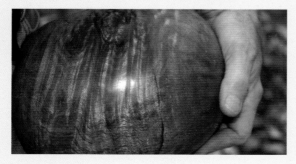

Applying an oil finish

I achieve an oiled surface by starting the oiling process immediately after the form has been shaped and sanded, and *before* I begin to hollow out the form. The oil will not harden in the green wood's fibers. Instead, it lubricates the fibers enough to prevent surface checking from heat produced while cutting the form's interior. It also helps the fibers from becoming contaminated by dust and debris over the time it takes to cut the interior, which is why I am very careful not to touch the wood's oiled surface with my hands while making the piece.

It may be necessary to apply, with a rag or sponge, several coats of oil to continue to lubricate the fibers while turning the interior. Though it may not sound sophisticated, I apply the oil only where needed... generally on the end grain. However, once the form has been hollowed to a thin shell, I apply an even coat of oil to the entire surface and hang the piece up in the room to dry. Because the walls are so thin, it generally takes only a few days to dry both the oil and the wood.

While the piece is drying, I add additional amounts of oil daily to the surface areas that continue to soak it up, but not to areas where the pores are full. Adding oil onto oil is pretty unnecessary, although sometimes hard to prevent. It's not important how many coats are applied, but how the wood will accept the oil.

Once the wood fibers are dry, the oil will polymerize and become hard, leaving a rather crusty surface residue from previous applications. At this point, I buff the excess oil residue off with a 6"-diameter stitched-muslin buffing wheel and brown Tripoli. Depending on the piece's size, this can be a laborious process. It is important to cut away the excess oil evenly on the wood's surface so the finished surface doesn't appear streaky. You must also be extremely careful, especially on lighter-colored woods, not to burn the surface by holding the form in a stationary position against the buffing wheel.

The final step is to even out the surface by buffing with an unstitched 6"-diameter wheel. This removes any built-up Tripoli residue that can form on the surface from the previous polishing and creates a lustrous, glowing surface with a slight sheen.

Spray acrylic lacquer

I use spray acrylic lacquer when I want a textured surface on a non-sanded wood. Oak is a rather raw and aggressive material, so I have preserved the raw wood feeling by leaving an unsanded, off-the-gouge surface protected with spray lacquer. When stroked with the palm, the surface feels like coarse sandpaper and sounds like a raku surface on a ceramic pot. It is a subtle finish, because unlike a glossy "what you see is what you get" finish, this surface asks for the interaction of three senses: sight, sound, and touch. I also use spray lacquer on decomposed spalted wood (see "Finishes for spalted wood" on page 229).

I use Krylon UV-resistant matte finish, which is sold at art supply stores. This spray coating dries to an invisible coat and doesn't change the wood's color, but protects the surface from handling and enables you to vacuum away household dust using a brush attachment. Care must be taken that you don't overspray the surface, or it will become shiny and look like plastic...which is what the spray is.

Raku pots

The reason I have always been attracted to raku finishes in ceramic pots is that they speak directly to the material of clay in its most natural state; that is, objects that are formed, fired, and are ready for use. Native American ceramics were my first exposure to pots created with this type of wood-firing process. Even when the pots have been decorated with burnishing or paint, the resulting effects speak honestly about the material being used. Wood shares that same inherent quality as clay in that its true beauty comes from within. The difference is the huge variety of species, colors, and patterns that wood provides. The similarity is in choosing a finish that reflects the nature of the material without trying to make it look like something that it is not.

Ash yields particularly good sandblasted surfaces because it has soft spring and summer grain that is easily removed. With the addition of bleach, my intent was to create a uniform, almost ghostlike surface to emphasize the lineal qualities of the object's design.

Sandblasting

Sandblasting has become a common technique over the past few decades. It produces a wonderfully neutral, matte surface on woods like ash and oak, which have very strong contrasting grain densities between spring and winter growth. Woods that don't have this delineation in fibers, like maple and birch, will get a sandpaper-like texture if sandblasted, but they won't have that deeply etched, swirling-wave quality illustrated by the annual growth rings in the tree. Blasting heavily spalted woods with sand can produce surfaces that are often very coarse and exciting. I use an inexpensive blaster from a department store, and bags of sand are available at any local industrial supplier or most equipment rental agencies. I take my blaster outside my studio and blast away. The only problems are I have to practically dress up in a hazmat suit to protect myself and that I lose all of the sand.

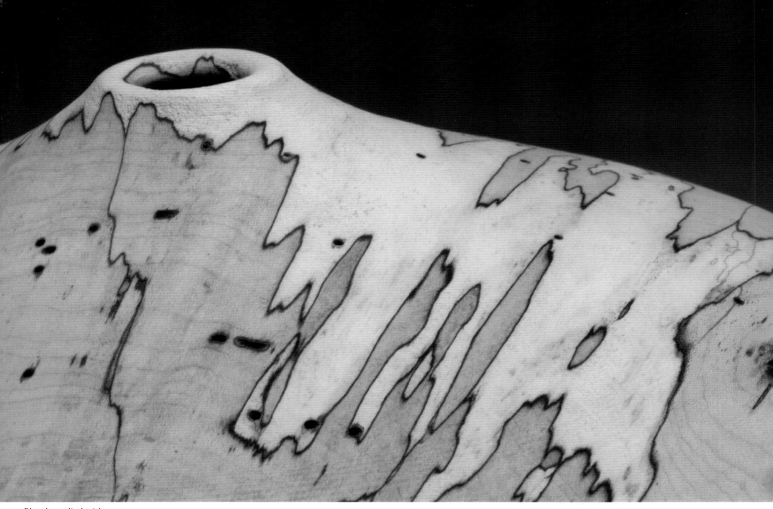

Bleach applied with a fine brush adds great drama and contrast to a finished piece.

Bleaching

Bleaching, as you might have guessed, lightens the color of the wood surface. I use Wood Bleach, a brand-name bleaching product sold through Sherman-Williams paint stores. Wood bleaches come in two parts (A and B) that are mixed equally. Bleach has a watery consistency that makes it easy to swab onto wood with a sponge, cloth, or brush. The consistency also makes it difficult to control bleach in tight quarters, because it runs. In detailed areas, it helps to apply bleach with a small brush. You can use as many applications as necessary. The more you bleach, the lighter the surface. Just be sure to allow each coat to dry before adding another coat, and always clean your mixing containers as you use them. There can be a yellowing effect on some woods, so it helps to put on several applications of the B component.

Wax

I do not use any waxes on my pieces now, although I did use wax back in the 1980s. This may be somewhat controversial, because buffed-on wax leaves a beautiful surface. The problem is wax attracts moisture over time and turns the surface dull. I once saw a piece of mine in a museum in Little Rock, Arkansas, that had a waxed surface... and it was covered with a light mold. The reason I was waxing my work was I fell into the trap of thinking I was supposed to use wax, because that's what woodturners did. After that hard lesson, I haven't waxed a piece since.

Bleach safety

Keep in mind that once the bleach parts have been mixed, they create an active chemical that will burn whatever it touches. You must wear eye protection and rubber gloves. In my shop, that's not a guideline, it's a rule!

Burning and burnishing

I had a student some years back who was doing excellent work in the studio, but he was rather young and quite shy. I was having trouble getting him really charged up. On the last day of class, I grabbed a propane hand torch and started burning one of my old hollow forms. Well, this kid took one look at that and just lit up like a house on fire. He ran and got all of the bowls he'd turned over the weekend and started burning the hell out of them. It was wonderful.

Burning is fun! Considering the many hours of energy and stress involved in making the perfect hollow form, putting the torch to the wood is almost a cathartic experience. Green wood is especially fun, to burn. The combination of moisture and elastic fibers can produce some very dramatic changes in the surface, and a good bit of steam, too.

When you are burning the pith or end-grain areas, cracks that didn't exist while you were making the piece will suddenly appear. It's not uncommon for a whole section adjacent to the pith to rise up as much as ½" from the surface. In most cases, these elements will settle back to their original positions after the piece finally dries out, and sometimes, cracks will close completely even though they remain quite visible. Nevertheless, it's a wonderful reminder of how much tension is locked inside wood fibers, and of the exciting things that can happen when that

Cautions to observe while burning

When burning, there are a few rules to follow. Don't do it inside, and clear debris from the immediate area, which I did not do during this brief photo shoot...shame on me. Two of the less obvious cautions are not to burn on a windy day, as it's harder to control the flame, and NEVER leave a charred or burned piece of wood sitting outside unattended. I did it once, not realizing there was a tiny live ember somewhere in the edge of the rim. I came back an hour later and the piece was gone. Only a pile of ash was left! It never hurts to squirt your pieces down after they've been burned, just in case.

Burning and burnishing

Burning a piece can be great fun, in my opinion. It's always interesting to see what results you get!

To burn a piece, use a propane hand torch and have at it. Make sure you've cleared all of the debris away from around the object—unlike the setup pictured here. Always undertake this finishing technique outside.

After burning the piece to your heart's content, apply brown Tripoli to a stitched buffing wheel.

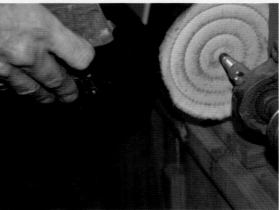

Burnish the piece on the buffing wheel until you have knocked off most of the char.

tension is released under the heat of the torch.

There is no mystery about the process of burning wood, but you do learn a lot of things as a result. For instance, it is critically important to turn the vessel walls to a consistent ⅛"-thick. Any thicker, and the torch accelerates cracking in the surface; any thinner, and the fire either raises a ring around the form, burns completely through it, or both.

You must accept that the heat of the torch *will* create cracks in the wood. If you don't want cracks, don't pick up the torch. I have learned how to predict where cracks will appear and to control them as they develop, but it does take practice with the torch. Experiment with the distance of the flame to the surface, with the intensity of the heat when working with either propane or MAPP gas (which is hotter), and the pace as you move the heat over the wood's surface. And, yes, I have gone through a number of pieces developing this skill. The most discouraging experiences were when I inadvertently turned an uneven wall thickness and a visible band developed around the form where the wall was thinner.

David Ellsworth, *Black Pot-Dawn, #3*, 1999. Burned and burnished ash; 9½" high x 5¼" wide x 5¼" deep. This piece, inspired by the rising dawn, has a transparent surface created with burning, sanding, and polishing.

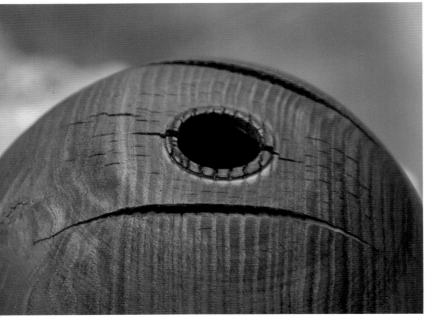

Burning the pith and end-grain areas will cause cracks. Sometimes, the cracks will close up, and sometimes they won't. It's one way to add texture to a piece!

Burnishing a charred surface

To finish charred surfaces, I usually burnish them. To do this, I load my 6"-diameter stitched buffing wheel with a heavy amount of brown Tripoli and then apply the wood directly to the wheel's surface. The Tripoli cuts down the char's bulk and gives the surface a somewhat dull polished look.

The next step is to *flash burn* the lanolin and wax residue left by the Tripoli. For this, I use the radiant heat off the side of the torch flame, holding it about 1" away from the wood surface rather than pointing the hotter tip area directly into the wood. I then buff the entire surface with a clean unstitched buffing wheel, and the piece is complete.

Sanding a charred surface

My series titled *Black Pot-Dawn* evolved from my observation of that magical moment between the dead of night and the early period just before daylight when the atmosphere in the sky becomes slightly transparent. My intent with these pieces was to produce a transparent glazelike effect, similar to a ceramic glaze, where the wood's lighter tones appear to emerge from beneath and through the burned surface. I cut the pieces from the crotch area of large ash trees so I could position the intense grain patterns of the crotch figure within the swirling patterns of the surrounding grain.

To create this transparent effect, I begin by burning the entire surface to a heavy char, then sanding back through the char in the area of the figured grain. This is the most exciting part, because I can play with the relationship between the burned and sanded areas to draw the entire piece together into a visual composition.

I begin by sanding the charred surface with 320-grit paper using a very soft 5"-diameter, 1"-thick foam disc. The process cuts through the char to expose the wood's lighter natural color. I select the areas to sand at my own discretion. If I want more light areas, I sand more of the char. If I want more dark areas, I burn more. Once the visual effect is reached, I flash burn the surface using the radiant heat as described above and evaluate the final results. If I like it, the last step is to buff the entire surface with a clean, unstitched buffing wheel.

Finishes for spalted wood

My selection of finishes for spalted wood depends totally on the condition of the spalting. If the wood is still solid, as in *Spider Pot* (below right), then I will use an oil finish the same as I would with a nonspalted wood. If the surface is heavily decomposed due to the spalting, as in *Maple Pot* (bottom), then I do not sand at all. I spray on a light coat of artist fixative, which is an acrylic lacquer normally used for charcoal and pastel drawings.

In cases where there is a combination of solid and decomposed surfaces, I often use oil on solid areas and spray on decomposed areas. I apply the oil first, then the spray, so I can remove any overspray in the surface's solid areas with a buffing wheel.

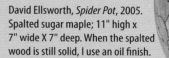

David Ellsworth, *Spider Pot*, 2005. Spalted sugar maple; 11" high x 7" wide X 7" deep. When the spalted wood is still solid, I use an oil finish.

David Ellsworth, *Maple Pot*, 2006. Maple; 10" high x 11" wide x 11" deep. Collection: Jane and Arthur Mason. When spalted wood is heavily decomposed, I refrain from sanding and instead spray on a light coat of artist fixative.

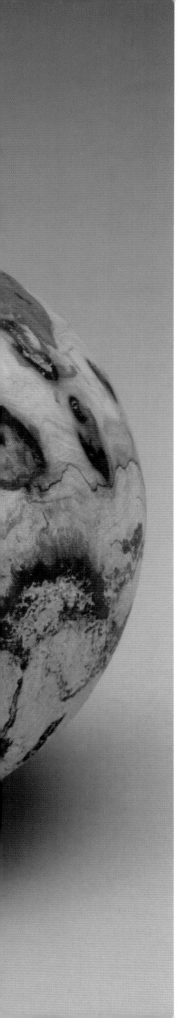

Drying Green Wood Vessels

During my years in turning, a number of mysteries about the "proper" way to dry green wood have evolved. Because mysteries generally evolve from a combination of curiosity and a lack of reliable information, I understand the amount of confusion that surrounds the subject of how to work with green wood. It could be green wood just doesn't seem to fit very well into the lexicon of conventional woodworking wisdom, especially when it comes to controlling the drying process. A moisture meter will tell you there's a certain amount of water in the bowl, but not if the bowl is going to crack when it starts to dry out. Just about the time you think you have it all figured out with one species, you try another, and the rules change. Then there's the problem of end grain versus face grain, and the differences between trunk wood, root wood, branch wood, bark, and all of the things furniture makers don't have to deal with because they get their wood from a store. Here, I'll discuss how I came to discover the mysteries of green wood, how it dries, and some drying methods I use to prevent cracking and checking.

David Ellsworth, *Hickory Pot*, 2006. Hickory; 3¾" high x 5" wide x 5" deep. The lower half represents chaos, with its mottled and pocked spalted surface. The smooth sanded solid wood in the upper half represents order. The meandering line is symbolic of man's restless journey, while the scale of the opening speaks of the need to protect mystery in life.

Discovering the free energy of green wood

When I started working with green wood, I didn't know these problems with wood even existed. Like everyone else, I had worked plenty of dry wood. That was easy. You did your technical thing and the wood did its thing, which was to sit there and be pretty. And it was.

But as soon as I began to explore working with green wood, everything became a challenge. I made a piece one evening in 1978 in my Colorado studio (at 8,500 feet), and the next morning, it had twisted all up and was sitting on the floor on its side. I was thrilled. Sometime later, I took the hint and did a piece out of red oak burl that had a round base and no foot. When it had finished doing its thing, I put it down and it rolled around until it found its own base. "My God," I thought, "what have I been doing buying wood from a store when this is like working with free energy in the palm of my hand?" I immediately developed a philosophy that dry wood was dead, while green wood was alive. I was naïve, of course, and later regretted how I expressed my epiphany because it was misinterpreted as a slam on all my friends who worked with dry wood, even though it wasn't meant that way. Anyway, I wasn't far off the mark when it came to the working aspects of this newfound material.

Then there were these questions: How do I try to *control* this movement? How do I design for it? Control is what woodworkers have always imposed on their materials in order to execute designs, but I didn't want control: I wanted free expression. I wanted a relationship between an idea and a material through a process. I wanted movement and gesture. I wanted ideas to evolve *from* the work rather than be imposed *on* the work. I wanted wood to become the *perfectly*

David Ellsworth, *Red Oak Burl*, 1980. Red oak; 6½ " high x 7" wide x 7" deep. Red oak burl has wonderful characteristics of stress and color throughout. This piece began as a sphere, with the entrance hole in a natural bark inclusion. Once dried, it took on its own shape and character.

imperfect material it is. And how could I achieve it if the material always stays the same? Initially, I had a great deal of difficulty trying to explain this approach to my customers, because all they were interested in was how thin the walls were and that, "Oh, by the way, you couldn't put cereal in it."

Of course, what I didn't realize in these early exploratory years was I was developing a skill that would ultimately give me a measure of control within my forms that I hadn't been looking for in the beginning. Instead of fighting this control, I eventually learned it came as a natural evolution from information to knowledge to wisdom. The more information I gathered by working with the materials, the more knowledgeable I became about the entire hollowing process, and the wiser I became in developing forms that satisfied my ever-growing aesthetic.

How wood dries

So how does green wood dry? What happens, and what factors have a say in how the wood moves? Besides moisture content, the fiber's mass, tension, and elasticity are the main players in the drying process. As well, the wood species you're working with, the climate you live in, and even what part of the tree the wood is from will all affect how the wood dries.

Mass, tension, and elasticity

Once you accept the fact wood does move, you also learn wood moves in a predictable manner. In a bowl or vessel, as the face (long) grain dries, it contracts and pushes the fibers of the end (short) grain out. The reason it moves relates to the amount of tension that exists in the fibers and how much mass is present, which is basically why veneers crinkle and boards crack. The last thing you need to consider is while dry wood has rigid fibers, green wood has elastic fibers, and it is these elastic, supple fibers that allow the wood to release tension when it begins to make the shift from green to dry. So there you have it. Mystery solved, at least in theory. In practice, the

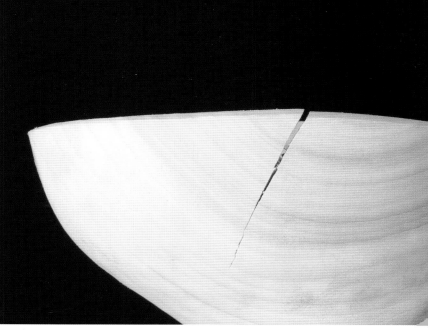

A crack in a poplar bowl due to uneven wall thickness—¼" at the rim and ¾" at the base. The rim dried out faster than the base, which caused it to lose its elasticity and crack when the base began to dry.

combination of mass, tension, and elasticity of fibers can make or break your piece...literally. For example, if you turn a green bowl that has a wall thickness of ¼" at the rim and ½" at the base, you're looking at a 100% increase in the mass at the base over the top. Equally obvious is that the rim will dry out before the base because there's half of the amount of material to dry. But what's most important is when the rim does dry, the fibers lose their elasticity and become rigid. So, when the base begins to dry, and the face-grain fibers shrink and the end-grain fibers move outward, the poor old rim is sitting there in extreme pain because it can't move with the rest of the bowl. Boom! Now you've got a cracked bowl. To successfully dry the bowl described above, you slow down the drying process so the fibers in the rim don't dry out and become rigid before the entire bowl has had a chance to release its tension.

Another example would be to turn a green bowl with a superthin wall of ¹⁄₁₆" throughout. Now take the bowl outside and set it on the dashboard of your car at noon on a sunny day. Give it an hour and watch it move as it dries, but notice it doesn't crack. Why? Because at ¹⁄₁₆" thick, there isn't enough mass in the bowl to get in the way when the tension begins to release itself and before the fibers become dry and rigid.

David Ellsworth, *Platter*, 1977. Walnut; 15" diameter x ½" high x ⅛" thick. This piece of wood was bone-dry when I turned it and suffered no distortion. However, if dried too fast, the extra dense fibers in the crotch area would shrink faster than the long-grain fibers and warp the platter.

Species

The next step in understanding how green wood dries is to recognize that while all species share many common properties, no two wood species are the same. Each species possesses a unique mix of characteristics—including strength, figure, cell structure, and fiber size—and each of those elements affects how the wood dries. If you imagine wood fibers as being a bunch of soda straws packed together, you can see some fibers are large in diameter and hollow with a lot of space between them and others are fine, with little room between them. Ash, poplar, hickory, and white oak all have large diameter hollow fibers with large gaps between them, while other species, such as lignum vitae, boxwood, ebony, and sugar maple, all have fine fibers with little room between them. The latter take longer to dry simply because it's more difficult for loose water between fibers to escape and evaporate.

To add to the mix, most tropical species also have heavy concentrations of resin. The more resin, the less room there is between the fibers for water, and the harder it is to control the drying process. The presence of resin is quite interesting. I'm not convinced woods like lignum vitae and cocobolo ever fully dry. It's not safe to use them for segmented work, because the glue doesn't stick to the resin. As well, I have some older bowls in these species where the resin has squeezed through the finish as fibers continued to shrink over time. The amount of moisture that remains in these bowls almost seems irrelevant to the drying process when the dominant factor controlling fiber movement in these species is the resin content.

Parts of the tree

Beyond species, not even two parts of the same tree are the same. The jobs and stresses of each part create different behaviors during drying.

Trunk wood experiences I've had are probably different from other turners because I prefer working the wood green. Turning hollow forms—my specialty—is far more difficult to do with dry wood because of the fiber's rigid and brittle nature. The green wood's moist, limber fibers are easier to cut and help reduce vibration that develops with the long, thin-shafted tools I use. When I do stumble on a dry log, I prefer to cut it down into smaller sections to make smaller forms. That said, if I did have some masochistic reason for drying out a large log, I would cover the ends with several coats of wood sealer, store it in a covered area of my studio that is even in temperature and away from moisture, and simply wait ten to twenty years. I presume that, at that point, I would be older and wise enough to realize I should have cut it down into smaller blocks and turned them green in the first place.

It is perfectly acceptable to turn a hollow form green and with thick walls, then re-turn it when it dries, in the same manner that you would double-turn a bowl or a platter. This is not my method, but I know turners who do it and make quite wonderful forms.

Limb wood tends to split easier than trunk wood because of the extreme tension limbs sustain just to support themselves as they grow. The fibers in limbs are more compact, which means less room between fibers and less opportunity to move evenly during drying.

"The next step in understanding how green wood dries is to recognize that while all species share many common properties, no two wood species are the same."

Root wood is softer and more flexible than trunk wood; otherwise, the roots would snap in a high wind while trying to hold up the tree.

Crotch wood has the densest and most tightly knit fibers of all because it has to be superstrong to keep the limbs from splitting open.

Burl wood, although not necessarily harder than trunk wood, has interlocking cross grain in a structural pattern that makes it extremely strong and elastic.

Spalted wood, whose fibers are being decomposed by natural fungi, can have varying densities that cover the entire range from solid wood to total punk.

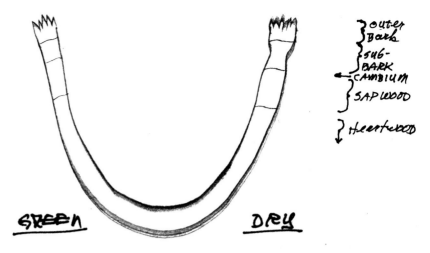

Sub-bark shrinks more than the outer bark as it dries. This cross-section of a bowl with a bark edge at the top shows how the fresh-cut side (left) is plumper than the dry bark (right).

This year-old leg on my wife's studio beading table was made of freshly cut beech. It's a good example of the role Mother Nature can play in overall design; the bark and the tree are actually different materials separated—noticeably so here—by the cambium.

Bark acts somewhat like the roof surface on a house because if you penetrate or remove it, you expose what's underneath. What's beneath the bark of trees is, of course, the sapwood, and by removing the bark—easily done when the wood is green—you expose the sapwood and potentially accelerate the drying process. Cutting the tree in the winter when the sap is not running will minimize the separation potential. And, of course, you can always glue the bark in place with superglue, as long as you don't mind stains in the end grain. We often forget bark and sapwood are different. They dry at different rates and shrink differently. Also, woods like ash, poplar, and walnut have a thick sub-bark between the outer bark and the sapwood, and this sub-bark can shrink as much as 30% more than the outer bark and sapwood that surrounds it.

All of these areas of the tree are desirable as turning materials, and as long as you observe the relationship between mass, tension, and the fiber condition, your success rate in drying our objects from these various parts of the tree will go up.

In other words, to successfully dry green wood, you must first understand why the wood does what it does. Then you can create an environment where the changes it needs to make can occur gradually. Let's look at some methods for doing just that.

Drying methods and tips

Like everything else, intuition, common sense, and a little experience (OK, sometimes a lot of experience) play a huge role in learning how to dry green wood. I also understand how people who have grown up in urban areas might find this intuitive factor daunting. It was easy for me because I have been cutting, splitting, and drying firewood since I was a boy. I knew the cracks on the end grain meant that the log was ready to chuck into the stove. But for those who don't have that experience, here are a few very generic, intuitive drying tips that might help, along with my favorite conventional and unconventional methods for drying vessels turned from green wood.

The two ideas I rely on are 1) when in doubt, slow the process down, and 2) cut samples and experiment. Slowing the process is the fundamental principle of air-drying wood, although few of us have that kind of patience, which is why we build wood kilns. Kiln-drying controls the rate of moisture loss so the wood doesn't shrink too quickly. The only way to know how a piece of wood will dry is to cut small samples and watch them dry. In general terms, soft woods, or those with large-diameter fibers, are easier to dry than hard woods with dense or resinous fibers.

Drying green bowls in brown paper bags helps prevent cracking. The bag creates a controlled atmosphere that allows moisture to slowly evaporate into the air, slowing down the drying process.

The brown paper bag method

One way to create the environment for slowing down the drying process is to place the object into a brown paper grocery bag. The bag acts like a moisture barrier. Assuming there is less moisture in the air of the room than inside the bag, the paper will absorb moisture from the wood, allowing the moisture to slowly evaporate into the atmosphere of the room and pulling more moisture from the bowl to the bag's surface.

In the meantime, the moist atmosphere inside the bag allows the thinner areas of the bowl to absorb the moisture being expelled by the thicker areas. The tension in the wood can then be released gradually because the fibers are able to shift from elastic to rigid uniformly throughout the bowl rather than in a single location. Again, what is most important is the shift needs to be gradual rather than sudden.

The wet shavings method

Adding wet shavings inside a paper bag sometimes helps if you're working with dry woods like ash or hickory, especially when the object has uneven wall thicknesses. In effect, you're introducing a small amount of moisture to help balance the moisture content between the thick and thin walls. This will help prevent the thin areas from drying out too quickly. Just be careful to use this trick with a light hand. Don't pack shavings tightly against both sides of the bowl, because it will deter any drying and cause mold to grow. Also, a ½"-thick bowl with 4" of shavings around it is actually a 4½"-thick bowl. And it will take an unnecessarily long time to dry out.

Adding wet shavings to a paper bag will help slow the drying process enough that even varying wall thicknesses should dry without cracking. Don't add too many shavings, or the piece will dry only from the exposed surfaces and cracking may occur.

The dog food bag method

The brown paper bag trick works very well in moderate climates, but in dryer climates, more layers are required to slow down the rate of evaporation from the bag's surface. In such situations, try using multilayered dog food bags. Regularly check for mold inside the bag and replace the bag if mold occurs.

The plastic bag method

Desert climates require the use of plastic bags, especially to store green turning blocks and logs before turning them. When drying a turned object in a plastic bag, keep it in a cool location and turn the bag inside out daily. This will allow moisture condensed on the interior surface to evaporate and be replaced with new condensed moisture. The object is dry when no more moisture appears on the interior, or when the object no longer loses weight.

The plastic sheet method

In less-severe dry climates, you can use sheets of plastic to dry the wood. Simply drape the sheet over the object, leaving some openings at the edges for the exchange of air. Flip the sheet over daily so the condensation that was collected on the undersurface of the sheet can evaporate. The bowl is dry when no condensation forms.

The wood sealer method

When double-turning a bowl (rough-turning to a thick wall, drying, then re-turning to a finished shape), coat at least the exterior of the form with wood sealer and store the bowl upside down in a cool location on a nonmetal grid. This allows air to flow beneath the form, and the nonmetal grid prevents rim staining. Drier climates may also require coating the interior surface. Again, a bowl will dry much faster with a ⅛"-thick wall than with a ½" wall, and a ½"-thick bowl in a paper bag may easily dry out in only a week. You can experiment by cutting slabs of green wood in different thicknesses, placing them in a paper bag, and seeing how long they take to dry. Otherwise, just make a few bowls and see what happens.

How to tell if a piece is dry

One quick way to tell if a piece has moisture in it is to hold it against your cheek or the back of your hand. If it's cool, it still has moisture in it. Tapping with the surface of a fingernail (not the tip) is another good way, as dry wood has a distinct brittle ring to it. Both methods require a bit of expertise in knowing what to feel for and what to hear, but this comes with experience.

I will often use my antique scale to weigh pieces as they dry because it helps me understand the percentage of moisture loss in species between green and dry, the rate of evaporation, and how a workpiece feels when it stops losing weight and is dry. If I'm drying a light wood like poplar and it feels heavy and cool, I don't need a scale to know it's not yet dry. On the other hand, if it's a dense piece of cocobolo, it may lose 2 to 3 ounces in a day or two, but take two weeks to lose the next 2 to 3 ounces. This is when I use the scale, to be sure the wood stabilizes over an extended period of time.

I believe experience and instinct play important and reliable roles in learning about the drying process. I suppose I could use a moisture meter, but I don't much care for poking little holes in my pieces, and I wouldn't know what to do with the numbers anyway. Numbers are relative, but relative to what? Do they mean the same in a dry climate as a humid one? I don't object to using these gadgets when drying wood if I'm going to make dovetail joints, but a moisture meter only gives you the numbers. It doesn't teach you anything about the drying process, or the difference in how the wood feels when dry, or how to adjust the drying process as you shift from species to species. In other words, drying wood when making bowls and vessels isn't as much about formulas as it is intuition and experience.

The scale is a useful tool to help you to establish the rate of drying for any species of wood.

This log shows end-grain cracks from drying too fast. The same kind of cracks can appear in a bowl if it is oversanded or simply spun for a long time on the lathe.

Dealing with heat checks and cracks

This shot of a log's end grain illustrates the problem of drying too fast. Now, imagine overheating a bowl by sanding at too high an rpm, or imagine the amount of moisture a bowl would lose by simply spinning on the lathe for hours and hours. In both cases, you get the same problem. If heat checks occur in the end-grain fibers of a bowl or vessel while it's being turned, don't panic...and don't grab the superglue. Wood yawns, and these checks will close down naturally—sometimes even completely—after the object dries. But if you pack these heat checks with superglue, not only will the end-grain fibers become stained, but also the checks won't be able to close down later because the glue will be in the way. Instead, they'll simply crack further. Besides, the glue will not stop cracks from getting larger in green wood. One solution is to wrap 2"-wide clear packing tape or shrink-wrap over these areas to prevent further evaporation and checking while the piece is being made. In all cases, I deal with the cracks after the object has completely dried and the fibers are stable.

Dealing with varying wall thicknesses

Bowls and vessels with varying wall thicknesses are the most difficult to dry successfully. Whatever method of drying you use, try to slow the process. Avoid extreme changes in temperature and humidity, including protecting the piece from air-conditioning and room heat sources. Cooler is better. Near the floor is best.

Alternate drying methods

If waiting around for green wood to air dry isn't your speed, or if you need a special method for a special piece, you may want to try boiling or "nuking" (a.k.a. microwaving). These methods share one thing in common: They drive out the loose water between the cells and explode the walls of the bound cells, allowing more moisture to be released than would occur through regular drying. The result is drying occurs quicker. Boiling and nuking seem to neutralize the hard and soft areas in the fibers so there is much less potential for cracking. There is a sacrifice in using these methods. Some of the chatoyant glow in the wood is lost as a result of exploding the cells. Curly, quilted, and figured woods still look very pretty when cooked, but they simply don't have the same three-dimensional chatoyant shimmer in the light. To learn more about chatoyance, read about it in Chapter 15, "Sanding," on page 210.

Boiling is my method of choice for drying pieces made of heavily decomposed spalted wood. Without the proper drying techniques, spalted areas actually fracture or pull apart rather than just splitting (see photo on page 239, top). I also use the boiling method when I know that cracking could occur from extreme tensions in the wood.

This is the propane burner setup I use for boiling bowls. For this setup, you need a galvanized trash can, a couple of cinder blocks, some heavy-duty steel rods, a cylinder of propane, a long rubber tube, an 80,000 BTU propane burner, and some water to boil.

As to equipment for boiling, I first solder the seams in a 30-gallon galvanized trash can so it won't leak. Then, I place the can on a steel grate or steel rods above an 80,000 BTU propane burner and put enough water in the can to cover the piece. Because my pieces have relatively thin walls (¼" maximum), I have no formula or schedules relating to the size of the piece and the amount of time it should be boiled. I just stick it in the soup and let it go for a couple of hours. If the walls of my pieces were thicker than ¼", I would have to boil them longer. After boiling, I carefully roll the piece out of the can and let it stand until it cools down. A ¼"-thick-walled bowl usually dries in about two days, with no cracks in the solid heartwood or the spalted regions.

Nuking, or using a microwave to dry out green wood, is a method with which I have no personal experience, so I won't attempt to pass on any information beyond what others have passed to me. Namely, do plenty of experiments with samples of different thicknesses and different species—and use someone else's microwave oven.

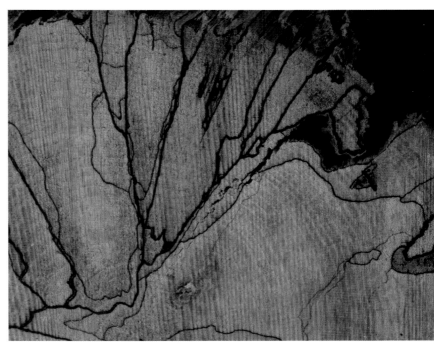

The fractured grain in this spalted wood could have been avoided if the wood had been dried with an alternate method. Boiling and nuking neutralize the hard and soft areas so there is less chance of fracturing.

The real problem with drying

Finally, I should say most turners simply don't realize that many of the problems they have drying their turnings don't actually occur during the drying process. We tend to overlook the fact that drying problems originate from the excessive amount of time spent working an object on the lathe as we labor, cut after cut after cut, trying to create that perfect shape. When working green wood, this overcutting ends up spin-drying the object's surface. You can see it when you look at the rooster tail of moisture on the lathe, the floor, and the ceiling. Then, there is the heat produced by oversanding. Fortunately, the more overall experience you gain, the more skillful and efficient you become with both your cutting and sanding processes. And with this greater skill level comes a reduced amount of time you spend spinning, cutting, and sanding.

In truth, the most valuable lesson you can give yourself is to take the time to enjoy the learning process by practicing on nonvaluable materials, even if it means losing a few pieces of wood along the road. Remember: it's only wood.

David Ellsworth, *Stratum Pot #3*, 1997. Spalted sugar maple; 13" high x 13" wide x 13" deep. Collection: Yale University Art Gallery. Gift of Ruth & David Waterbury. This finished piece features heavily decomposed spalted wood directly adjacent to solid wood, yet the piece was safely dried without cracking by using the boiling method. Boiling is an excellent way to neutralize tensions in the wood so spalted wood doesn't crack.

Ellsworth on...

Teaching

The only thing that parallels the satisfaction and intensity of my engagement in the making process is sharing that experience with others, especially through teaching woodturning. I think of teaching as a fair exchange between teacher and student. Because I'm primarily a workshop teacher, I have the advantage of working directly with small groups where these exchanges become possible. Teaching woodturning requires four basic elements: creating a safe space, knowing your subject, and having the ability to think like a student throughout the instruction period. The final step is simply to tell your own story.

For me, teaching is just as engaging and interesting as the making process itself.

Create a safe space

Creating a safe space comes in two basic forms and begins from the moment a student walks into the teaching environment.

The first form involves the physical space—specifically, the use of safe equipment, proper lighting, an emphasis on safe procedures, and an absolute minimum exposure to sawdust or other airborne materials. This includes proper dust collection, but it also means minimizing the use of toxic or allergenic woods and finishing materials. Also important is orientation of equipment so half an airborne bowl doesn't strike another student.

Creating a safe space also includes emotional safety. Make sure students are never made to feel embarrassed for making mistakes. Nothing will stop the learning process faster than a teacher coming down on a student for something the student can't yet do or doesn't understand. Part of the teacher's responsibility is also to protect students on all levels, including racial, religious, or sexual harassment.

Know your subject

One of the best ways a teacher can present ideas and information to students is to follow the exact same approach he or she takes to making something, and in the exact same order. This way, the student sees the chronology and the logic in the teacher's methods. It is also helpful to understand other methods besides your own.

Teachers often overlook that by doing something in a specific way, they give the impression that there is only one way. To prevent this, present various approaches to a problem and compare the way different tools work to make the same cut. Students can then add new information to their existing experiences without feeling they have to throw out what they've already learned.

As well, this "my way is the only way" perception can be the first step in creating dependency in a student. It is natural, of course, for students to be drawn to a particular teacher or subject. Yet it is important for teachers to create opportunities during

the workshop for students to develop a sense of independence so they learn to solve problems on their own. Ideally, the goal is to transfer ideas and working methods from teacher to student without ownership, so that with time and practice, students develop their own turning styles.

Think like a student

The idea of a teacher thinking like a student relates directly to the cliché "too much knowledge is a dangerous thing." I can have all the knowledge and experience in the world, but if I don't know how to communicate it, I have no business being a teacher.

Try to put yourself in the role of the student and ask, "What's coming out of my mouth?" "Is my message getting through?" "Is there a better way?" And most importantly, "Does what I'm showing relate to the students' interests in turning wood?" Thinking like a student reminds us we all receive information differently. We can be visual, verbal, tactile, conceptual, or any overlapping combination in between. By presenting information in different formats and approaches, I am able to better communicate my methods to more of the class.

It is also important to be receptive to how students present information to me. It is important to hear what they have to say with the same value I hope they are listening to me. This also helps me learn about how different people approach similar subjects.

An example is measuring the depth of a bowl. My way is very low-tech. I simply use anything lying around that's reasonably straight and long enough to reach from the rim to the bottom of the interior. But this method might befuddle an engineer, who would be inclined to use a ruler, because the incremental marks reflect his own experience, namely, measuring the distance from point A to point B. Both of these methods work, and both will give the same result in locating the depth of the bowl. The lesson is that by acknowledging the value of both approaches to this task, I validate the student's way of solving a problem. Additionally, a line of communication has been opened that might otherwise not have.

Thinking like a student helps to keep me fresh as a teacher. There's nothing worse than getting in front of a group of students and sounding like a broken record. One way to freshen my delivery is to ask my students how and if what I'm presenting relates to their own experiences. What if a student has experiences with a tool I've not yet worked with, and gets the same results? I'd definitely like to know about that.

I also work with students with varying skill levels. Some are quite experienced, most are beginner level, and some have never even turned on a lathe before. By having this mix within each class, students are able to reflect on the experiences of one another. Working with students at different experience levels also helps to reduce the competitive element that can develop so easily within small groups.

Tell your own story

Considering the breadth of the woodturning field as we know it today, the demand for new teachers will continue to outgrow the number of new subjects there are to teach. That is, in twenty years the number of people around the country teaching open-bowl turning will increase while the subject itself will remain relatively the same. However, the personalities of the teachers are different, as are their approaches, methods, styles, and intents. What each teacher brings to the subject is vital to the continuing interest in learning to turn a bowl. My point is each of us knows our own story: what we like to teach, how we teach, and what our students expect to learn. What we don't know are the stories of our students. If I am going to be effective as a teacher, I want to establish a comprehensive learning situation so my students get more than just the mechanics of how David Ellsworth turns a bowl. As such, I need to provide an opportunity for my students' stories to emerge.

Engaging strangers with meaningful subjects over a short period of time requires trust. Woodturning workshops simply don't give a lot of time, so the best way I have found to establish trust is to break down the classic hierarchical slope of the teacher knowing all and being "above" the student. If we break down

this slope, the line of communication and learning can flow both ways.

Providing meals is a great way to discover your students' stories. Fortunately, my wife, Wendy, and I both love to cook. Mealtime is a time to relax, but also a time to get away from the intensity of working on the lathe and begin to explore other things. These other things can be anything from life experiences to politics to religion.

Teaching methods

Equally important to the how of our teaching methods is the what. What, exactly, are we giving our students? Is it simply the mechanical skills of manipulating the tools? Or could we combine technical skills with the design skills? If we consider turning wood a centering process, we could focus on helping our students develop the gift of self-expression.

Experience yields confidence, which naturally leads to personal pride. While all people share similar attributes, they obviously do not always share the same interests. Students could be interested in any piece from the humble fountain pen to a bold piece of art. Developing ways to understand and appreciate our differences will do more to advance the creative elements in woodturning at all levels than continuing to learn to how to produce what has already been made.

In conclusion

I realize this book is primarily about providing answers, yet I hope it has also raised as many questions. In doing so, each of us will challenge the *unknown* as well as the *known* within our work and ourselves. And it is from this approach that we will provide the framework for the future of this field.

One only has to look at the wonders of the work being produced today to recognize how our lineage and the learning processes have evolved through inspiration and engagement. Turning wood is a very engaging sport. At the very least, it seems to draw the best from those who play the game.

Glossary

Bevel: The surface on the end of the gouge that intersects with the flute to form the edge. When making finish cuts with a gouge, the bevel touches the wood and supports the edge during the cut. The bevel makes contact with the grinder during sharpening.

Burl: An aberrant, knoblike growth that can occur on a tree's root, trunk, or limb. Burls can form with either onionlike layers or in a cross-grain structural pattern. Either type creates stunning visual beauty when used in decorative furniture and turnings.

Burr: The micro-sized, sawtooth-like surface that forms on a tool's edge when grinding. Generally honed off with a slipstone on spindle tools, bowl turners may or may not retain the burr on their gouges depending on personal choice.

Buyer: Someone with the interest, desire, opportunity, and means to purchase a turned wooden object.

Chatoyance: A shimmering visual effect seen in the polished surfaces of curly and figured woods. This cat's-eye, almost three-dimensional illusion occurs when the undulating structure of grain fibers breaks up and returns incoming light rays so the brain perceives the surface as coming from multiple directions.

Chuck: A clamping device used for attaching a piece of wood to a lathe. Modern chucks have four jaws of various sizes designed to hold many shapes of objects.

Collector: Someone with the interest, desire, opportunity, and means to purchase a second turned wooden object.

Cool sanding: A way to power-sand wood with less heat to minimize wood fiber damage. Cool sanding involves softening the foam back that holds the sandpaper and using a slower lathe speed or, in some cases, rotating the object by hand while sanding.

Dig: The undesirable effect of catching the tip of a tool in the spinning wood, often resulting in either redesigning the object or junking it.

Divot: A groove or depression left in a piece of wood, generally caused by a dig.

Double-turning: A two-step process for creating a wooden bowl from green wood. First, the rough block is turned to a bowl shape with a thick wall. After the bowl dries, it is re-turned to a desired wall thickness and finished. This method is used to prevent the bowl from cracking during drying.

Faceplate: The most secure method of attaching a piece of wood to the lathe. The faceplate attaches to the wood with screws, and then is threaded onto the spindle of the lathe.

David Ellsworth, *Maple Pot*, 2007. Spalted sugar maple; 9" high x 10" wide x 10" deep.

Ferrule: Placed over the end of the tool handle, the ferrule provides support to the union of the tool's handle and shaft. Ferrules are generally made with copper or brass pipe, but nylon cord tied in a knot and coated with superglue works just as well.

Gouge: A chisel-like tool with a curved edge. Gouges come in many shapes and are used for turning spindles, bowls, and vessel forms.

Grain: Refers to the color, pattern, and direction of the fiber growth. Grain fibers grow parallel to the tree's growth and are laid out similarly to a pack of soda straws, where the straws' sides would simulate face grain and the straws' ends would represent end grain.

Green wood: Fresh-cut wood that has yet to dry and whose fibers are malleable and limber, as opposed to dry and brittle. Green wood is easier to cut, making it a perfect material when learning to turn. Green wood will crack as it dries unless properly managed and stored.

Interior-finishing cut: The final cuts used to finish the inside of a bowl. Can be made with a gouge or a scraper depending on the wood's condition, moisture content, and/or personal preference of the maker.

Jam chuck: A chuck threaded to the headstock and used to support the upper region of a bowl or vessel so the foot, positioned toward the tailstock, can be shaped and finished. Most often homemade from plywood, PVC pipe, or solid wood, jam chucks are made in many diameters and heights to fit the turner's needs. Open bowls can be placed over the jam chuck's rim while hollow forms can be placed inside the chuck.

Lathe: Similar in concept to the potter's wheel and the bow drill, the lathe is a primitive power-carving tool that is more than 5,000 years old. A close cousin to the metal lathe, the modern wood lathe supports and rotates a wooden object while the operator cuts and shapes it with additional hand-held tools.

Maker: A descriptive term of both affection and compromise, but with very little baggage as compared with *artist* or *craftsperson*. The term *maker* is inclusive of both artists and craftspersons whether they be self-taught, apprenticed, or school-trained; isolationists or egocentrists; highly creative, or just mildly confused.

Natural-edge bowl: A bowl whose rim utilizes the shape of the surface of a log or other part of a tree. Natural-edge designs can be used for either decorative or utilitarian bowls. Also called *natural-topped bowl*.

Nib a.k.a. nubin: A term referring to the small bit of raised wood that appears at the bowl's center when the interior waste wood is removed. Nibs tend to occur either as result of an incomplete cut, or possibly the intersection of the tool's tip and the floundering focus point of a pair of trifocals.

Parting tool: A rather thin-bladed, blunt-tipped scraping tool most frequently used in spindle turning, but also at times for working in the area of the bowl's base.

Pith: The first annual growth ring that forms the center of the tree. The pith area is quite prone to growth stresses and is, therefore, generally eliminated from the bowl's design. Vessel makers are known to take liberties by incorporating the pith within their designs.

Punky: A natural state of decaying wood determined by a woodturner to be somewhere between moderately useful and totally useless. See *spalted* below.

Resin: A solid or semisolid substance found between the fibers in many woods, but particularly noticeable in pines and tropical woods. Resin presence is often greater than actual moisture content, making some woods difficult to dry.

Roughing cut: The initial step in turning a block into a bowl or vessel using a gouge. The roughing cut removes all the extra or irregular surfaces.

Scraper: A heavy-bodied round nose tool used to remove wood when making spindles or bowls. Scraping tools are not as efficient as cutting tools, but are considered easier to use when making finishing cuts in a shear-scraping position on fine-grained dry wood. They do not work well on green wood.

Scraping cut: A cut performed with the edge of the gouge perpendicular to the cutting surface.

Shear-scraping cut: A cut used to finish the bowl's exterior when using a gouge or the bowl's interior when using a scraper. The shearing action is achieved by positioning the edge of the tool approximately 45° to the surface being cut. On the bowl's interior, the cut begins in the center of the base using a scraper and works out toward the rim. On the bowl's exterior, the cut works best when it begins at the rim and progresses toward the base using a side-ground gouge.

Skew (a.k.a. skew-chisel): A spindle-turning tool used for both roughing and finishing cuts. Sometimes referred to as a tool with an attitude, the skew can be somewhat difficult to master, but the reward is a super-smooth surface often requiring little or no sanding.

Slicing cut: A cut that fluidly removes waste material during shaping of the form. The front third or half of the tip on the side-ground gouge is used to remove wood in a manner similar to peeling an apple.

Spalted wood: A fungal decomposition of cell structure that is Mother Nature's way of turning a dead or dying tree into the forest floor. Spalt manifests in warm, moist climate conditions and produces brown or black zone lines highly favored by woodturners for their decorative patterns.

Woodturn: A nonword often, and incorrectly, used to describe the process of spinning and cutting something attached to a lathe, as in "I'm now going to *woodturn*." In truth, one does not woodturn any more than one glassblows, claythrows, or fiberweaves. The correct usage would be: "I am now going to turn wood."

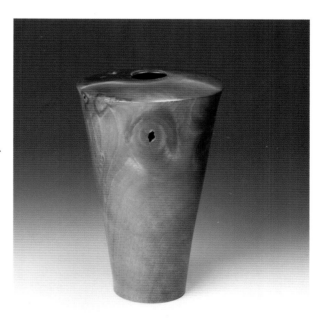

David Ellsworth, *Vase*, 1978. Claro walnut burl, 7½" high x 3½" wide x 3½" deep.

Resources

ABRANET SANDING DISCS
Abranet Finishing Discs and Interface Pads
P.O. Box 360275
Cleveland, OH 44136-0005
(216) 631-5309
www.homesteadfinishing.com

ASSORTED ACCESSORIES FOR WOOD AND METAL
ENCO
400 Nevada Pacific Highway
Fernley, NV 89408
(800) 873-3626
www.use-enco.com
customer-service@use-enco.com

McMaster-Carr
P.O. Box 4355
Chicago, IL 60680
(630) 833-0300
www.mcmaster.com
chi.sales@mcmaster.com

MSC Industrial Supply Co. Inc.
75 Maxess Road
Melville, NY 11747
(800) 645-7270
www.mscdirect.com
cust_service@mscdirect.com

BUFFING WHEELS AND POLISHING COMPOUNDS
Hagstoz Jewelry Supply
709 Sanson Street
Philadelphia, PA 19106
(215) 922-1627
www.hagstoz.com
info@hagstoz.com

CRAFT SCHOOLS OFFERING CLASSES IN WOODTURNING:
For a resource listing of over 36 national and international schools and private workshops where woodturning is taught, go to the following link from the American Association of Woodturners:
http://www.woodturner.org/resources/schools.cfm

DC MOTOR DRIVES
Woodco Products
5507 55th Avenue S.
Seattle, WA 98118
(206) 723-8487
www.woodcousa.com

FACEPLATES – TOOL RESTS
Bill Kuhlemeier
Sea Horse Custom Fab.
486 Banks Chapel Road
Ranger, GA 30734
(706) 334-4057

FACEPLATE SCREWS
Manhattan Supply Corp. (MSC)
See listing under "Assorted Accessories for Wood and Metal"
#14 x 1", Phillips Round Head
Cat. #87923447 - $20.12/100
#14 x 1 ¼", Phillips Round Head

McMaster-Carr Supply Co.
See listing under "Assorted Accessories for Wood and Metal."
#14 x 1", Phillips Round Head

FACEPLATE TAPS
Beall Tool Company
541 Swans Road N.E.
Newark, OH 43055
(800) 331-4718
www.bealltool.com
jrbeall@bealltool.com
1", 1¼", 33mm x 8tpi

GALLERIES
Cervini Haas Gallery
4222 N. Marshall Way
Scottsdale, AZ 85251
(480) 429-6116
www.cervinihaas.com
info@cervinihaas.com

Del Mano Gallery
11981 San Vicente Boulevard
W. Los Angeles, CA 90049
(310) 476-8508
www.delmano.com
gallery@delmano.com

Patina Gallery
131 West Palace Avenue
Santa Fe, NM 87501
(505) 986-3432
www.patina-gallery.com

rakovaBRECKERgallery
1855 Griffin Road
Dania Beach, FL 33004
(954) 924-9878
www.rakovabreckergallery.com
info@rakovabreckergallery.com

Sarah Myerscough Fine Art
15-16 Brooks Mews Mayfair
London W1K 4DS
United Kingdom
+44(0)20 7485-0056
www.sarahmyerscough.com
info@sarahmyerscough.com

Snyderman Gallery
303 Cherry St.
Philadelphia, PA 19106
(215) 238-9576
www.snyderman-works.com
Bruce@Snyderman-Works.com

GRINDING WHEELS
MSC Industrial Supply Co. Inc.
See listing: "Assorted Accessories for Wood and Metal."
100/120 Grit Aluminum Oxide
8" x 1", ⅝" arbor
Cat. #75941443.........$22.00

ORGANIZATIONS
American Association of Woodturners
222 Landmark Center
75 W. Fifth Street
St. Paul, MN 55102-7704
(651) 484-9094
www.woodturner.org
inquiries@woodturner.org

Collectors of Wood Art
(888) 393-8332
www.collectorsofwoodart.org
info@collectorsofwoodart.org

Wood Turning Center
501 Vine St.
Philadelphia, PA 19106
(215) 923-8000
www.woodturningcenter.org
info@woodturningcenter.org

American Craft Council
72 Spring Street
New York City, NY 10012
(212) 274-0630
www.craftcouncil.org
council@craftcouncil.org

SANDPAPER
(Auto body & paint suppliers)
Self-sticking 6" discs (220gr):
Norton #32374
Self-sticking 5" discs (320gr):
Norton #32371

SPRAY LACQUER
Krylon Acrylic
(800) 457-9566
"Crystal Clear" - #1303
"Matte Finish" - #1309
"UV-Clear" - #1305

TOOL STEEL
ENCO
See listing under "Assorted Accessories for Wood and Metal."

McMaster-Carr
See listing under "Assorted Accessories for Wood and Metal."

MSC
See listing under "Assorted Accessories for Wood and Metal."
Drill Rod: ⅜, ⁷⁄₁₆", ½" x 36"
¹⁄₁₆" and ³⁄₁₆" square 10% cobalt tips

VACUUM CHUCKS
Bill Grumbine
1587 Siegfriedale Road
Kutztown, PA 19530
(610) 248-7661
ultradad@enter.net

VACUUM PUMPS
Surplus Center
P.O. Box 82209
Lincoln, NE 68501
(800) 488-3407
www.surpluscenter.com
Cat#: 90048A315, ¼ HP, 220V - $89.95

VERTICAL SOLUTION
Don Geiger
2606 N.W. 170th Street
Newberry, FL 32669
(352) 472-5035
dongeiger@cox.net

WOODTURNING EQUIPMENT AND SUPPLIES
Craft Supplies, USA
1287 E. 1120 Street
Provo, UT 84606
(800) 551-8876
www.woodturnerscatalog.com
service@woodturnerscatalog.com

Packard Woodworks, Inc.
P.O. Box 718
Tryon, NC 28782
(828) 859-6762
www.packardwoodworks.com
Packard@alltel.net

Robust Tools, LLC (Robust Lathe)
3376 Mound View Road
Barneveld, WI 53507
(608) 437-4748
www.turnrobust.com
deb@turnrobust.com

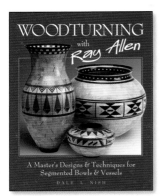